T0204565

More Praise for
Stewardship in your Family Enterprise

Wealth is an amplifier. The larger the family, the more crucial communication and governance becomes not only for the business, but also for the family. Dennis Jaffe does a wonderful job addressing the challenges and outlining the tools and techniques needed to help families sustain wealth across generations.
Dirk Jungé, 4th Generation Family Member,
Chairman & Chief Executive Officer of Pitcairn

Dennis Jaffe has always had the knack of delivering real wisdom about families that is actionable and results oriented. This book is organized in a way that allows the reader to go directly to the topic at hand to learn what they need and apply it immediately. It will be on nightstands of many family leaders.
Kaycee Krysty, President and CEO, Laird Norton Tyee

Many books in this field dwell on 'horror stories': family wars and failure. Dennis Jaffe provides a welcome focus on what works, with decades of practical experience and reasoned thought to back him up. You will profit returning to these pages again and again, no matter what size your family enterprise is.
Keith Whitaker, Managing Director,
Family Dynamics, Wells Fargo

Dennis Jaffe has devoted his career to helping business and wealth owning families have it both ways — enjoying meaningful, enduring, relationships as members of a cohesive family and being responsible stewards of their assets. For families wanting to prosper emotionally and financially over generations, Dennis shares his wisdom and his faith in our ability to work together and be successful regardless of the challenges.
Lansing Crane, former Chairman and CEO of Crane and
Company, 5th generation family business

Jaffe's book is an inspirational journey of understanding and hope for all of us connected to a family enterprise — whether as a member in a family enterprise or as an advisor. Jaffe's genius is in taking a complex subject matter and presenting the material in such a way as to make each reader feel smart. Stewardship in Your Family Enterprise captures the magic and possibilities of shared family wealth. My only regret is that this book was not published 20 years ago.
James Olan Hutcheson, Founder, ReGENERATION Partners
and Recipient of Richard Beckhard Practice Award, Family Firm Institute

A comprehensive and in-depth discussion of the real issues families face as their family business matures and subsequent generations become employees and owners. I am deeply impressed with Dennis's approach to governance issues, resolving business conflicts and developing future family leaders. Required reading by a truly exceptional counselor and consultant in the family business field.
Bill Messenger, President, Aureus Inc

Its clarity and comprehensive scope will appeal to business-owning families, but there's considerable food for thought for family business practitioners as well.
Amelia Renkert-Thomas, Principal, Withers Bergman

Dennis Jaffe has been at the forefront of innovative thinking for a generation of academics and consultants who study and work with families and their businesses—helping them govern in better ways, work in better ways and love in better ways. Stewardship in Your Family Enterprise represents the culmination of Jaffe's learnings on this multi-faceted topic.

He has pulled all of the insights he has gathered together himself and written about so many times over the years and he has joined those insights with much of the knowledge others have added to the field in the last 25 years into this single guidebook for families, for business owners, and for the consultants who serve them.

This single volume brings together the best thinking about families and what helps to make them successful as they move from one generation to the next, as managers of successful businesses and as stewards of the many treasures that make up each family. For anyone who cares about family businesses and how they successfully move from one generation to the next, Stewardship in Your Family Enterprise is now the essential first stop. It is Family Business 101, 201 and 301 all rolled into one place.
Norm Boone, Chairman, Mosaic Financial Partners

Many of the concepts and issues identified strikes a chord with the current generation of Asian business owners who needs support and guidance on how to tackle these issues. One would get a much better understanding and how to move forward after reading the book.
Thomas Ang, Credit Suisse, Singapore

Dennis Jaffe has written a "must-read" book that serves as a comprehensive guide and invaluable resource for family members striving to understand the dynamics and impact of wealth in the context of a family enterprise. Stressing the principles of leadership, teamwork and stewardship within a family structure, Mr. Jaffe leverages his unique background to suggest practical tools which help families better understand and communicate their values, and overcome challenges and barriers that stand in their way. Concise, articulate, and profound, this book can help families of all kinds learn from past mistakes and enable them to proactively construct a stable and focused foundation for the growth of future generations.
Allison Taff, Director, Family Office Services, Silver Bridge Advisors

All wealthy families can benefit from the generous wealth of advice and information in this book. Dennis Jaffe has been a pioneer in this emerging, complex field, and has organized the topics: each stands alone, making it immediately useful to a family wanting to learn how to cope better with a specific challenge--or just to read a topic of interest.
Barbara Hauser, family advisor, author of International Family Governance

This book is a must read for families who want to develop both their wealth and relationships. Especially next generation family members will hugely benefit from it.
Jozef Lievens, Managing Director, Institute for Family Business and FBN Belgium, Professor, HU Brussels

ALSO BY DENNIS JAFFE

Dennis T. Jaffe Ph.D.

Stewardship In Your

Family

Enterprise

Developing Responsible Family Leadership Across Generations

First Edition. January, 2010
Reprint. September 2014

Designed by Alden Bevington
of Pioneer Imprints
www.pioneerimprints.com

ISBN-13: 978-0692295649

Library of Congress Data Available Upon request

Printed in the United States of America

10 9 8 7 6 5 4 3 2 1

 Contents

Preface

Practical Tools for Sustaining Family and Business Across Generations

As difficult as it may be to raise a family or to run a business or manage complex investments, combining them is many times more difficult. Sustaining a family business or a portfolio of diverse family assets is one of the greatest challenges a family may encounter. It is the reason that most family businesses fail to survive into the third generation and that the family adage "shirtsleeves to shirtsleeves in three generations" has become so common. It's not easy to manage one family business, let alone multiple family enterprises. The elders want to establish a family legacy of wealth and success as a source of pride and livelihood for future generations. They know the odds are against them, but the vision of continuing the family enterprise across generations is so powerful that often they are willing to do the immense work needed to overcome the obstacles to success.

Despite these obstacles, family wealth creators overwhelmingly want to see the family continue together into the next generation as owners and stewards of a shared family enterprise, in whatever form. Although the promise of continuing a business into the next generation is usually not the only reason people start a family business or garner wealth, the wealth creators' attention eventually shifts from the present to the next generation. But no matter how well-intentioned they are and how serious about the next generation, they may avoid taking the steps necessary to ensure the family moves forward together or even deny these steps are needed. Their efforts are too little too late, leading to the many documented disasters in succession.

Why do families want to continue working together as a family? Family members across generations trust each other and genuinely like being together. They may rightly think that the business or the family's portfolio of shared assets is likely to bring more to the family if it is managed by the entire family as a whole than if it is split into portions that are the provinces of various individuals. Moreover, the family sees the business and its resources as a source of meaning and focus.

Peter Block introduced me to the notion of stewardship about 20 years ago. He referred to an attitude about wealth and personal relationships that considers not just self-interest but also the impact on current, and even future, generations. When a family has created wealth, the question arises, What do we want our wealth to do for us, as a family, and also for the world? They want to pass wealth and their family enterprises on to the next generation, but also they have a sense of what they want the wealth to do for their heirs and what they want the heirs to do with the wealth. They want more than to give them the ability to spend and live nicely; they want the wealth to be used for the greater good. This of course includes the livelihood of the next generations, but it also includes the next generations' passing on a family legacy to their employees, the community, and the world. In order to create a mind-set and value of stewardship, the family must do more than establish rules for their estate and for the family-business inheritance; they must instill specific values, attitudes, skills, and practices in the next generation. My personal goal for this book is to help families accomplish this. Families with wealth are important because they can have a major impact on many people.

I have tried to create a useful guide for overcoming the real challenges that confront families as they journey through generations on the road to family wealth stewardship. This book provides practical steps, lessons, and techniques for dealing with the complexities faced by families with such shared assets as businesses, investments, property, and foundations, among others.

The book is not arranged as a narrative that you must read from start to finish, but rather as a number of short topical selections, each focusing on an area of practice that will help you sustain your family business or family wealth. Each selection is designed to stand on its own, as a lesson in a particular area with examples and practical action steps, or Keys to Success, that a family can take in that area. You and your family may select topics of interest in any order, as each selection can be read as a standalone prescription for a specific challenge. You, as a family member, will find some selections that speak directly to your particular issues and some that you will want to pass on to your parents, siblings, or spouses. In the book's seven parts, you will find more than 50 lessons for managing the complex and trying, but entirely predictable, transitions, transactions, crises, and concerns attendant to operating a successful, growing family with several shared assets.

Who This Book Is For and How It Can Help

Dealing with shared money is a common challenge for all families. In this book, I focus on the problems of families who have been extraordinarily successful, creating wealth by starting a business or accumulating multiple investments and real estate. A successful, wealthy family faces complex difficulties that other families do not. Family members have to deal not only with inheritance, but also with the question of whether the next generation will share family assets or divide them. Some assets can be divided neatly, but not those such as a single business or wonderful vacation home. The possibility for conflict over who will control and benefit from a business or from a vacation home's use and income is well known. Parents want their offspring to share such family resources, but siblings and their new spouses and families may find that a tall order.

If the family assets are considerable and if there are many children or branches, the issues the family will have to resolve are even more complex. Family members will have to learn to work together and create rules, agreements, and activities to help them do this, not only today but going forward, as the family and its enterprise progress through generations. To help them address the combined challenges of living harmoniously as members of a family and living productively as people who work together to sustain their wealth, I share many tools and practices used by families who have successfully managed these competing demands and developed and operated very large, long-lived, and successful family enterprises.

Family businesses are the backbone of the world economy; perhaps 90 percent of all the businesses in the world fit into this category. Many of them begin with sweat equity from several family members, who pitch in because they know, care for, and trust each other. Alternately, a business may become a family business when an owner, whose children are grown, wants to include some of them in the business and wants to pass the business on.

In recent years, the definition of a family business has expanded. Quite often, as a family crosses generations, they sell their operating business or diversify into a holding company for the various assets they own and manage together. As a family moves into the second or third generation, the single business can evolve into a series of family ventures, each with different managers and leaders. The family wants to remain united, but rather than being united around a single business, they want to stay together around a number of family ventures. Like other practitioners, I call these families **enterprising families**, to denote their interest in creating multiple family enterprises that not only create wealth but also express the family's values and vision. Some selections here deal with the transition to an enterprising family, but *rather than focusing on the business end* of selling or diversifying, they focus on the many ways that *a family* can build a partnership when they own and manage several shared assets.

An enterprising family must perform a delicate balancing act. It must balance the needs and desires of the younger generations with those of the elders. It must balance the need for prudent and thoughtful management of assets with family ties. And it must divide assets, resources, and leadership positions—in the family and in the business—fairly among all family members. Personal relationships and problems rooted in family dynamics may clash with the stark issues of power and control over assets. An enterprising family must perfect the ability to develop and sustain caring *family* relationships as well as productive *working* relationships.

Good family relationships are not the same as good working relationships, and members of a successful enterprising family must develop both. In fact, members of an enterprising family must achieve what are called **dual relationships**—relationships between people who have both a family relationship and a business relationship with each other. A boss can fire an employee; however, if the employee is related to the boss, are there additional issues the boss must consider before taking this step? Say the boss is the father, and the employee is his oldest son; does this change the boss's ability to fire him? The act reverberates from the business to the family and back again. Consider three siblings who, as family members, are each slated to inherit one-third of the family's assets. Now consider that one of them has been the manager of these assets for many years; another has a successful career as a professional; and the third has chosen not to work but rather to be supported by the family's wealth. Is it fair to pass the wealth on to these family members in equal shares? Or should the differences in the siblings' commitments to these assets and the amount of time they've spent working for the family ventures be taken into account? After the parents pass the estate to their children, the potential for conflict looms large.

This book will help you face the challenges that arise when families work together. A family-business relationship is based on family ties, which invariably are emotional, unconditional, and informal. But business is about accountability, performance, and formal roles and responsibilities. When a family has a business or manages shared assets, it is likely that at times the family aspects of a relationship among family members will conflict with the business aspects of this relationship. A father may discover that interacting with a son in his business is different from interacting with a business partner to whom he is not related. A brother and sister may find that the closeness they shared growing up hampers an effective adult working relationship, in which they need to depend on each other in ways that are very different from those they relied on as children. This does not mean that family members must leave behind their family relationships. However they must learn to determine what is appropriate for a certain situation and be versatile enough to apply this learning almost instinctively in order to manage the constant shifting between family and business relationships that the various arenas of their lives require. This is not easy.

The family faces even more layers of complexity as the second generation grows up. First, they have to decide whether to keep the business or to sell it, and if they are giving it to the next generation, they must decide who will own it. A critical question each generation must confront is, Do we remain unified and manage our family assets together, or do we divide them? If they sell the family operating business, is there any reason for family members to remain together as a shared economic unit, investing together, or should each now go his or her own way? What is the basis for a family partnership if the family business is gone? I have found that families discover many reasons for remaining together; among them are forming or strengthening personal bonds, enjoying the financial benefits of investing together, and providing meaningful ways for family members to work together.

The challenges are not over, however, when a family has made the decision to remain together as an entity involved in any number of projects and endeavors. Another challenge facing families is that over generations what began as a set of trusts and entities to protect and help the family can become burdens that stifle them. Trusts or other legal documents that give subsequent generations little or no control over their inheritance and hold them hostage to the family end up creating a generation of eternal children who are helpless, dependent, and confused. However if a family works together to craft family governance agreements and practices that allow for each generation's review, both the generation that created them and later generations will be more likely to adhere to them, manifesting the family's values and goals in their family and business relationships with each other and in their business, or financial, decisions. When subsequent generations are given control over their inheritance and are encouraged to familiarize themselves with the family governance agreements and structures—especially if these allow them to make responsible amendments when a changing world requires it—they are more likely to become responsible, diligent adults, empowered, active, and engaged in charting their own future.

As each generation of young people grow up surrounded by family wealth, the elder generation must determine the most-effective way to pass on their values to their heirs. How can parents motivate their children to develop their own expertise in various areas and make a commitment to useful work when they have grown up surrounded by family wealth? How can the family avoid making a transition from successful and hardworking family wealth creators or generators to a group of relatives who are merely consumers and may deplete the family's wealth in a single generation? Families can do specific things collectively to develop the skills of the next generation and inspire young adults to make the best use of these skills and of their own unique talents.

To sustain a family enterprise, a family must focus on engaging the next generation. The family as a whole has to prepare them to take on leadership roles and to keep their family legacy alive and healthy. This is not a financial or legal activity, but one that combines personal, emotional, and vocational development. Throughout this book, I will explore many ways successful enterprising families are developing and supporting the next generation in their journey to become family leaders.

In the stories of these families who have learned to work together by applying such practices—whether in the process of leadership succession or in other aspects of the creation of a robust enterprise that has thrived over generations—I have, for the most part, used fictitious names and changed details to protect the families' privacy. But because I have learned a great deal from my work with them, I would like to thank them for their indirect collaboration. In some cases here, I have also drawn on the examples of families whose stories have been in the media, or whose members have spoken publicly, so if you recognize a family name, I am using information from the public record.

My Journey with Families

I am not a financial adviser; I work with families on the personal and relationship aspects of family business and wealth, helping them actively manage family dynamics and development as well as business development and governance. My work lies at the intersection of family therapy, psychology, and personal life planning; business management and strategic planning; and the emerging field of family-business governance. Along with others in this developing field, I continue to synthesize principles and ideas that span several professional fields and disciplines focusing on personal and business development.

I have worked for nearly 40 years not only with families who have owned a family business, but also with families who have a family office or multiple family assets. Together with the family members, I have confronted the challenges related to family succession, developing new leadership, and creating the infrastructure to sustain their family wealth in all its forms across generations. My personal mission is to help families unravel unnecessary conflict, overcome their helplessness and actively define their values and purpose, guiding them in the search for the most-effective way to manifest their vision in the world. A wealthy family has the resources to make a critical difference in a world that sorely needs their involvement.

I work intensively and over the long term with families who want to carefully navigate these transitions. I have developed principles and best practices for successfully managing the shift from one generation to the next, including preparing the next generation to take over. While many families will seek out a consultant or adviser to help them, many more will find that with a book like this to guide them, they can work on their own.

I want to share a bit about my personal career and the aspect of it that included my own life journey with families, which led to the work I'm doing now. While I work with the family's businesses and financial ventures, the heart of the family is the foundation and core of what I do; considerations of it inform every practice I suggest, every tool, action, and technique I employ. My efforts encompass multiple people and generations as I try to help families in their search for a balance that enables them to grow and thrive in a difficult and challenging world. This balance requires harmonizing the needs and aspirations of the many individual members of the family with the desire for a shared entity, "the family." As one author noted, the family is a "haven in a heartless world," when it works. But family can also be a source of pain, frustration, conflict, and injustice. As frequently as they use the terms *love* and *caring*, thought leaders and practitioners in the field employ the terms *warfare* and *dysfunction* when talking about family relations.

The work that led me to where I am now began with my seeing families in times of extreme conflict and stress between generations during an era when it seemed as if the entire country was sizzling with such tensions. In the turmoil of the 60s, I worked with runaway youth. They were hurt, wounded, and angry, but also were sincerely trying to find their way in a world that did not respect their sense of justice and self-worth. When I was barely 20 myself, I opened a runaway house and crisis center designed to be a place where young people could reconcile with their families in a safe environment that allowed them to be heard but also encouraged them to listen to the concerns of their parents. Later, my work grew to encompass families with inherited wealth as I became involved with young people in religious cults who wanted to give away their wealth to their gurus. I watched deep feelings and complex interests surface on both sides as parents and children tried to reconcile their differences and began to become keenly aware of how short-term and long-term decisions could have profound consequences for all involved. Engaging with these families was a deep learning experience for me. I recognized the many ways that family members could define what was right—and had to if they were to find harmony in the family. During this period, I also worked with families facing the ultimate crises of death and chronic illness. In all these situations, it became clear that probably the most important factor in resolving a family crisis was bringing all the people it touched together and inspiring them to search for ways to successfully address these complex issues and diminish or dissolve the pain that accompanied them—and doing this with people who were not disposed to compromise or listen to each other. I also became involved with various family advisers, trustees, and financial consultants, who often felt helpless to intervene.

In graduate school, I studied management and sociology, where I discovered the world of business and the human challenges of planned and unforeseen change. I learned that a business is a vehicle to achieve human purposes, as a family is, but the two are very different in the talents and human qualities they value and in way in which they focus on end results, as well as the end results they applaud. This was a significant awareness for me, and not one easily come to. I also learned skills and tools from the emerging field of organizational development (OD), which had grown out of the idea that the most-effective organizations are those in which people at all levels are meaningfully engaged in decisions and planning and are characterized by relative openness, transparency, and information flow across boundaries. The field has been especially successful in helping individuals develop authentic communication and in bringing teams and small groups together to learn, plan, and govern themselves. The ideas of collaboration, openness, and organizational learning seem to apply equally well to the family. My organizational consulting helped organizations going through major changes—mergers, implementation of such changes, fast growth, or downsizing—engaging people in the transition so that the experience became more positive.

These two strands—building shared purpose in the family and in the organization—are the twin building blocks of my work with family enterprises. How did these two disparate cultural settings—families and corporations—ever find common purpose? The breakthrough occurred in the early 80s, when a small group of visionaries from a range of disciplines who worked with a hybrid entity called a family business gathered to see if their work had any commonalities that could benefit from interdisciplinary sharing. I was invited to a workshop held at the University of Southern California on this topic, and my first reaction was, "What is a family business?" I'd worked with families and with corporations, but I'd never thought there was any connection between the two. I was not alone. No business school or management research mentioned family business, except derisively, to denote that a certain business was not run on rational business principles. While almost all businesses were family businesses, the conventional wisdom was that the family did not belong in the business, and if it involved itself with the enterprise's daily operations, it was creating a setting for disaster.

But the field of family-business consulting was launched, and its pioneers were able to discover the reasons families naturally organize themselves into family enterprises to work together. Practitioners and thought leaders in this burgeoning field also looked at how the family could be a resource adding great value and longevity to a business, as well as how the existence of family conflicts and the process of moving between generations could lead to destructive conflict and disintegration. I am proud to have been part of this productive dialogue for nearly 30 years.

In the past decade, a new element entered this new field of family businesses, which is reflected in this volume. At first, the field was about family business, seeing the family and the business as co-equal, overlapping entities. The truism arose that most family businesses fail, because after two generations nearly all of them came to an end. But this was misleading, in that when a family sold or shut down a business, it did not necessarily represent a failure. Some things come to an end. For example, we would not say that selling the family home is a failure, as there are other conditions that lead family members to want other houses. Similarly, watching the evolution of a family, we see that the family may amass a great deal of wealth from a single business within a generation, but over time the family's interests in and management of its family wealth may diverge and diversify into more than one venture. Looking at family business, we progress to looking at the family who uses its wealth for many purposes, such as multiple ventures, developing its human capital, and serving the community and the world.

My work evolved from working with families alone, to working with family businesses, to working with families as they evolved over generations into multiple "family enterprises." Just as the family business has its time, so a unified extended family may not exist after two or three generations. But the small number of families who have amassed great wealth have reason to maintain family unity over generations. Even if they sell the original family business, they retain trusts, shared investments, and a family name and legacy that have meaning and value. They are also prone to conflict, crossed purposes, and difficulty in aligning interests and managing their organizations and financial affairs together over generations. So, today I once again work with multigenerational families, but now they are families who wish to align the individual and collective purposes that are made possible by their wealth.

This book was written over about seven years, with contributions published in a number of different magazines and journals. It presents concepts, practices, and pathways that I believe will be helpful for a family who has significant wealth and wants to have the most positive impact on their heirs, as well as on the community and the world. It is therefore about family stewardship, that is, what happens to wealth rather than how one goes about acquiring it.

In this collection, I have tried my best to unify the tone of the selections and write primarily to an audience of families struggling with these intergenerational concerns. Although my audience includes professional advisers who want to understand these families—and some of the material was originally written specifically for advisers—I have edited and rewritten these pieces with the family in mind, addressing their challenges directly. While reviewing the selections for this book, I found that because I wrote them at different stages in my work in this field, my concepts and messages may vary slightly, reflecting the development of my understanding. I have tried to keep my terms and usages consistent, though since the family enterprise is so complex, that is not always possible.

How the Book Is Organized

The book is organized into seven parts, each with several selections that include concepts, lessons, and tools. Each selection presents stories and relates the experiences some families have had with various techniques and practices. Each one invites you, as a member of an enterprising family, to join this exploration of ways in which successful enterprising families address the complex challenges of sustaining their family assets, growing responsible children, and working together to make shared decisions. Because each selection is intended to stand on its own, and some of them were written at different times, there is some redundancy across them. However, I have tried as much as possible to make the tone, the ideas, and the Keys to Success clear, consistent, and most of all, practical and useful.

Part 1 — The Delicate and Complex Nature of Family Enterprise and Family Wealth introduces the family enterprise as a system, an interconnected series of activities and elements with multiple purposes and members. The book begins by looking not at the family *business*, but at family *wealth*—what constitutes it and how a successful family typically views it. Then we look at the family enterprise and the challenges a family must face if it is to continue to sustain the enterprise across generations. It is helpful to begin with this section before delving into others.

Part 2 — Effective Governance and Decision Making presents the key elements necessary for the creation of an organizational structure that will ensure the family successfully manages shared assets over generations. To manage the complexities of family, business, and shared wealth, a family must create explicit agreements. The lessons in this section focus on creating a mission statement that encapsulates the family's vision, principles, and values; setting up a family council and governing board; and creating a family constitution.

Part 3 — Building Communication and Resolving Family Conflict focuses on the ways in which the legacy of family relationships affects a family enterprise. Many things that otherwise a family can manage fairly easily are difficult when family members have to go off to work together. This section provides tools with which families can build communication and resolve conflict through open, direct, and respectful conversations about money, wealth, and business.

Part 4 — The Rocky Transition from First to Second Generation examines the predictable and unavoidable transitions a family enterprise faces as the business and the family grow and evolve. This section looks at the inevitability of transition and explores some key choices, including those regarding leadership succession, that a family must make proactively to ensure they are prepared to address the possibility of change when it arises. In addition, it examines how these decisions affect the entire extended family.

Part 5 — The Personal Challenges of Succession looks more deeply at how different stakeholders, inside and outside the family, are affected by the selection and installation of members of the next generation in various roles and responsibilities. Succession is a process not just of anointing a leader, but of choosing and aligning all interested parties.

Part 6 — Developing Leadership and Teamwork in the Next Generation presents some of the challenges that evolving family enterprises face as they seek to develop and channel the skills, capabilities, and commitment of the members of the next generation. If the family's enterprises are very successful, it will take a special family member to continue to manage them. This section presents guidelines to help the enterprising family develop diligent and committed family teams in each generation who will be prepared to take over the responsibilities of family stewardship from their elders.

Part 7 — Creating Stewardship of Family Wealth shows how parents can ensure their children are prepared to deal with the emotional and the practical aspects of family wealth. This section explores ways in which the family can develop the many forms of family capital presented in Part I. In addition, it shows how various forms of family wealth affect each family member and suggests ways in which the family and its members can give back to their communities.

Acknowledgements

Prior Publications

Many of the selections in this book were originally published in some of the most influential and thought-provoking magazines available for enterprising families. They were written at different times and for different purposes, but have been edited for consistency and as much as possible, to eliminate redundancy.

I want to thank these publications for allowing me to reprint selections from my work as a cohesive whole in this volume so that it may reach a wider audience. For a number of years, beginning at its inception, *Families in Business* provided a platform for my writing in this area. For four years, I wrote a column titled "Working with the Ones You Love," for this wonderful publication, and many of these columns are included here. I want to thank the *Journal of Financial Planning* and the magazine *Family Business* for publishing several of the selections. *The Journal of Wealth Management* allowed me to publish revised versions of articles written with James Grubman and Fredda Herz Brown, included in the section on family wealth.

Some of the selections were co-authored by colleagues, whose contribution and ideas are equal to my own in the selections they co-authored. These colleagues include Fredda Herz Brown (*Becoming an Enterprising Family, When Succession Crosses Genders, Overcoming Entitlement and Rising a Responsible Next Generation*), Sam Davis (*The Independent Family Board, The Serious Business of Family Philanthropy*), and Fran Lotery (*Nurturing Talent Across Generations*), all from Relative Solutions, and James Grubman (*The Dilemmas of Acquired and Inherited Wealth, From Conflict to Clear Life Purpose: Coming to Terms with Family Wealth*).

It Takes a Village

The ideas and concepts that are filtering through this emerging field have been developed by a growing community of practitioners, whose professional experience spans many family enterprise–related fields of service. In the last 30 years, work with the human and personal sides of the family enterprise has evolved from a small group of pioneers into a global community of practitioners who are looking beyond finance and business to see the deeper personal issues that motivate and characterize families who own and operate enterprises. I have been a part of this community since it began and have collaborated with many people on projects, seminars, and work with client families. I want to thank some of them below for their support and contribution to what you read here.

First, I want to acknowledge two important partnerships. Through my involvement with the Aspen Family Business Group and work with David Bork, Joe Paul, Sam Lane, and Leslie Dashew, I learned a great deal. More recently, I was part of Relative Solutions, and Fredda Herz Brown, Sam Davis, and Fran Lotery added to my capability and knowledge. For nearly 30 years, I have been a professor at Saybrook University, which has provided me with professional support and a scholarly community that allows me the freedom to grow and develop across several fields.

Other close colleagues have been friends, critics, and guides as I worked and learned. They include James Grubman, Laurent Roux, Linda Mack, Kirby Rosplock, Tom Livergood of the Family Wealth Alliance, Norm Boone, Joanie Bronfman, Jim Hutcheson, Carmen Bianchi, Steve Goldbart and Joan DiFuria of Money, Meaning and Choices, Jack Moore of the National Association of Corporate Directors, Mike McGrann and Tim Habbershon of Telos Consulting, Keith Whitaker, Glenn Ayres, Kristin Armstrong, Ricky Mercado, Kurt Rauzi, and the group of families, advisers, and professionals who brought me to South Australia as Thinker in Residence to work with them in 2007.

The Family Firm Institute has been my home base for learning since it began, and I have attended its conferences, read its journal, and maintained a network of colleagues who have helped me learn and grow. An emerging organization, the Collaboration for Family Flourishing, has begun to help me expand my work from that in which the family business is at the center to that which focuses on the multigenerational family. The seminal work and personal and professional support of Jay Hughes, and of colleagues like John Warnick, Peter Evans, Michael and Bonny Hartley, Bill Messenger, Katie Kinsey, Patricia Angus, Hartley Goldstone, Tom Rogerson, Bente Strong, Lee Hausner, and Barbara Hauser, to name a few, have enriched my work immeasurably.

A book is more than a piece of writing. It is the work of wonderful craftspeople who shape it and make it shine. I would like to thank two people who have made incredible contributions to what you are about to read. George-Thérèse Dickenson took the rough manuscript and worked through my clumsy phrasing and confusing phrasings, and made them clear and elegant. I thank her for a wonderful edit and the integration of all the disparate selections. And when she was done, Alden Bevington, of Pioneer Imprints, was on hand to design the book—its type, its look, and its cover, and to place the words into a package that reflects the tone and message. Thank you, Alden, for making this book a reality.

And finally, I would like to thank the other inhabitants of my household, my wife Cynthia and my son Colton, for putting up with me when I was working on this book over the years.

 **Part One**

The Delicate and Complex Nature of Family Enterprise and Family Wealth

My first task is to set the stage for what is to come by articulating the nature of the complex entity that is the family enterprise. The best way to understand the intricacy of the family enterprise is to recognize that at its core is an extended family, developing across two or more generations; I call this an **enterprising family.** The history of the family enterprise—from the initial generation of wealth creators to siblings who marry and create their own families to a third generation of family branches dispersing and adopting different styles, values, and perspectives—is that of an extended family, or as those of us in this field sometimes say, a clan. Although the family enterprise engages in serious business and financial activities, the major relationships are first, and primarily, those of several generations of family members. A *family enterprise* is a *business* facing the challenge of succession, but as well as being business owners, managers, staff, and the like, the key players are *family members*, so family relationships, roles, and generations must be taken into account when examining the enterprise.

The drama of family history and emotional dynamics is played out on the stage of the family enterprise, which may comprise shared assets and large fortunes as well as one or more businesses or financial entities. Although the family's closeness and connection give them clear advantages as business partners, they can also be liabilities. Within view of other immediate family members, family branches, and the community, the family members must, for example, gracefully accomplish the transition from one generation to the next in the business as well as in the family while at the same time dealing with the death of the patriarch. Although discussing the situation openly prior to death would clearly aid in the transition following a death, family members in the next generation find it difficult and awkward. They worry that they will be viewed as greedy. Is it any wonder that they hesitate to discuss such issues with their father or family?

Enterprising family transitions are never straightforward. Business and generational transitions often involve loss and are complicated by the unique characteristics of the family enterprise (the complex transitions, the semipermeable boundaries, and the like). The family members have to contend with back steps and side steps as they try to face the necessity of change in areas in which their various financial and business assets intersect. However it is possible for the family enterprise to anticipate—and therefore to prepare for—these twists and turns because they are inevitable for all families. If family dynamics are dealt with sensitively, intelligently, and transparently, the fact that they affect both the family relationships and the business relationships can be an added benefit to the family enterprise. Learning to deal more effectively with the family not only helps its members strengthen their relationships, but it helps them move forward with the *business* of the family, in ways that also preserve the *family* connection.

The family enterprises serve multiple purposes for the family. First and foremost, they generate wealth for its current and future generations. This wealth gives the family members choices and options that are not available to less-affluent families. As we will see in the following selections, a family's wealth is more than just its money. Family wealth also has to do with the way the family opens doors to opportunity, reputation in the community, and creative pursuits. The challenge for a family who has created wealth is to decide what purpose the wealth will serve. This decision is not made by one person, or all at once, but rather is a set of intentions and actions that involve all family members' learning, sharing, and deciding together over many years. This section introduces dramas experienced almost universally by multigenerational families of wealth and defines the basic concepts that are the building blocks of sustained family success.

1.1

From Founder to Successor: Lessons from Nineteenth-Century Wealth Creators

The great fortunes of the nineteenth century were often dissipated in the transition to the second and third generations. Yet more than a century later, some of these families are still known for their family wealth. This selection presents some of the best practices that can be gleaned from the experience of this earlier cohort of wealthy families. These practices from the past have been adopted by some of today's enterprising families who want to duplicate the achievements of these special families from past centuries.

The United States is facing a generational crossroads as trillions of dollars in new wealth generated at the end of the century is being passed down to the next generation. The elders (and not-so-elders) who created this "new" wealth are beginning to confront the question of legacy: What will the impact of all this wealth be on society and on the families of those who initially generated it?

Enterprising families can learn something from looking at the business patriarchs of the previous century and at the hundred-year impact of some of the great fortunes from the nineteenth century. That era produced some great fortunes that accumulated very quickly. The new industrial wealth was seen very differently from the "old" wealth of the landed families of the time. As today, some of the business titans and their families wanted nothing more than to be accepted in polite society. Their heirs were known more for their parties and houses than for their accomplishments.

Some families pursued different paths; they focused on re-creating their family legacy in each generation. The outcome can be seen in a continual compounding of their net worth—even as the number of family members increases geometrically—as well as in the creative pursuits of the members of succeeding generations, in society, the arts, and politics. The successful families built their foundations for the future in three areas: developing next-generation leadership for their legacy business, creating a family philanthropic mission, and developing positive values and processes for family-member development and participation.

Creating next-generation leadership in the legacy business is the greatest challenge facing a family. Families fail to successfully meet this challenge when they treat running their business as a prize to be won by the most assertive child. In each generation, a business faces new hurdles, and the family must develop its leadership talent. One exemplar of a patriarch who effectively developed leadership is Judge Thomas Mellon, patriarch of the family who owed several public corporations and banks. Judge Thomas was a tough businessman but a dedicated and thoughtful parent to his five sons. As shown in his autobiography, he made time to respond to each son and early on assigned each an area of responsibility and a limited degree of autonomy in that area. His sons were all successful in cooperatively developing the family's assets, and included Andrew Mellon, who became one of the most acclaimed U.S. secretaries of the treasury. Judge Thomas was willing to let go and cede control to his sons when they were ready. In contrast, Henry Ford's mentorship of his seemingly competent and dedicated son, Edsel—which consisted of demeaning him and second-guessing him—some say, led to Edsel's early demise. Despite this unfortunate episode, when Henry's grandson Henry II took over and enlisted the help of a professional brain trust known as the whiz kids, the company not only recovered but grew and thrived under his third-generation leadership.

Rupert Murdoch is an example of one of this century's very tough and controlling entrepreneurs who takes time to mentor his two sons. He has assigned his sons positions of increasing visibility and responsibility in his empire. We also see quiet successions this century, like that of Brian L. Roberts, son of Ralph J., co-founder of Comcast Corporation and its CEO for 46 years. Brian worked with his father for many years and is now the company's chairman and CEO. While most entrepreneurs have big egos and personas, it seems that the key to their success is having patience with and respect for the potential successor, as well as clearly exhibiting interest in him or her, rather than seeing him as a competitor or threat.

With the vast fortunes have amassed and perhaps some guilt or misgivings about their immense size or how they came to be, some families feel pressured to develop a social or philanthropic mission to guide them. After making a fortune, a family often finds it hard to feel motivated or empowered by making still more. The heirs of some entrepreneurial giants have guided the family into this terrain. The most famous and successful shift occurred in the Rockefeller family. The devout and eccentric John D. Rockefeller (JDR) was widely derided during his life for his business practices. His son, known forever as Junior, took the less visible role of stewarding the family into diversified investments and philanthropy. By creatively drawing on the trust and tax law to shelter the family from inheritance taxes, he created enormous family trusts for successor generations while also developing a vast network of social and philanthropic ventures.

Junior is the model for a second-generation heir who does not follow the father into the family business, but rather diversifies and creates a broader family mission. He created the family office, which not only managed the family's investments and trusts, but also offered a springboard for each of his five sons to develop their own set of interests, including running a bank, developing one of the first venture capital firms, and becoming vice president of the United States. By setting up private foundations, focusing on clear goals, and recruiting talented players, he fostered social innovation in a broad set of areas: science, the arts, the environment, and education. In fact, his example shifted the family's image from "robber barons" to social stewards. Family members were not pushed to go into any particular business but rather were encouraged to use their wealth to make a difference in society. His leadership was less flamboyant and visible than that of his father. He carried on the family legacy by redefining its vision and spending most of his career implementing it. He was a steward for the third generation, who followed him with their own larger-than-life successes.

Today, the closest example of this evolution can be seen in the emerging career path of Bill Gates. Though his children are young, he has begun to shift his family's fortunes from his base in Microsoft Corp. to stewardship of family philanthropy and service. Interestingly, while he is one of the most successful entrepreneurs in history, he can also be viewed as the heir to a successful and wealthy family with a tradition of social service. His father, a corporate lawyer, has been a key adviser in developing his foundation, taking on some aspects of the role Junior played for the Rockefellers. Other business leaders of recent times—Gordon Moore, David Packard, and William Hewlett of Silicon Valley, for example—have seen their heirs and fortunes move toward philanthropy.

The example of the nineteenth century is that the health and "soul" of a family is sustained when it attends to both its financial and its social mission over generations. Sociologist Paul Schervish, who has studied the life paths of families of great wealth, finds it natural for an enterprising family to move into a range of areas including politics, the arts, and social service. The challenge for a growing family of wealth is to create a mission, a set of family values, and support for not just a few leaders to emerge but each family member to find his or her own vocation in life, which builds on the opportunities offered by the privilege attendant to being a member of such a family.

Finding a binding reason for remaining together as a family is another key task for a multigenerational enterprising family. The family founder is often larger than life, living in a grand mansion that can become a source of folklore and a reason for staying together. But each generation of a family must find a new reason for unity or the family's fortune will simply be cut into pieces and spread among the heirs. To remain integrated, each generation must answer the question, Why are we together as a family? Many families find a reason for staying together in their family traditions, religious beliefs, and values having to do with service and community.

One tradition that seems key is the family gathering. While the rationale for an annual gathering may be social, families who have remained together find that other activities can be part of their get-together. They can share financial information and the state of the family's various ventures. They can educate each other. They can share activities and successes of family members. In effect, the family as it grows becomes a much like a village or community that comes together periodically to cement the bonds of its citizens.

A recent book by Adam Bellow, *In Praise of Nepotism,* details the positive ways that families pass on their skills in many fields and specifies how some families become very clear about grooming heirs to take on important roles. While there is a continuing debate in the United States about whether this is fair, Bellow suggests that the desire of parents to see their children succeed is so much a foundation of society that we cannot imagine a world in which successful parents do not want to promote success in their children. Bellow suggests that when nepotism is accompanied by accomplishment and competence, when it is used to open doors but not necessarily to guarantee success, it in fact serves a positive social purpose.

Amassing a fortune often takes place relatively quickly. The challenge for a family today is to take that fortunate event and make sure that the next-generation leaders pay attention to the family's wealth, stewarding it across generations and learning how to turn their good fortune into a family tradition that nurtures each generation and develops a positive vision for the family that goes beyond its legacy business.

1.2

True Wealth:
The Stewardship of Family Capital

This selection defines the multiple types of wealth that can be developed within a family. It shows that family wealth is much more than just financial. It also offers an outline of the key areas a family can explore when trying to answer the question, What is our family wealth? This selection previews the six dimensions of family wealth that are explored in this book.

Affluent families today find themselves confronting some new—and very unexpected—challenges. They are concerned about the ultimate fate of their fortunes and the future of their family. What effect will an inheritance have on their children, and how will their family and the things that they care about fare in the hands of the next generation?

In the broadest sense, estate planning involves helping families pass on their wealth so that the next generation uses it wisely and well. Passing a pile of money on to heirs is not a complete solution, as we see from the predominantly sad stories of lottery winners. Heirs must be prepared to receive their wealth and learn to use it according to the values of the family. They must inherit not only financial wealth, but also many capabilities, connections, and resources to help them achieve the highest and best purposes of their financial inheritances.

While the term *wealth* commonly refers to money, there are in fact other types of wealth that can be inherited. One can inherit social position, intelligence, qualities of character, a family network of friends and associates, and access to resources. I have defined six potential sources of value, or what I call capitals, that can be transmitted to future generations. A family who explicitly focuses on developing all these types of capital has positioned itself to sustain, and develop **True Wealth.**

The figure on the following page summarizes the elements of each of these types of capital, and how it is manifest within a family.

Capital	Definition	Expressed as
Spiritual	The mission, values, core purpose, and shared meaning that together are the foundation of the family and inform its approach to wealth and its members' relationships to each other	• Understanding the deeper meaning and purpose of wealth in the lives of family members • Family mission & values statement • Telling the family story to the next generation • Talking together about values and what is really important
Financial	Resources to reinvest and support a comfortable lifestyle, and ability to manage and sustain investments productively	• Creating clear and realistic expectations among the heirs • Teaching all heirs values and responsibility about managing wealth • Generating a sense of responsibility and capability to support the long-term strategy
Human	Developing in each heir the character, skills, and identity necessary to understand how to manage wealth, find important work, and live in a complex, difficult, and demanding global environment	• Initiating age-appropriate discussions about money with each heir • Building self-esteem and identity independent of having money • Helping heirs develop a sense of purpose for their lives • Ensuring the heirs develop skills and ability needed to make one's way independently
Family	The ability to stay connected within the extended family, to compromise and work together, and to create caring, positive, and productive relationships	• Generating respect and trust by regular communication • Healing past misunderstandings and hurts • Developing the ability to listen and learn from each other
Structural	Structures to manage the family wealth, to make decisions, to get competent advice, to manage family businesses or investments, and to steer the assets in a volatile environment	• A written family constitution • Regular meetings of family councils, assemblies, and boards • Accountability and clear communication to beneficiaries
Societal	Commitment and a sense of respect, compassion for and connection to the suffering and concerns of others; providing service within one's community and using resources to support the future of the planet	• Manifesting the family's values in the community through action • Involving all family members in service and philanthropy

The Six Dimensions of Wealth

- ## Spiritual Capital

Defining and keeping in touch with the deepest values that express the nature of the family. Coming to terms with the deepest and most important questions in life. Creating congruence between family wealth and inner values.

Spiritual capital is put in place when a family

- Understands the deeper meaning and purpose of wealth in their lives
- Has a mission and values statement
- Tells the family story to the next generation
- Talks together about values and what is really important

It seems strange to use the words *spiritual* and *capital* in one phrase. What are they doing together? Spiritual capital—the values and principles that the family stands for—is the basis of and informs all the other forms of capital. Spiritual capital is how the family defines and lives its values and core purpose, and weaves together all its activities to create a sense of meaning for individuals and the family. Spiritual capital is put in place when a family looks beyond its wealth, asking what it means for them and how they want to use it. It represents translating the family's success so that it fits their original dreams, informing their success and that of future generations with the family values, and recognizing the potential value that pursuing one's dream has to each generation.

The meaning of your family wealth

The overriding "spiritual" question for a family is, Why are we passing on our wealth to our heirs? What do they want their resources to do for their children and heirs? A core concern is finding the balance between using resources for **consumption** and **stewardship** of the wealth so that the wealth can continue to grow and be passed on to future generations. Some heirs regard their inheritance as a *legacy* that they must pass on to the next generation, others as a *gift* of fortune, and others as what they are *entitled* to. These are value questions that the family should guide an heir to answer, not leave to chance.

Defining the family mission

The family mission is the philosophy of the family, what it stands for, why, and how it carries out its basic operations. It sets standards, expectations, and boundaries. When a family has shared its story, it can crystallize the core idea and values into a mission statement. This can be a paragraph or a longer statement. It defines what the family stands for, what their wealth and business is for in a deep sense. What is the family's purpose and how do they express it? It may include the reasons behind that purpose and perhaps even parts of the founder's story. It is a living document that can be amended and added to by each generation as long as any changes to it are crafted thoughtfully and with consideration for the generations that have come before. It should be a source of pride that offers direction to each heir as he or she grows up and not just an empty statement on the wall.

Telling the story of the family spirit

The founders of a family often have a dream and a set of guiding principles. If the founders carefully set them down, these principles can form the foundation for sharing the family wealth through several generations. Using video for example, the family founders can present their dreams, values, and ideals, and preserve them for the future. The family history gives life to each generation's values and aspirations, defining the unique way they will pursue the family legacy. If a family has overcome adversity or struggled, its current fortune can be accompanied by the memory of their dedication to something more. By telling the story to each generation in turn, and adding to it, the family will sustain the memory and honor the commitments of the past.

Deep sharing about things that matter

In the end, values and purpose are communicated by action, not words. As a living guide to action, telling the story is not enough. A family has to have a tradition of shared activities that express their values and times that family members can learn about them from each other. Family gatherings are fun and important, and successful enterprising families who pass on wealth have regular conversations about what family members are doing that matters and how individuals are acting on their shared values.

- **Financial Capital**

Sustaining and stewarding resources to reinvest and support a comfortable lifestyle; the ability to manage and sustain investments productively.

What the family must do to sustain its financial capital:

- Create clear and realistic expectations among the heirs
- Teach all heirs values and responsibility about managing wealth
- Generate a sense of responsibility and capability to support a long-term strategy

A wealthy family can pass on to its heirs a substantial financial foundation for a good life. Along with the financial resources comes the responsibility to manage them capably and sustain them for the future, as well as a financial strategy and structure for investments. An heir does not just get a bunch of money. Along with funds, he or she gets a mechanism for investing them, values and expectations about what to do with them, and resources and support structures to help manage them. These must be communicated and taught, not simply buried in financial reports.

Clear and realistic expectations

Families have begun to ask the question, How much do we want to pass down to our heirs? Some very wealthy people have decided that they want to pass on to their children enough so they will be comfortable and able to do what they want in their lives, with the bulk of their fortunes going to serve some other purpose. Others pass on wealth with no strings or with expectations that are far from clear.

Responsibility, financial literacy, and stewardship

A generation ago, there was a paternalistic approach to inheritance. Trustees and advisers were expected to take care of the next generation and their wealth. This created a sense of dependency in the heirs. Heirs today must be prepared to manage wealth not by being given parental figures and unbreakable trusts, but by being taught how to handle investments and make decisions and by being schooled in the responsible use of them. They must learn basic financial oversight and management, so they can exercise knowledgeable and prudent oversight of their investments. If you inherit money, but do not inherit the capability to understand what you have and the sense to use the advice of professionals, the risk of losing it is high.

• Human Capital

Developing the skills, capability, and character of each heir to understand how to manage wealth, to find important work, and to live in a complex, difficult, and demanding global environment.

A family develops human capital when they

- Initiate age-appropriate discussions about money with heirs
- Build self-esteem and identity independent of having money
- Help heirs develop a sense of purpose for their lives
- Help heirs acquire the skills and the capability to make their way independently

Human capital is the development of responsible people, whose values, skills, and motivation enable them to use inheritance wisely and productively.

This form of capital cannot arrive in a lump sum, but is developed over many years, starting early. If you start late, you will build on a faulty foundation that can cause the whole edifice to collapse. It takes much more than good intentions to develop human capital; it takes a great deal of investment and time.

Conversations about money

Developing human capital begins around the house, in the early years. To develop human capital, a family must deal with money and its meaning at every stage in raising children. Children learn about money and about the family's status through a lot of small messages not only from family, but also from friends, school, guests, and the community.

The family must review how money is viewed in the home:

- Is it a source of nurturing, a substitute for being together?
- Is it given out of guilt when parents are not fulfilling their roles?
- Is it a sign of how important a person is?
- Is it connected with service to the family, as in doing chores and fulfilling one's responsibility to the family?

Wealth and identity

Inheriting money has a curse, the dark side; it can disable people, isolating them, causing shame about what they have or arrogance or a sense of unworthiness. The discovery of personal identity in heirs has been compared to a journey during which an individual must go out into the world and find out who he or she is alone, away from family and the family name. The major challenge in development of heirs is to balance a sense of responsibility with their sense of entitlement.

Personal development

A family should have a set of expectations about education and development and should clearly define their expectations of young, growing family members. What levels of achievement are expected of the young? What skills and knowledge should be developed? Young people need to know what is expected of them and to receive guidance and sometimes "tough love" to direct them. As a young person grows, offering unconditional love and support is not the way to develop the individual's self-esteem. A person has to demonstrate his or her capability and meet specific established standards. Self-esteem is not about being loved; it is about feeling that one can do something important and worthwhile and demonstrating that to others.

Money and work

Human capital is expressed by your heirs when they become mature, responsible, satisfied, and productive adults. Young people of wealth have difficulty developing a firm sense of who they are: Are they more than their money? What can they do to be productive if they do not have to work? They need help learning that to feel significant, people have to do something that matters, and that the selection of a vocation is not just about making money. The young heir has to find a way to do something important.

• Family Capital

The ability to stay connected within the extended family, to compromise, to work together with family and others, and to create positive and productive relationships with others.

A family develops family capital when

- It generates respect and trust by regular communication
- It heals past misunderstandings and hurts
- People are able to listen and learn from each other

One's wealth is deeply connected with one's family. The family has a web of relationships with each other and a place in society. If your parents went to a prestigious school, you will have less trouble than most people getting admitted. You inherit the family name, reputation, connections, and status. These create an incentive for wealthy families to remain connected, but they can also add challenges—in the form of past feelings, continued dependency, and difficulties in personal development—that the family must work actively to overcome.

The keys to building a reservoir of family capital are quite simple: Families must know how to express respect and affection for individuals, and they must have mechanisms for resolving conflicts so they do not fester or poison the family's shared interests. Siblings want parental approval and attention. These feelings never go away, nor do the major and minor hurts of divorce, deep disappointment, or bad judgment. Family capital is the ability of the family members to build the inner strength that enables them to overcome hurts and disappointments and to advance beyond the emotional underbrush of their upbringing so they can act reasonably together as adults.

Building positive communication

The ability to communicate is a critical step. Family capital swells with family members' ability to talk with each other directly rather than through others when there is a problem. Avoiding the conflict and the person with whom you had a disagreement and holding on to the feeling of hurt, resentment, or disappointment may feel better in the short term, but it can have disastrous effects on the family, the business, and of course, the two people with whom the argument originated. Being able to let go of painful hurts is necessary as well. A family must have a place and time to talk things through. When children are at home, the dinner table or evening can be a time to talk about what is on people's minds. As families grow up they must make time to talk, especially if they share a business or investments. Family capital is strengthened when a family has regular family communication and regular **family meetings**. Forming a **family council,** in addition to the more-formal **family boards** and financial structures, can be a first step toward developing clear policies and practices.

A family, like any significant entity, has to create a mechanism to address and resolve conflicts. This begins with a commitment to coming together and sharing differences. The family must master the ability to resolve conflicts without escalating them. Disputes about money, salary, ownership, and investments are often connected to family issues and past family history. In order to move ahead and sustain wealth, a family must master the ability to compromise, to see that win–lose dynamics are not really appropriate in a family. If one person loses, everyone loses.

Reconnecting as adults

As families grow, the patterns of being together can be sustained. A family should have regular shared activities so that they can continue to know each other and have fun together. These shared experiences form a foundation of connection that is needed when there are tragedies, tensions, or deep hurts that need to be addressed. A multigenerational family is like a community; relatives may not know each other at all, but at their best, they share a common core of values, heritage, and ways of being together that allows them to overcome disputes and make shared decisions that respect each set of interests and concerns. Large families maintain their connection through various forms of family reunion.

• Structural Capital

Governance structures to manage the family wealth, to make decisions, to get competent advice, to manage family businesses or investments, and to steer the assets in a volatile environment.

A family develops structural capital when it has

- A written family constitution
- Regular meetings of family councils, assemblies, and boards
- Accountability and clear communication to beneficiaries

Over time, more and more people enter a family. From a nuclear family, children grow up, marry, and have their own children. As members increase, the need for governance structures to manage decisions and administration of wealth grows. There should be a clear mechanism for making decisions and implementing them. The governance and management of a family's shared assets, investments, and philanthropic endeavors are both personal and financial tasks. As a family of siblings moves to the third generation of cousins, they cannot work as a single group, and they do not know each other as well, so it's more likely that conflict will arise. Governance structures make these relationships clear and diminish the likelihood of dissension.

The family constitution

Governance structures create clear paths for family members to participate in wealth management. At the center of them lies a formal family constitution that sets up agreed upon procedures for how the family participates in governing its wealth. Many families have given the benefits of wealth but rather than allowing beneficiaries to participate in its management establish provisions for trusts and trustees to "take care of things."

Written agreements about governance can help family members know where they stand and how to take action. They clarify the following issues for heirs:

- How the family uses and allocates its resources
- Family priorities, resources, and strengths
- Expectations and responsibilities of family members
- Basic ground rules for family participation and income
- How a person gets involved in the management of assets or family business
- How one advances in the business or family office
- How family members are paid in the business
- Guidelines for ownership, succession, and inheritance

Family councils and boards

A structure is more than a written agreement. A family can have trusts, wills, and other documents but still not function as an organization. There must be explicit family gatherings, with clear rules, in which family members can talk about issues and concerns; resolve conflicts, which always arise; and make decisions. There are **three key structures** that a family can put in place as the number of people and the amount of shared wealth grow, and each one has a different purpose.

- A **family council** is a formal or informal gathering of family members that meets regularly to deal with issues of the family. It makes decisions either by consensus or in an advisory fashion. The council is a place to talk about concerns, to be heard, and to air issues.

- The **shareholder gathering** is a regular meeting of the family owners, similar to a corporate annual meeting. As a group, they create a Shareholders Agreement, which communicates to the board the needs, concerns, and values of the shareholders.

- The more-formal structure is the **family governing board/s,** which govern/s the family's investment or investments. The board is made up of family members and a specific set of representatives that act for the family members they represent.

These structures exist in name only in many families. After being carefully crafted, they are often hung on a wall, never to be looked at again. For them to really work, they must be reviewed often and their steps followed; there must be continual communication within the family; and each family owner should have access to complete information about each of the structures. While family owners can receive clear communication, they have responsibilities as well. They must keep the information confidential, and they must understand that their participation has limits.

• Societal Capital

Maintaining one's wealth with a sense of respect, compassion, and connection to the suffering and concerns of others, taking a place of service within one's community, and using resources to support the future of the planet.

Families create societal capital when they

- Express their values in the community through action
- Involve all family members in service and philanthropy

Every wealthy family is visible in the community. Their societal capital relates to how they use their standing, and the influence that goes with it, to make a difference. They are citizens, and they stand for something. What does the community see when they think of your family? That is your societal capital.

Citizenship and community leadership

Wealthy families and individuals are part of a wider community, and how they express that involvement is an important aspect of what their wealth means. The basic fact about wealth is that the family has more than enough, and the community knows this. The choice a wealthy family must make is how to give back. In generations that inherit wealth, very often personal identity and work are expressed through community service rather than commerce. Community service through the family's philanthropy is one way members of inheriting generations can make their mark on the world.

Family philanthropy

While individual members of a family may make their own decisions about giving, wealthy families often organize a family foundation through which they visibly serve the community. The various forms of a family foundation are not just vehicles to give money but means by which heirs can be involved in how their money is used and can help the groups and services that they care about. It is also a way to express the family's leadership in the community. A family can have means by which they give large amounts to the community, but there is also a need for individual family members to express their own values. Effective social capital is expressed in both individual choices and collective family choices.

The example of service

Service is more than giving money. Often visible time and leadership in a community group or service means more than giving money. When family members work in community groups, they show their commitment and their capability. Many heirs can be found in public service through elected office—from local school boards to the Senate. When children are growing up, it is easier to teach them about service by giving them an example of helping than by giving money. When a family begins to practice service together, they show that this activity is as valued as making or managing money and that pleasure can be derived from service as well as consumption. It also offers an example that service can involve real work and can be a valued way to contribute to the community. Many heirs choose to dedicate their work to service as a way to make the most important contribution that a family can make to the community.

Developing Family Capital Through Family Conversations

I have presented a model of six types of wealth that a family must develop if it is to preserve its assets and thrive through generations. Families that find ways to develop human, financial, family, structural, societal, and spiritual capital will find that they have created a foundation for their wealth to grow, provide satisfaction, and do good over the generations. It will create a fabric for the family to get together, hold to its ideals, and take action.

Developing the six types of capital in your family and heirs is not an overnight process. It takes careful intention and many years of work. It begins with awareness—noticing how many elements there are and then holding conversations about how they apply to your family. There are several things you can do to begin to develop more types of capital in your family. Consider these issues from your own perspective. Then, one by one, involve other people.

Keys to Success: How to Develop Family Wealth

- **Ask yourself.** Look at the various types of capital and given your current life stage and place in the family, define some personal steps you can take to increase your own personal "capital." List the areas in which your family might increase the family wealth.
- **Talk to an adviser.** It is helpful to talk to someone you trust who has some distance from the family and some expertise in these areas. Seek out an adviser and talk about your various tasks, challenges, and options. You can find out how other families manage these and what other options and choices might be available to you.
- **Talk to other family members to air and clear up issues.** In every family there are areas of misunderstanding, even difference, and confusion about wealth and inheritance. You can seek out other family members and ask them questions and share your concerns to create an optimal relationship for the future.
- **Hold a family meeting to increase family communication.** Any family member can call the family together for a discussion. You don't have to be the patriarch or the matriarch. By airing issues in your family and initiating a discussion, you are acting as a family leader and beginning a process that in itself creates family capital. You might look at some of the areas about which you feel there are differences and create an environment in which family members can share their differences without feeling pressured to force an agreement.
- **Define the family mission, values, and constitution.** If your family chooses, it can go on to explicitly define what it wants across the generations. It can create its own family mission statement and constitution. This will take several meetings and a lot of work in between them.
- **Create an ongoing family council and family board.** Ultimately, a family can create governance structures that define regular paths for discussion of issues, making decisions, and carrying them out. This is a sustained, long-term, and often difficult process, involving many advisers and much patience and sensitivity, but its payoffs can last for generations.

1.3

The Family Dramas of Succession and Inheritance

The challenges of family enterprise have been the stuff of many dramas, real and fictional. This selection defines some of the predictable dramas that arise when a family is in business together or has considerable wealth. To avoid the tragedy that makes for a good play, families must create communication skills, family agreements, and structures that help them negotiate boundaries and resolve the deeper issues facing them. As every family business faces forces of globalization, growth, diversification, and competition, each family must also resolve its own dramas related to legacy, inheritance, succession, and family justice. Despite great cultural differences in family enterprises, certain major family dramas seem to be universal.

One of these archetypal family business dramas is the conflict between the confident and powerful patriarch and the sons and daughters who struggle to find a role and a place. This is often a source of negative emotional energy that casts a shadow over the business. Freud used the Oedipus myth, reinforced by many legends of royal sons ending their father's reign, to dramatize a violent model of family succession. In Freud's view, the bloody tale of sons plotting to overthrow their father, take up his authority, and split it among them was a developmental paradigm. In this paradigm, sons go through a stage of life in which the feelings behind such actions predominate. Some sons do not grow out of them and instead became stuck experiencing them over and over in later relationships. The theme of sons' jealousy and rivalry for power appears in the biblical tale of Cain and Abel, as well as in the story of Joseph and his brothers. The feminine side of mythology, on the other hand, provides scenarios of nurturing and fertility, collaboration and partnership, personified in the Earth Mother.

Family business offers a grand stage for mythic behavior. If not completely universal, certain mythological themes are common: A patriarch has built a kingdom with many subjects (employees), buildings, and visible achievements.

The royal trappings can be seen in vast corporate headquarters, grand board-rooms, corner offices, and even in the corporate name. Like a monarch, the family business leader is in absolute control of his kingdom, and he likes it that way. The sons and daughters know they will inherit the kingdom, but they are forced to wait, without power or authority, until succession occurs, often not until their father's death.

Business people strive to make decisions based on rational self-interest. But the emotional currents of a family, usually established when the children were very young, can lead to behavior, feelings, and choices at odds with good business practice. The family emotional reality can't be ignored or by-passed. The emotional center of a family enterprise must be addressed before it can deal with business realities.

Parents' Quest for Legacy

Family-business founders have two legacies they want to preserve: their family and their business. But these may be in conflict. In a recent talk, an Asian entrepreneur was asked about the balance between work and family. He made it clear that his family had to make sacrifices, and one of them was to cope with his absence. He was married to his business.

A business founder may want his children to follow in his footsteps, but most often under his terms—"the way I've always done it." A son or daughter must be a follower, not an innovator. A parent-founder may continually see problems in his child-successor. Henry Ford, for example, would not allow his son Edsel to take over his company and thwarted his efforts until Edsel's untimely death.

If the child is talented, the battle between parent and child can be intense. One bank founder recruited his very capable son from a larger bank, ostensibly to have him take over. After a dozen years, the son began to take initiative, but the father undermined and overruled him. The son finally decided he'd had enough and secured an attractive job elsewhere. Only then did the father realize the son was serious and begin to yield real power to him, but it was difficult for the father really to let go. In the end, the father started yet another business.

Despite these examples, fathers and mothers tend to have soft spots for their children. In many family companies, employment serves several nonbusi-ness purposes. It can be a way to give something to children who may not have received the personal attention and nurturing they needed earlier in life. A couple who have had to struggle for success can now ensure that their children never have to face poverty. But children who receive wealth without restraints often feel entitled to it and lack motivation to work or achieve a goal. Sheltered from responsibility, the heirs feel no sense of confidence that they can make their way in the world without the family job.

A child who is aimless, or having problems with drugs and alcohol, can be a prime recruit for a job in the family business. The business serves as a baby-sitter or a social welfare agency. In several enterprising families, a child like this, who has a title but no accountability, becomes a drain on the family and on company morale. If this person gets fired because the company encounters financial difficulties, is sold, or decides to bring in a professional manager, a seismic battle within the family often results.

Heirs' Search for Identity

Second-generation children often grow up revering "the founder," who seems larger than life. What can they ever do to measure up? One heir to a family fortune said his only desire was not to be the first in the family to make a mistake. In his view, there was nowhere to go but down. Often parents don't fully appreciate this struggle.

In the traditional pattern of personal development, children grow up and seek their own paths. But when a family business is in the equation, going one's own way is often taken as rejecting the family. One heir stated the dilemma this way: "Myself or my family; either way, I lose." But the patriarch often uses subtle bullying to entice a child to join him in the company. "How can you not come into the business?" the father asks. "Where could you possibly do better? Where could you rise more quickly?"

In some family firms, family and work appear to be in harmony, and places in the business are assigned to reflect family hierarchy. The Ferragamo family, designers and manufacturers of fine footwear, under the direction of the founder's widow, Wanda Ferragamo, placed each of the six children in a different division of the company. In other families, notably those in the Middle East and India, each heir is given the managing directorship of one business. The family manages a portfolio with places for each heir—some units large, some small and struggling. Of course in reality, only one or two of the businesses in the portfolio really make money. The rest merely preserve individual self-esteem.

A family business whose founder or co-founder is a woman often exhibits a more harmonious variation on the royal theme. The son of Estée Lauder, Leonard, found great success as the company's operations manager before becoming CEO. After Donald Graham served a long apprenticeship at *The Washington Post*, his mother, Katharine, gave him the reins. Both of these companies have since gone on to third-generation family leaders.

An heir can find his or her identity inside the family or outside. It is a crucial choice. If the whole family is turned inward—looking to the parents for power, acknowledgment, or significance—who is keeping an eye on the marketplace or the customers? Many families lose focus or effectiveness when they turn excessively inward. On the other hand, if the children prove themselves in another venture before joining the family business, they will acquire a sense of inner strength and will not obsess about being acknowledged by Dad or Mom.

The Need for Teamwork

The challenge for heirs does not just involve personal identity. Sons and daughters must forge a team to run the business. While all of them may not be in management, frequently they all inherit some part of the ownership, and they all may serve on the board. The siblings must learn to work together and overcome their family-based rivalry.

A patriarch can make it difficult for siblings to be a team. In many families, the heirs have a deep individual relationship with the patriarch but little or no business relationship with each other. In one family of seven children, the father died suddenly, and they found they had no history of working together or even seeing themselves as a team, because all their work had been conducted in intense relationships with their father. It took them several years to learn to compromise and coordinate their widely divergent experiences.

If the business has less space at the top than there are candidates to fill it, a struggle may ensue. Each family member feels that he or she is competing with the others. Some families feud openly, and some plot in secret, like royalty of the feudal era. Many founders do not clarify their plans for the future, setting their children up for conflict when the founder is no longer around. In one family, each son and son-in-law felt that the patriarch had told him that he would be the chosen one. Only when they compared notes years later did they discover something was awry. They have since been able to create a team among themselves, agreeing to run the growing business together until it is sold.

In one large business, the oldest son had been working diligently for the company. The "kid brother" had a more erratic history, but finally began working in the family firm. The parents made it clear that all the children would inherit the business. They also wanted the two sons to work together. The kid brother had the same dream, but oldest brother felt his years of service and hard work made him the leader. The parents had difficulty dealing with conflict, so when they passed on, the two were left to deal with the situation. Their challenges: Should there be one leader or co-leaders? Should one brother work for the other, or should the older brother buy out the younger? For the first time, they could not rely on Mom and Dad to regulate their relationship.

The Pursuit of Family Justice

Family feuds, which today tend to take the form of lawsuits, are always in the news. In one of the longest and most costly suits on record, the two sons of Johnson & Johnson heir J. Seward Johnson sued their father's third wife, who had inherited the bulk of his estate. What was at stake was not so much the cash but the feeling that the children had never really been loved or acknowledged by their father. The revelations were highly painful and personal. Why do such fights go on so long and so publicly? This is no mystery to those of us who understand that the parties' hurt is so strong that the only way they can feel validated is if the opposing family member loses. Heirs link the estate or the business to their own feelings of deserving it, being entitled to it, or having been wronged by the parents.

One son who had worked in the family business with his father and sister was outraged when the father picked his sister as the CEO. Though he had only a minor role in the business, he expected to be a full partner. When she took over, his sister's first act was to fire him. But he was a one-third owner of the business and member of the board. Negotiations began for the business to buy his share—which would make him very, very wealthy—but he spurned all offers because he didn't want to make his sister rich by selling his stock to the company at a discount. He had no funds of his own and lived in a small apartment, but his anger at his parents and his sister kept him from doing what was in everybody's interest. His real intention was keeping the family hostage, not getting free of them.

Families link inheritance to a sense of family justice, which unfortunately involves siblings'—and generations'—radically different perspectives. What seems fair to some is considered a betrayal by others. Because the feelings often come to a head on the parent's deathbed, the loss adds to the pain. Parents feel they can't do the right thing for everybody, so they often choose to ignore the conflict and let the next generation fight it out.

Other important factors involve recognition and favoritism. Eldest, second, and subsequent children arrive at different stages in the parents' lives and thus are treated differently. A slight or hurt may be magnified when there is an overall feeling that parents are not physically or emotionally available. One daughter said she took a job in the family business in order to finally have a relationship with her father. In another family, a son who worked in the business kept trying to please a father who had no idea that his approbation was an issue.

Given the power of such family dynamics, enterprising families must take great care to anticipate and respond to them with clear communication and compassion. What do families who are successful in resolving these issues do differently from those who are conflicted? They tend to find ways to talk about the concerns before they flare up. In different ways, each member of these families has learned to let go of hurt feelings. He or she has shifted the focus from receiving benefits from the family to meeting external challenges.

Keys to Success:
Moving Between Generations in Family Enterprise

Here are some strategies to keep family dramas from overwhelming your business:

- **Meet as a family.** Isolation tends to lead individual family members to work at cross-purposes. There are many questions that occur to children about the family as they grow up. What is our money for? What do you expect from me? What is the future of our business? What does the family stand for? Every family should come together at regular intervals, in a fairly formal manner, to discuss such issues. Every effort should be made to be inclusive and to talk about difficult issues. The purpose of these talks is not to make decisions but to learn about each person's desires, welfare, and future plans.

- **Have concrete discussions about the business between parents and children.** Relationships between parents and offspring cannot be only public and collective. Time must be allotted for one-on-one conversations, especially about legacy and individual expectations. These conversations are especially important between business owners and heirs who work in the business because they involve expectations and the future. I knew a father who was concerned about his son's attitude and work ethic. His son, age 23, had just graduated from college, and the father assumed that he was planning to take over the business. The son, however, thought he was just working there to take some time off to decide what he wanted to do with his life. The two spent hours together each day discussing current work situations and some family issues, but never discussed this tricky subject, thus neatly avoiding any sensitive areas.

- **Create family guidelines to channel expectations.** In a clearly written document, specify the senior generation's expectations and values—what they want their heirs to carry on. It can take several forms: a comprehensive document called a family constitution or a shorter mission statement, which includes the family's vision and values. It might include specific policies for family employment and sale of assets and compensation or just values statements. At any level of specificity, the guidelines create a stick in the ground that heirs can use to align their expectations.

26

Family dramas and psychic patterns cannot be ignored. However, they lose some of their bite when the family faces them directly and tries to act without being caught in their power. To preserve a family and business legacy, family members must find ways to share the positive power of working together without falling victim to emotional pitfalls.

Behind the business in every family enterprise, there are family dramas of legacy and succession. The family business provides a place where the next generation seeks identity, validation, or justice from their parents and siblings. The challenge for a family enterprise is to recognize this, and harness its positive elements, while minimizing the negative and self-destructive conflicts that can destroy it.

1.4

Stakeholders of the Family Enterprise

Understanding the family enterprise begins with examining the complex roles that family members may fulfill in various family ventures. In order to avoid difficulties in the enterprise and conflicts among family members, each family member must understand and clarify the specific role he or she has in the ownership and management of the family wealth. Many family disputes are caused by confusion about which responsibilities accompany an individual's role. This selection outlines the family and business roles that will be recognized and regulated in selections to follow.

As the family grows, persons who joined it through birth and marriage need to learn their roles and responsibilities in the business. Along with the family, the business grows, or the family diversifies into a large enterprise, comprising several companies, real estate, philanthropy, and community service. Within a generation, a family can become a complex matrix of businesses, professional and charitable ventures, and people, in which control, ownership, and benefits are dispersed among many individuals, often who have competing interests. Each person has his or her own idea of what the enterprise should do for him and what he thinks he can do for it. The family is surrounded by a veritable army of employees and advisers who want the best for the family, but must take into account their own personal concerns and desires. In this way the family enterprise resembles a state (and, in fact, some family businesses are as big as a state).

Each family member has a role and status as a family member. An individual may be son, daughter, cousin, brother, or in-law, each of which carries with it a history and expectations. Growing up in the household of the family who owns the business, a scion may come to expect certain benefits, such as income, support, and access to resources. The family role evolves and changes as the presumed heir grows up and forms his or her own family unit. While it may have been so when the individual was young, family membership no longer automatically guarantees a corresponding role in the family enterprise. Yet many family members believe that there is (or should be) a connection, and some make assumptions about what being a member of the family entitles a person to. Although generally the family members who think this way aren't aware of it, this connection is usually self-serving and is not always in line with legal or business realities.

The family enterprise (consisting of the legacy family business, as well as related shared family assets, such as real estate, investments, and philanthropic vehicles) is an arm of the family, but it cannot be run like the family. A family member can participate in each enterprise in a variety of roles—for instance, as employee, director, leader, or owner, among others. Each of these roles entails different rights and responsibilities. This is a difficult lesson for a family member. When a son talks to his father, it is hard for him to remember that he is also an owner talking to a director, or a manager talking to his boss. In a family enterprise, interaction is made more complex because people may have relationships that encompass several roles.

To help a complex family make sense of this, I would like to specify the most common roles in a family enterprise. In the leadership role are the **directors**. The people who manage the various entities are **managers**. **Beneficiaries** may or may not be **owners**. And finally, **advisers** are not family members but offer the family their expertise for a fee. A person in any of these roles may or may not be a family member. I will delineate each of these roles, suggesting that an individual within a family enterprise be clear about which role he or she is inhabiting when engaging with another. When a family member begins an exchange by saying, "I am speaking as a director of this business, not as your father," he can avoid a lot of conflict and confusion.

Family members grow up with different degrees of entitlement having to do with family assets. In different ways, and for different reasons, young people in a family believe that the family wealth is "theirs." They benefit from its resources, and in so doing, they tend to assume that they have some power to make decisions about family assets. They grow to expect this will last forever. But they must discover that although they benefit from the family's wealth, in fact, they have almost no rights to anything. If they also inherit ownership, they will be able to make some choices about their assets. But these will be limited by the existence of prior agreements and structures, like trusts, that regulate relationships, responsibilities, and decisions.

The difference between the status of beneficiary and that of owner has to do with the rights that a family member has to make decisions about her assets. A beneficiary may have ownership, but the responsibility, control, and oversight over the asset lie with another person. An owner has limited discretion. Owners have the right to sell their ownership, but within the limits of a Shareholder's

Agreement. Unfortunately in many families, these agreements are misunderstood or out of date. Family owners often do not know what is in these agreements or understand them, especially in relation to how an asset is to be valued when sold and whom it can be sold to.

A family owner (or beneficiary) has to understand that there are different degrees of "having" family wealth. One can get income from an asset and from the family wealth, but this does not necessarily entitle a family member to any power or control over what to do with the asset that provides the wealth, other than limited rights of ownership regarding sale. While many people are absolutely fine with having the benefits of wealth with no power or responsibility, others feel deeply disenfranchised by this, especially in relation to those who have more involvement and control because of their roles as managers and directors.

Some families create a very clear boundary on these matters—defining an elaborate process for entering the family business and moving into the role of manager. Several things confuse the occupancy of this role. First, there is confusion about its relation to ownership. There is no inherent formal relationship between working for a family enterprise and having ownership; a family member may work for a family business and not be an owner, and an owner may not work in the enterprise. A family manager must learn to be an employee, receiving a salary for his or her work, having her performance evaluated, and answering to a supervisor (not her father or other family members who may own the business). Because of the presence of the family, family business owners find that they have to make many aspects of employment clear to family members, so that the family member doesn't attribute additional perks, power, or status to her employment.

Who has the power over the business? This belongs to a board of directors, whose role is to oversee the asset, making sure its overall operation fits the intentions of the owners as a whole. The board sets the direction and hires the leadership. The family member who is the majority owner (or who holds the voting shares of the company) is a director. The board also often includes other key family owners, usually from the older generation. Some family enterprises have begun, like public companies, to appoint independent, nonowner directors, who offer a deep wisdom and experience. When the ownership is in a trust, the directors are the trustees, who may or may not be family members.

The director role has been likened by Jay Hughes to that of a tribal Council of Elders. In a large or diversified family enterprise, the directors must make decisions about its future. They look at the emerging leadership of the family and assess whether the new family leaders, usually in the role of managers, are ready to move into directorship. The directors cannot live forever, and hence they face the challenge of setting up an orderly process of succession. They must decide when a member of the next generation is ready to become a director.

Some of the complexity of family business has to do with issues that affect individuals who have more than one role. For example, how does a family manager or director act in situations in which she has additional self-interest? Many families face situations in which, say, a family member may want to act as an independent investor in a family venture or get a fee for services to the family. The directors must evaluate these situations and be transparent with all family members about their decisions as to whether this is appropriate for a family member and whether they will allow him or her to invest or receive a fee for services. Family members together make up a collective entity, the family enterprise, whose life transcends these individual roles. In order for the whole enterprise to operate smoothly, its parts must communicate freely and often, not only passing on information, but also exchanging ideas and feelings about what is being done in the business. In a family, these exchanges are often purely advisory, but there is a greater need for education and communication in a family enterprise than in other business enterprises.

There is one final role, that of the adviser. The adviser offers expert knowledge to various parts of the family enterprise and is often an individual who has a long-term and special relationship with a family leader. The issues family members need to keep in mind regarding the adviser role are two: It must be clear to whom the adviser gives advice—who is the client?—and the line between offering advice and taking responsibility for it must be respected and maintained; in an advisory position, the individual does not have to take responsibility for it. Many advisers get drawn into roles as managers and even directors. Often a family relies on an adviser to the extent that the adviser appears to be running the family enterprise. However, the efficacy of the adviser role can be diminished if a family member does not think that the adviser works for him or her or does not understand what the adviser is proposing.

Family members and others in a family enterprise are joined together in complex interlocking roles, and they need to be sensitive to their roles in the family. A family member must understand the limits of his role, and those with control and responsibility must understand whom they work for. When working with a family who owns an enterprise, I find that from time to time clarifying the family stakeholder group with whom I am meeting, and their role/s within the family enterprise, is helpful in framing our conversation.

Part Two

Effective Governance and Decisionmaking

Governance is a common term that is much misunderstood. At its core it is about who is responsible and who makes decisions; it is about power, opportunity, and accountability. For a family with wealth, the question of who has the power and who makes decisions is crucial. Very often, this is not talked about or even thought about. The family founder, usually the patriarch, has the power, and holds on to it until he passes it on to a successor. But that paternalistic model does not work for today's complex families. There is rarely a single person who can take on the complex tasks of leading a family in the second, third, and successive generations. The diverse activities and functions of the family demand many types of leaders. Also, the modern ethic of family, and that of business, involves less authoritarian rule and more collaboration. The journey to define family governance is one in which the family learns how to work together as a team, with each family member having a voice and an appropriate and clear role in the various elements of the family and its multiple enterprises.

The siblings and their spouses of a second generation form an extended family, but they usually have not learned to act as partners who own a large and challenging business. A family may have their estate plan and legal agreements in place, but they may not have really made clear to the second- and third-generation successors the way in which the family will operate as a business entity. To do this, they need to create a family and enterprise governance system, by undertaking the tasks outlined in this section. The legal agreements create rules and structures that may feel exceedingly rigid and controlling to the people in the family. While the rules were set up *for* the family, if they are not designed and understood *by* the family members, it will feel as if these rules and structures control the family, rather than support it.

Every individual in an enterprising family has multiple roles. As well as being owners and family members, some are also employees, with incomes dependent on the family business. This raises questions that governance agreements and activities help answer:

- Who should oversee the work and set the salaries of employees who are members of the family?
- Who will be on the board of the business, and how are they to be selected?
- How will the board work with the family owners?
- What are the expectations and rules about family employment?
- How will profits be split between reinvestment in the business and distribution to owners?
- How is future leadership determined, with several families and outside employees all involved?

These questions lie in the realm of governance. For a family of owners, who may or may not be involved in operating roles in various family enterprises, the work of governance is to define the principles, policies, and decision-making procedures of the family as a whole. Governance is important in the oversight of all businesses, but it has a special significance in family enterprises, because the key stakeholders are also family members, and therefore decisions must include consideration of the family, as well as the business, dimension. A rivalry between cousins, or brother and sister, may stem from the family history but be played out as, Who should be the business leader? Members of a family who have grown up together have to learn how to act as owners and business partners while at the same time learning how to manage their parallel lives as relatives.

Governance helps the family deal with this complexity on a structural level. It sets rules and defines structures for making decisions. Family enterprise governance includes the business and the family missions, legal agreements, authority and decision-making structures, and the rules and practices that regulate the activities of a complex enterprising family.

Of course every business legally must have a board of directors and articles of incorporation that specify who the members will be and how it operates. Too often, even though these structures exist in name, they are not realized in the operations of the enterprise. Often the articles aren't specific enough or don't deal with the most important issues. They address business issues but don't deal with the family tensions that will inevitably arise. Or they may define a board, but not say how the board is selected or what the rules are for representing different family constituencies.

The board of directors, or governing board, and articles of incorporation of a family venture have an important role, but there are additional aspects to family governance. First of all, the family must decide what they want their business ventures to do for them, that is, their **core purposes**. These have to do not with good business management, but with the guiding values, vision, and goals, or the mission, of the ventures for the family. The family must specify which family members are part of that process of defining the mission. Is it the older generation only or will some members of younger generations participate? When can the younger generation make changes to an agreement established by the older generation? These questions must be decided by the family ownership group, or family council as we will see later. If the family owners are the decision makers here, they may or may not listen to the views of other family members, such as young adults or spouses, who although not owners may be in the future.

As we will see, a family does not naturally learn how to get together and decide these things. Family governance usually includes a document, often called a **family constitution,** that makes explicit the mission of the family, its various business and financial ventures, and how the elements of the enterprise are governed. It specifies how the family gets together, what it does, and how decisions are made.

Family enterprise governance gets more complex and explicit as the family grows or as the number of business entities multiply and their size increases. A family with two generations and one operating business can have a simple structure. But as the third generation grows up, and the family diversifies into other areas, the family must evolve a set of rules to govern interaction. What can a family member expect, and how can he or she participate in the management and decisions about the family holdings? This is especially important when family members are no longer connected through the original business or are geographically dispersed. It is tempting for a family to think they can hire a lawyer or professional to draw up these agreements. But my view is that such generic agreements do not represent the real voice of the family. If the family does not participate in creating them, they will not be comfortable following them, or worse, some members may strongly disagree with them. I advocate having professional advisers work with the family to help them create family operating agreements that define family governance. The key outcome for the family is not the document itself, but rather their learning how to work together and develop the ability to harmonize divergent views.

While there is not a one-size-fits-all governance model for a family, a complex family typically will fare best with at least two major governing bodies: a family council, which represents and defines the desires and intention of the family, and a board of directors, which ensures prudent decisions are made for the benefit of the family owners.

One of the functions of governance is defining how each entity works, what its purpose is, and how the council relates to the board. Another aspect is specifying the roles, rights, and responsibilities of each family member in his or her roles as owner, family member, and employee.

The **family council** defines, organizes, and regulates the personal elements of the family. A family with several assets will likely have many activities to coordinate. They need to keep the family, with all its discordant voices, united in support of its various enterprises. As each new generation grows up and new people enter by marriage, the basic values, rules, and legacy must be revisited—to ensure that they are clearly stated and understood, as well as shared by the new members and if necessary, revised to accommodate the new members' views. And there must be a means by which family members can come together to learn about them and make the decisions that have to be made each year to keep the family moving forward. Regular meetings of a council are important because as the family grows, the pressures to split up and separate into individual family units become greater. The family governance structure may also include task forces and other subgroups charged with organizing certain family recreational and educational activities.

While each individual entity is important, the family has to see governance as the center of its work together. As the owners of a family enterprise, the individuals together are much *more*, and much more *complex*, than a family, which can be informal and freewheeling. Because of the many business ventures and the potential for conflict, the enterprising family must formally organize its governance. Without governance a family not only may face extreme conflicts as the generations shift, but also may lack the structures, and likely the ability, to resolve them.

This section of the book addresses the elements that make up family governance; it presents key structures and practices that successful families create to manage their wealth across generations and shows how they fit together. It examines ways in which the family defines its mission, the soul of governance. If the family has not agreed on what and why, it can't begin to consider how. The following selections also present the key elements of a family council and board of directors.

2.1

Strategic Planning for the Family and the Business

A diverse family with several generations cannot continue to operate as it did when it owned a single business run by its founder. As new generations emerge, and the business needs and climate begin to change, the enterprising family must plan for its future. The planning process does not involve only business and financial strategic planning; it must also take into account the needs and nature of the emerging family. This selection offers ways in which the enterprising family can begin to go about creating effective structures for putting their goals into action by creating a planning strategy that considers both family and business drivers. In addition, it presents and examines the primary components of this two-pronged strategy.

For a family business—often a family's most precious asset—surviving successfully into a second generation is highly problematic. I have identified a model of how the family can enhance the chances of survival by engaging in a two-dimensional planning process:

The **family** must determine its wishes for the future by defining its goals and values for the business, rules for family participation, plans for development of young family members, and policies for ownership transfer. By convening a **family council**, the family can make its wishes clear and explicit.

The **business** can develop an active **board of directors,** or governing board, that generates a strategic plan for the business future, linking the family shareholders' needs with the business challenges and realities.

To help ensure a healthy future for the business, the enterprising family might consider engaging a financial planner who can assist in both levels of planning.

Balancing the Concerns of the Family and Business

The most important "member" in a family's future may not be a person at all; rather it may be a small or large business entity, or several of them—that is, the family enterprise. It can take many forms, a restaurant, small manufacturer, or a large public company or family office that acts as a holding company for multiple ventures, among other possibilities. Whatever form it takes, the family's business looms large in planning for the enterprising family's future. In doing estate planning, the business owner may be concerned only with who will inherit the business and how it will be transferred. However, proper strategic planning for the future of a family business must include consideration of two dimensions: the family's desires and intentions for the business and financial planning for the business future within the context of the evolving economic climate.

Statistics gathered by the Family Firm Institute (www.ffi.org) suggest that a family firm has only a 1 in 3 chance of surviving into the second generation. Yet few business founders believe that their business will be the one to fail. They often don't see the ways in which family considerations can overwhelm business realities nor are they aware of their own lack of renewed focus on the business after intrusions of family dynamics. These are primary reasons so many family businesses fail, and they arise from a unique quality of the family business: People from different generations of the same family may share management and ownership in the business and, therefore, must work together. Not every family member inherits ownership, and not every family member works in the business. But those who do, or want to, often base their decisions on personal rather than business considerations.

Families and businesses often have different criteria for making decisions, and this can negatively affect the business. If a family member's qualifications aren't high on the priority list of an individual who is responsible for hiring, for instance, he or she may decide to employ someone simply because he is a family member, which can lead to an unqualified employee's having major responsibilities. No matter how carefully it is done, dividing income from a family business among successors also can lead to conflict. In a family, parents usually want to treat their offspring equally; a business usually pays according to the job level and the employee's performance. Is compensation for those siblings who work in the business based on family criteria (i.e., all paid equally) or on the work they do (i.e., various jobs valued at different rates, according to the market)?

Similarly, family authority is often defined by birth order, whereas in the enterprise a particular family member may have different seniority, capab and fit. Can a younger sister supervise her big brother? Can one sibling other? Furthermore, complications may arise because family members w owners are entitled to dividends as well as their salaries. Individuals find selves in value conflicts between demands of the business and the family. scenarios must be anticipated and planned for.

The key strategic planning challenge for the family business is negot the boundary between the world of the family and the world of business. family can make agreements covering these areas and the places in which intersect, and can understand and agree on why the agreements are neces the possibility of destructive conflict is diminished. To navigate these tric eas, the family can use the two overlapping, interrelated—but quite differ planning teams introduced above.

The first is a council of family members, whose task is to deal with th "business of the family," including developing a new generation of family members, regulating the family members' involvement in the business, and aligning the business with the family's plans.

But the family council alone cannot design the future of a strong family business. The planning process must also address business realities, helping the business develop and innovate along paths that are sometimes difficult for a family. This is achieved by convening a proactive business board of directors.

The **family council** expresses the will of the family. The **board of directors** represents the needs of the business. Different elements of planning are carried out by each of these groups.

All members of the council are also members of the family (frequently including in-laws, young adults, and family members with no connection to the business); the board contains the representatives of the family owners responsible for the oversight and development of the business. Some family members may be members of both groups, but each group has its own function.

The Work of the Family Council: Strategic Planning for the Enterprising-Family Future

Planning does not come naturally to a family. Family members spend a lot of time bumping up against each other and trying to find quick fixes, fast ways to restore family harmony. They develop such habits as avoiding issues, denying problems, and keeping secrets from each other. If an issue is controversial or upsetting, families often learn not to talk about it, or to talk with everyone except the person involved. Even members of relatively functional families often limit their communication with each other, which can impede the planning process.

siblings, perhaps spouses—must gather to craft answers to these questions, a process with which the family may not be familiar because the family members who own the business and the few members who work in the business tend to take care of the enterprise by themselves. In this case, a business adviser may have to convince the family that they need to convene as a council to discuss these issues.

The act of getting together may itself challenge the family's established communication and power structures. If a family is divided about which sibling should become the next CEO, for instance, or if certain family members don't want to talk about who is being paid what by the business, they will resist coming together to discuss the future. Some business owners will say, "This is my decision, and mine alone, so why should my children be involved?" Even if this decision is the sole province of the owners, given the potential for controversy, the family needs to discuss the plans for the future and hear and react to those formed by the founder.

The family council must plan to secure the future of the family enterprise in four areas:

- Mission and values
- Next-generation development plan
- Guidelines for family involvement
- Ownership and transfer policies

Mission and values

Planning is based on assumptions and predictions, and many family business owners make assumptions that may not be correct. For example, if a family has a thriving business, the owners assume that the next generation, their children, want it to continue and want to be partners in its ownership and management. But this may not always be the case; some family members may want other things. They may want to create their own businesses or pursue other careers, and they may want the family's money to support them as they move in these directions.

Before deciding the fate of the business, the family has to define their own future goals—each individual's and those of the family as a whole. Where does the business fit in? What does the business stand for? While, as we've discussed, the family must learn to approach such questions as a business, it's essential that they recognize these questions encompass more than just business considerations. The family must look at its own values—those about generating, spending, and saving wealth, and those having to do with how the family wants to be remembered in the community.

The family council can explore the values and intentions of the older generation and the talents and desires of the younger one, both for the short term (the present) and for the long term (the future). Conversations about values, money, and desires won't be as effective if the family does not take a broad and far-reaching view, looking at their life goals with an eye toward the future. This life planning prepares them to tackle the tough questions about the business and its future, because if the family members understand one another and agree on values for the business, the family has a framework for deciding how the business should run.

Next-generation development plan

When you ask an enterprising family what they want from their wealth, most often they state that they want their children to have good lives. They are concerned their children will not find a focus or will live only to spend the family's wealth. To begin to achieve the useful, worthwhile, and fulfilling lives their parents envision for them, young people in the family can each be asked to formulate a **personal development plan**. Creating this will not by itself bring the future into focus, but it will raise questions that will help the next generation begin to clarify their desires. By bringing into the mix information that may not have occurred to the individual family member, these questions can take the individual beyond the obvious choices. If the youth is having difficulty creating such a plan, he or she might consult a career coach or counselor.

Working in the family business often becomes the path the children just think they want or feel compelled to choose. Too often, entry into the family enterprise is an unconscious choice, which young adults make for the wrong reasons—such as obligation or because it is easy. Some members of the next generation simply do not think beyond the family business. They enter without outside work experience and soon feel (or actually become) unsuited for work anywhere else. They are trapped, and the business is trapped with them.

When planning for the future, the family should ask the heirs to think about what they want to do with their lives. The family business should be presented as a choice, one among many, that the heirs may select if it is appropriate. Each family member should have the challenge, and the opportunity, to develop his skills in any way he sees fit. The family should consider how it supports the job and career choices of family members and encourage them to think beyond the family business. Going into, or staying in, the family enterprise too often is like never leaving home.

It is not only the younger generation who need a development plan; but the elder, the business founder, also needs to look at his or her personal development, specifically in terms of what she wants to do with life outside, or apart from, the business. When the founder has a personal development plan, it is easier for her to make the tough decision to disengage from the business, and truly let go. Unless she finds someplace meaningful in which to put her energy, she will be back.

Guidelines for family involvement

Is the family for the business or the business for the family? The family must decide how to treat family members who want to work in the business. This includes setting rules for entry: What does a family member have to do to get a job? How is compensation determined? How is performance evaluated? What perks are available to family members? Do all employees get cars or credit cards, or just family employees? Do all family members get cars as gifts? What about a house? The family whose members want to give gifts to each other has to learn the difference between gift giving as a business matter and gift giving as a personal matter. If there are no guidelines or rules for such areas, conflict is inevitable.

The family council sets clear expectations for entry into the business, reinforcing that working there is not a right, or a form of family welfare, but a privilege for someone who is accountable to the family for results. This must be made clear to family members before they develop an unwarranted sense of entitlement.

As a family grows and its business develops, the family must make its attitude toward these matters more explicit. Most families develop rules that establish job qualifications and move toward paying market rates for employment. But in the business's early stages, when it really is an extension of family, individuals may get into the habit of using the business as a means of garnering perks. Once family members are accustomed to receiving extras—like season tickets—it is hard to stop this practice without those affected feeling it is "unfair."

A family who wants to grow its business across generations should develop a family charter or constitution that states the rules and expectations in these areas. Strategic planning includes a plan for how family involvement will unfold.

Ownership and transfer policies

As a family grows, family owners and other family members may need income from the business, and the business may need capital for development. It is important to establish guidelines for deciding whether the enterprise should retain earnings or increase family member distributions. Families have harmed the long-term development of a venture by having no process in place to deal with family members' sense of entitlement, especially when more and more family members felt entitled to a certain level of income.

Many family-business founders want nothing more than for their businesses to remain in the family. But they do not adequately consider such issues as the degree of ownership given to each member and the method for determining the inheritance, both of which are matters of some consequence to the heirs. Will they each inherit an equal share, or will the family members in management inherit more? What is the rationale for the difference? Who controls the business, and what are the rights of minority family owners? Will family members who inherit a smaller percentage of ownership receive any other assets? Can a family heir who has ownership sell his shares to another family member or to a nonfamily member? What is the procedure for doing this?

Each of these questions deeply affects the future of the business. One of the most important areas for planning is the priority assigned to each of these areas in terms of family management and ownership. While many families say they need to keep their options open, the family should consider whether they are more likely to stay together as an enterprising family or go their separate ways. They must ask about the financial needs of the next generation and how the business will provide for them. Many family businesses that provided a good income for one or two families cannot provide the same lifestyle for a half dozen.

The greatest challenge facing the family council is deciding whether to let go of control or ownership of the family's legacy business. At some time, a business will stop growing, and the family will have to ask itself whether it should diversify into other areas to provide greater opportunities for family members to grow their wealth more quickly. The family may feel obligated not to sell and therefore hold on too long. This decision rightfully belongs to both the council and the board of directors, each of which has important perspectives on the choice.

The Work of the Board: Strategic Planning for the Business Future

The primary task of the board of directors is to look at the business *inde-*

pendently from the family's needs. Its purpose—and usually its composition—is different from the family council's. The board usually includes the key business owner and may include family members who play key roles. But unlike the family council, it might also include key nonfamily executives and independent nonfamily directors or advisers including a representative of the key business owner.

The family council tells the family and the business how they want family members involved in the business and what values, rules, and policies they want the family and the business to follow. But while the family is looking after itself and is not focused on business concerns, the board must help the family see what is possible on the business end and what procedures it must follow to have what it wants. The family wants the business to be an engine for its livelihood, and the board will often have to challenge the family, sometimes even setting limits on pay, distribution, or family involvement. They also provide checks and balances so that family members do not go outside what is healthy or legal.

The board of directors focuses on four areas of strategic planning:

- Business renewal
- Capital needs—business and owners
- Key employees—leadership team succession
- Succession governance

Business renewal

Business development is often graphed as an S curve, starting slowly, then sloping upward for a period of fast growth. Over time, which can be from years to decades, the curve levels off and even drops, as the business matures. Business renewal involves reigniting the engine of growth to begin a new S curve that grows out of the tail of the old one. However, too many businesses flounder, decline, or go out of business, rather than innovating and developing.

The family business is particularly challenged by issues having to do with renewal. Over time, the very qualities that brought it success—loyalty, service, consistency, and persistence—can become liabilities, favoring the status quo over change. Rigidly following the family's values can make it difficult for a business to plan for change. The shadow of the founder, whose visionary energy becomes the will of the business, makes it difficult for successors—whether family or nonfamily—to let go of old ideas and people.

Business success depends on having a plan to renew and innovate, a staff that is dedicated to this, and the resources to make it happen. The board has to challenge the business for a development plan—and allow the best of the leadership to move ahead.

Capital needs—business and owners

The business faces competing demands for resources. The founder and family want their rewards, while the business needs capital for expansion and development. The business planning process must take into account these two sets of needs and manage cash flow, borrow to invest, or arrange to buy out impatient or unrealistic owners. The future of a family business often rests with a capital campaign that allows the business to gather the cash necessary to develop by recapitalizing family members. The younger generation often arranges to buy out their elders or their siblings. They may take on investors or offer shares to nonfamily employees. The family may shift its focus and begin to see itself not as tied to one legacy business, but as having a portfolio of investments.

Key employees—leadership team succession

Dealing with conflict inside the family about who will lead the business often precludes the family's paying attention to nurturing and developing nonfamily talent. Working for a family business is a delicate balancing act. Many highly capable leaders shun such enterprises, fearing there is no place for them at the top; they are concerned that their capability will be ignored in a highly political family environment. Too often, they are correct.

The strategic future of the business involves determining the next-generation leadership team—not just the top person, but also several capable people who are not clones of the founder and are young enough and dedicated enough to lead the company to the next level of development.

The care and nurturing of nonfamily executives is not just about paying them well. It is about making sure that as the generation shifts, power and authority is offered to nonfamily leaders as well as to family members. Many of the strongest family businesses represent partnerships between family and nonfamily leaders, each bringing their own strengths to the organization.

Succession governance

Succession of generations is not a single event. It often takes place over many years and involves a long period of cross-generational partnership. As life spans and careers lengthen, so do the number of years that two generations—or even three—work together. The board is often responsible for setting the terms of the shift between generations and monitoring each stage of the process. The presence of independent, nonfamily elders on the board, who are respected and listened to by the patriarch or founders, helps the founders manage the difficult process of letting go and allowing the next generation to take over. These elders must be available to intervene and assist in case an emergency results in the loss of a key member of the older generation.

The goal of succession governance is not simply selecting the next leader or setting the terms by which the new leader is chosen and ensuring they are followed. Rather, it is developing the talent, focus, and resources the business requires if it is to continue to be successful. This includes the board's being open to novel forms of leadership that may emerge and governance being versatile enough to allow for this. The talent, for instance, may be dispersed among family members or several managers, and a form of shared leadership may emerge. The members of the generation to whom leadership is passing often are in the best position to answer the question, Who should lead the business? And the older generation should recognize this. Rather than answering the question for them, the older generation may need to allow the next generation to resolve it themselves.

Planning in Two Dimensions: Start Today

To summarize, strategic planning for a family business is a **two-dimensional process**—looking at the business future and understanding that such future lies within the context of family ownership and control. The two types of planning can proceed either consecutively or concurrently. Both the family and the governing board look after the business, but each group has a different slant and set of concerns. The family often hears its own issues more loudly than those of the business, but a planning process has to ask how the family can achieve what it wants within the reality of its actual business.

The makeup of the family council and the board often overlap, with some of the same people serving on both groups. In addition, the choices one body makes affects the other. So the best path is for the two groups to interact in various ways, not just through one family leader or liaison, but through a set of clear communication links set up for this purpose. A financial planner can ensure the two groups work together smoothly and effectively.

A family who is several years from a generational shift should begin its planning process today. It must form a family council and make active use of its board of directors. In addition, the family must communicate its desires, values, and priorities to the board if the board is to be able to successfully plan for the future. Planning for the generational shift often continues over several years, with the groups working on their own but communicating and interacting frequently with each other. Because the family enterprise is such a complex system, a complex and multifaceted method of planning is necessary if it is to move successfully into the future.

2.2

Why Enterprising Families Need a Constitution

A multigenerational family is much like a tribe or small federation. While related by blood, by the third generation its members may not have the intimate connection of the earlier generations. Over time, the blood ties are looser, creating the need for a set of agreements and processes by which many free-and-equal family citizens can make decisions, select leaders, and define their shared interests. To succeed, an enterprising family must imitate a government by creating its own constitution. With this document, the members of each generation can understand the nature of the family and the rules and expectations that govern it so they can plan their lives and make choices that are realistic and well informed.

Every time an enterprising family crosses a generational barrier, the link between family owners and a strong and growing business becomes problematic. The family members will likely have many different relationships to the business: For some, it may be an easy place to find work; for others it may be a playing field to display personal achievement and add to the family's legacy; for still others it may represent a cash cow or a status symbol. Can the business fulfill all of these varied, and sometimes contrasting, agendas for all family members? This question becomes especially significant as the business evolves from one venture with a single owner to an enterprise with many family and even nonfamily owners.

Conflicts that arise in families who own and control businesses often have their roots in family members' and generations' varying expectations and understandings, which themselves are rooted in the messages the members of the younger generation receive from their parents. As a family grows more distant from the founder, the opportunity for mixed or confused messages becomes greater. What one parent will say to his offspring regarding succession and ownership differs from what a sibling or cousin might say to hers. How will the family arrive at a singe message for the heirs in each generation? Many wise families with large businesses create a master document for the family setting forth the family's core values, rules, and operating assumptions regarding its business and its wealth.

A business is based in formal legal agreements that set forth rules of ownership and business operation. A family also has agreements; they might be informal and may not be legally enforceable, but certainly they have personal and moral force for family members. For example, on the business side, they may address the ways in which the family should exhibit respect for employees or provide value to customers through a dependable good or service, and on the family side, they may establish policies regarding support for family employment or for new family ventures. Related to this is a question that we introduced above when discussing the family council: Is the family there to serve the business or vice versa? This is the core question of the purpose of the business for the family.

The EU had a long-running constitutional convention to create a charter for its Union. After the charter was drafted, it was rejected by two key members of the alliance. Although the EU exists regardless of whether it has a formal constitution, many European leaders believe that a guiding set of principles and agreements would be a step forward and are hoping to get ratification from their member countries. Like the EU, an enterprising family is a network of connected people striving for a common purpose to guide its future success as well as that of its members. A constitution, created by one generation but binding on future ones—and with enough flexibility to allow for new realities and directions—would help the alliance span generations. Moreover, its existence affirms that every new generation lies in the shadow of the past and must respect certain values, core agreements, and understandings from the family's history.

A family with many members and a large business—or a large enterprise comprising many businesses, diverse investments, real estate holdings, and a family foundation—may decide the time has come to link all these entities and create a master agreement to help guide the family for generations. Because each generation will have different interests in and desires for this association, families usually decide to draft a constitution when two or more generations are pondering their roles and connection to the family's enterprise. The purpose of creating a constitution is to get agreement in areas in which there are likely to be differences so that every adult family member can understand what he or she can expect, what the rules are for involvement, and how to derive benefit from the many sources of family capital.

Constitutions famously begin with constitutional conventions, in which key stakeholders gather together to define what they want. Traditionally, they are somewhat large and rowdy groups, which begin with significant conflicts until several leaders emerge who help the group forge consensus on key issues.

The family constitutional conventions we have seen are indeed large, boisterous, and emotionally intense affairs.

Who convenes them and who attends them? Like the family itself, the convention is not a pure democracy. The elders, who often have created the wealth and have greater control over it, are its key members. They form the upper house—the "House of Lords"—and hold the family's legacy and long-term memory. However, they are legislating for future generations, so the more that other generations are part of the discussions from the beginning, the greater the chance that they will agree and be comfortable living with the outcome. A good group for a family convention is a reverse pyramid, with key elders at the top joined by several members of the second and third generations who represent and are in touch with their generational groups. These gatherings are not a single event, but a process that seems to work best over a year or two of development, debate, experiment, and compromise, with informal contact between the meetings. An outside facilitator can help create a safe container for the debate, ensuring that all voices are heard, that conflict stays within bounds, and that the participants move from emotional intensity to a more rational and flexible way of thinking that results in working agreements. In fact, moving people out of rigid or stuck positions is one of the primary reasons the process takes several meetings, both formal and informal.

Setting the Stage: The Mission

Like those of their governmental counterparts, family constitutions begin with mission statements that present the family's vision, principles, and values and usually are drafted in a family meeting or with the family council. Much has been made of the need for both a family and a business mission. In Steven Covey's personal habits, in the qualities of a successful business proposed by Jim Collins in *Built to Last* and *Good to Great*, and in those characteristics and elements of enduring family businesses articulated by Danny and Isabel Miller, we see that long-term success begins with a relatively clear and simple statement of who the family is, as a family and as a business.

For an enterprising family who has prospered, the way in which the business affects the community and marketplace rubs off on the family, especially when it shares a name with the company. The business's good works may be attributed to the family's values, and its failings may tar the family's reputation. To ensure that these effects are positive, a family—as controlling owners—can set forth key values for the business that should be available to, understood, and adhered to by the leaders of the company, whether they are family members or not. These values may be a source of competitive advantage: Knowing that the family stands for them, customers feel they can rely on the company to embody them. The family constitution, through its mission statement, can make these values clear to subsequent generations of the family and to the employees of the business.

While the business's mission is relatively clear, the family's mission might not be. Each generation of the family must get together to ask, "What is our purpose relative to the business and to each other?" A family has a legacy and common history, but that does not dictate whether the family should remain together as an entity for another generation. What if members of a generation find they no longer have the talent or interest necessary to own or run the business? When do they sell, and how do they go about it? Since ownership is more than a question of return on investment, but also concerns the family's role in the community and employment of future generations, the entire family must be part of this discussion.

The family's mission should lay out what the family stands for—articulating its values and the ways in which they should be expressed in the business and in family members' relationships to each other and to the community—as well as how the family supports and regards the individual contributions of older and newer family members. What is expected of a family member? What are the responsibilities of those who inherit the family's name and assets? Many families define a **Family Code of Conduct**, which specifies how family members treat each other and how they are expected to act as citizens of the community.

The basic question facing the members of each generation is, How much do they want to be connected and how much do they want to be independent? This harkens back to the question about a family member's purpose relative to the business and to each other. Spelling out in the constitution the rights and obligations that accompany citizenship in the family enterprise will help future generations both grapple with this question and figure out how to deal with the repercussions of their answers. It is likely that some family members will be inactive shareholders. And faced with a large stake in a company that may offer no role for influence and not much income, they may decide that being a member of the family should not necessarily include owning part of the family's legacy business. Or family members may not be satisfied with their return from the business. Or some may think more capital is necessary to develop the business. Others may want the family to consider a sale. The constitution may not answer the questions that arise from these disparities in the ways in which family members view the business and their connection to it, but it provides a framework for resolving them by specifying how minority family members are treated or providing for them to sell some of their ownership to outsiders or other family members. In defining the rights and obligations of citizenship in the family, a family constitution defines the degree to which family members are tied together by their legacy and the degree to which they can pursue their desires as individual citizens.

Thoughtful Governance Yields a Good Constitution

Governance is thus the central feature of a good constitution. It specifies how decisions are made and how laws or rules can be created that bind the whole group. For a family, since different members and generations have different degrees of ownership, the democratic solution "one person, one vote" will not usually suffice (though for some families that is indeed the rule, regardless of how much ownership is held by each individual). The constitution defines how members of the boards of directors, both the boards of the entire enterprise and those of each individual entity, are chosen. It may specify term limits, retirement ages, and provisions for representing different family units or generations, just as a government provides for representation of provinces, states, or other entities. It could also specify which decisions—such as, say, the sale of the legacy business—require a two-thirds vote or whole-family consensus. The constitution may also provide for governance of philanthropic endeavors, inheritance of ownership, and the buying and selling of shares of various family entities.

It may also set out how the family supports or encourages new ventures. Some families, like governments, create a family bank that offers loans and invests in new ventures, some of them founded by family members. The constitution can also provide for a family CEO, a family leader who is different from the CEO of the family's business, who may or may not be a family member.

Furthermore, the constitution defines a wide variety of links between family members and the business, and between family members in general. It may, for example, provide for whole-family assemblies to be held every year or two so issues, concerns, and new directions can be discussed. This would be an appropriate place, say, for amendments to the constitution to be proposed. The constitution may also set forth clearly how a family member can become employed by a family entity—a business, foundation, family office, or investment—specifying what is required to get the job, how a family member is compensated, and how performance in such a position is evaluated. By creating clarity in these areas, a family can at least limit the possibility of conflict and misunderstanding.

The Constitution, a Gift to the Future

Creating a constitution that is understood and respected by all members of the family is a great achievement. Having such a document signals that the family has taken the time to clearly define who it is and set forth rules that will help each generation grow up and take on higher levels of responsibility and leadership in the family. The constitution recognizes that a large family with a large business is a considerable economic and societal unit. As such, it cannot be governed by legal agreements only, even when they are supplemented by informal understandings. Consolidating all the family's agreements and ironing out its members' differences in order to create a master operating agreement that covers the family's ventures and activities will undoubtedly move the enterprising family forward.

2.3

Defining a Family Mission and Crafting the Constitution

This selection continues the presentation of family governance, providing specific examples of how to develop the various key elements of a family constitution by linking purpose to specific policies and practices. Once a family decides that such a document is important, they need to begin to determine how to create one that reflects their own family uniqueness and to focus on what they want in it.

Governance is anchored in a series of agreements made by the family to bind the members together. While there are many individual documents, trusts, partnerships, and entities, the family needs an overriding statement that all members have a hand in creating and that defines the personal reality of their union as well as the family's legal and financial structure. They should integrate the numerous elements of their large and complex family in a mission statement of purpose, values, and organizing principles that explains the deeper intentions underlying their holdings and relationships. Good agreements supported by the family build a foundation for avoiding major conflicts among the areas of family, assets, and the community.

Family Missions

Agreements are anchored in a foundation of shared purpose. Ivan Lansberg, one of the first to map the governance structures of family business, observes in his 1999 book *Succeeding Generations* that to remain together the family needs:

> *a sense of common purpose—to look beyond what they own to discover a sense of mission, religious or political purpose, a larger purpose of what they are doing. It could be religious—God wants us to do it—or political—create jobs in the community—but this larger purpose frames what they do. Each*

member of the family needs to understand their personal role in the pursuit of that mission. The family can articulate 'what it means to me,' and people are motivated to serve in some way and are therefore involved psychologically.

One family mission statement reads as follows:

We are a family committed to our members and descendants being responsible, productive, well-educated citizens who practice the work ethic and make constructive contributions in the local community and the world at large. Each member is encouraged to develop and use self-supporting, marketable skills that contribute to the enhancement of their own self-esteem and independence. We urge family members to adopt lifestyles that are healthy, personally satisfying and at such a profile as to preserve the maximum level of family privacy, given the public nature of our business. We urge the continuation of the orientation of prudent, careful investing with a long-term view of outcomes so all our descendants of XXXX may enjoy the benefits of the foundation they built.

We believe clear, constructive communications are at the core of our long-term success as a family. We encourage all efforts to further harmony, develop humor and perspective on life, balance long-term concerns while enjoying the present; and to enhance communications, caring and amicable relationships among family members.

The mission provides a clear rationale for the family to remain together for further generations. It explains why the family is in business, how the family as a whole and its members will use their wealth, and what it stands for. The mission defines the core family purpose, usually in the form of a statement passed down from the founder of the business or family, beginning with his or her dreams and values and refined by successive generations as the family grows and diversifies. If the founder did not put the mission in writing, it remains for his heirs to do this.

The family must invest time and energy in creating or refining this mission statement. The statement, which articulates the family's vision, values, and purpose, guides the direction and behavior of the family, its members, and its organization/s. The vision is a picture of what the family wants to be in the future, as far ahead as 100 years. The purpose crystallizes what the family stands for and why it is important. The values are the core principles that detail what is important to the family in what it does and how it does it, often reaffirming the values of the founder.

From Why and What to How

A mission expresses intentions, aspirations, and ideals but does not say how they will be put into action. It does not offer specific guidelines that would eliminate disagreements about how to bring it into reality, what it means to individual family members, or how it should be applied in a family dispute.

Families like to see themselves as informal and free-form, so generally a family member's first response to the suggestion that an enterprising family take the time and energy to create a formal family constitution is that it seems utterly pointless. "Who needs one?" "We know each other well enough." "We can sit down and work things out when they come up." "My family knows where they stand and what to expect. I make the rules. Why put things in writing?" asks the founder.

In many cases, informality works fine, but as both family and business become more complicated, and pass through generations, one of the most important gifts elders can bequeath to future generations is a formal, written family constitution.

There is nothing more painful than a family-business disagreement, in which individuals expose old wounds and misunderstandings, with each side expressing deeply held and seemingly inflexible beliefs and neither seeming to listen to the other. The business is often a hostage and a bystander. By the time consultants are brought in to help, the family is at the end stage of a conflict that has been long in developing and in which feelings have become so bitter and rigid, and personal investment so deeply entrenched, that simple resolutions are no longer possible. If only the family had foreseen that it could come to this. If only the family could turn back the clock.

In fact, most family conflicts about business could have easily been anticipated. Their timing isn't predictable, but like a market downturn, these conflicts will hit at some point, and a family needs to be prepared. These disputes tend to fall into common categories—employment, benefits, leadership, relationship to the family—and often revolve around such questions as, Who will work in the company? Who will receive what benefits from the family assets? Who will have control? How can I separate myself from the family? Anticipating each of these and creating clear guidelines for decision making, which everyone supports, will reduce family pain, conflict, and poor financial management.

A family seeks agreement in many important areas: family council operations and appointments and roles for family representatives on the board of directors; conflict resolution for family members and branches, including how to clearly and explicitly define a conflict so it can be properly addressed; guidelines for making decisions about the family money and for how family members may sell their stock; and roles for family members. Often, a family has many agreements—trust agreements, buy–sell and shareholders agreements, and other formal legal documents—but the agreements either are not clearly understood by everyone or lack clarity about details. Creating plain-language agreements can help a family with multiple assets and generations organize and supplement the legal ones, providing clarity about family rules and the ways in which the family operates so members will have the information necessary to plan their own development paths. Some of these agreements are signed by the family or embedded in legal documents; others are morally and ethically, but not legally, binding.

A family constitution is a legal, or quasi-legal, guide for family behavior, decision making, and setting up the succession from one generation to another. Beginning with the mission statement, the constitution then extends the mission into practical action. It sets up a framework and a forum for a group of equals to deliberate issues, create policies and procedures, clearly define family members' rights and obligations, and make decisions about the important issues they share.

After articulating the mission statement, the constitution defines policies, rights, obligations, and agreements that cover the major ways the family works together and how its resources will be distributed. It includes specific agreements about employment, compensation, stock ownership, inheritance, and sale of family assets. Once set in motion, it can be amended, but it remains in force for future generations, and the members of these generations grow up comfortably aware of its boundaries and provisions. The first generation solidifies their commitment to the constitution by signing it. Subsequent generations are educated about it while they are growing up and asked to subscribe to its principles when they become adults.

Although there will always be uncertainties—such as who will decide to enter the business and who will lead it—the constitution's guidelines ensure that family members do not have to read tea leaves to understand what father, or mother, has in mind for them. Most important, a constitution is a foundation for maintaining trust within the family. By setting down rules, it offers each family member the security that comes with knowing what he or she can expect from the family enterprise—regarding position or role, decision making, and resources—as long as she operates within the established rules.

Elements of a Constitution

The areas that might be covered by a constitution include the following:

Owners Commitments, Rights, and Responsibilities

Central family values.

Values pertaining to how family members will treat each other and act in the world; values they want to see reflected in the business; how they will use their resources to benefit others; and what the family will do to enrich society and each other's lives. It often prescribes a **Family Code of Conduct**, as mentioned in the previous selection.

Guidelines for ownership, inheritance, and succession.

How the family will deal with issues of money and power, distribution of resources, and allocation of jobs, position, and authority in the business. What is expected of owners, and how ownership will be passed from generation to generation.

Responsibilities of family members.

Obligations of family owners, including participation in decision making, confidentiality regarding sharing information, treatment of employees, behavior in the community. Given the gift that family members receive from the family, this is a clear statement of what family members are expected to give to the family in return for being part of the whole.

Support for personal development.

How the family's wealth supports the education, aspirations, business ideas, and futures of its members. Can include specifics about support for education, personal travel, and even investment in new ventures.

Marriage and divorce.

Guidelines for participation by spouses in family governance and the business, and for protecting the business in the event of divorce. May define opportunities for employment and ownership as well as rules of inheritance for in-laws. This is how a family can present their desire for a prenuptial agreement to a prospective spouse—in the context of becoming part of the family's governance process.

Recreational assets.

Families often have vacation homes and other shared property. Policies govern their use, payment for upkeep, decisions about changes and maintenance, and when or how they can be purchased or sold.

Financial and Investment

Asset purchase and management.

While the board will oversee the asset management, the family will often have some values and guidelines for return, diversity, or social responsibility that they want the board to honor. These are often part of a family shareholders agreement.

Stock agreements: Buy, sell, and exit.

How ownership passes among family members, how stock is bought and sold, how its value is determined, and the limits to ownership. Defines how a family member can sell stock and exit family ventures.

Conflict of interest.

Individuals have their personal investments and businesses. This policy spells out the issues that might arise when family members have the opportunity to invest separately from the family. Specifies how much individuals need to communicate, how information obtained from family service can be used, and when an investment has to be offered first to the whole family.

Family Employment and Compensation

Employment eligibility; roles for family members.

Defines who will be eligible to work in the business, requirements for entry, entry process, and how jobs will be offered to family members. Many families, as they shift from being managers to governors of their business, want to clarify and limit the roles that are available to family members, to make sure that their business and financial activities attain the highest professional standards.

Employment preparation, compensation, oversight.

Generally family employment policies specify that the business takes precedence over family considerations and that a family member must attain a professional degree and work outside the business prior to employment. They usually include specifics about applying for a job, supervision, expectations of compensation, and accountability. They also define the standards by which family members get paid for work in the various businesses, the specifics of accountability, and the processes for evaluation. Because of the sensitivity of family employment issues, and the fact that family members are often owners, the board usually will oversee some elements of family employment.

2.4

How Clarifying Values Builds Focus for a Family Enterprise

With great expectations and enthusiasm, many enterprising families have begun to create values statements, both for their businesses and for their family. But too often the glow fades when after they come up with an elegant and inspiring statement, it doesn't seem to do anything. Creating value statements is wonderful, but they are a bit insubstantial. Looking at them closely, two family members may discover they have opposite views of what the values mean in action and how they should be respected. This selection will explain how families can most effectively ensure that their values inform their work and that their work embodies their values.

First, I must make it clear that values are not created by a values statement; they are already there and just need to be highlighted and recognized. They are created by people's *behavior*, though they aren't always clear or explicit. The purpose of the statement is to recognize, emphasize, and clarify them. But they are hard to find, because they aren't objects. They are principles and goals that underlie the way people treat each other and make important decisions. When a person enters an enterprising family or a family's business, he or she learns what is important to the family by observing what they do, how they act. Take, for example, a family in which people listen to each other, disagree politely, exhibit respect when talking with each other, and share a lot of ideas in a meeting without looking for cues from the person in charge. These behaviors indicate that the family values respect for people and their ideas. Values are shorthand for behaviors, and when a value is stated, it should be clear what sort of behavior is expected.

There is always a gap between stated values and actual behavior. Many values statements express espoused values that are, in fact, not backed up by actions. Harvard management researcher Chris Argyris notes that every company has a set of espoused values, which may be quite different from the values expressed in the company's actions. This is true for individuals as well. For example, some family leaders say they are open to new ideas, but they show little interest in what other family members have to say. The company appears to act very differently from what people would expect, given its stated values. The gap between actual and espoused values may be an unspoken issue that inhibits healthy expression and constrains the organization.

Values are part of the legacy that founders want to pass on to their family, employees, customers, and community, implicitly or explicitly. Over time, the values emerge from the founder's behavior, casting a huge and influential shadow over the whole entity. When a founder departs, his or her values are one of the strongest elements of her legacy. At the time of transition, it is important for the company that the enterprising family define these values, as a guide for successors and new people who enter the firm.

Defining values is not just a vanity exercise to celebrate the founder. An aspect of family businesses that makes them especially competitive is their ability to sustain a long-term commitment to these values. They can be depended on to adhere to them because of their stewardship and ability to look beyond the immediate bottom line. The Smucker family, who owns a publicly traded food-products company that bears its name, has a set of values that must be satisfied whenever a major corporate decision is made. When Malden Mills, a U.S. textile company, had a huge fire that destroyed its factory, the family owner was celebrated for pledging not to lay off workers while the company rebuilt. He put his business at risk to fulfill this pledge, in what turned out to be a futile attempt to put values above the bottom line, as the company failed. Knowing a company stands for something, like the quality of its products, is an important selling point that builds trust between owners and employees, customers, and the community.

Values are also a part of the fabric of the family who owns the company. Like a company, a family *stands for* something. These values are not voted on but come down as part of the legacy of the elder generations. A family may value the land, preservation of the traditions of its business, development of the capability of each generation, service to the community, or its religious and spiritual heritage. The place of the family in the community comes from what the family is seen as valuing.

This poses a challenge for succeeding generations. What if one generation disagrees with some of the previous generation's positions? For example, the public sense of sustainability of natural resources has evolved greatly over the past generation, and some members of the new generation may want to hold the family, and its enterprise, to a standard that is different from that to which it adhered in the past. The values of one generation sometimes need to be revised, and this may lead to conflict with the elders. Or as more people become part of a family, the original values may not be held by everyone in the family or may be seen by different people in different ways. So a family who has a values credo must place its values in a living framework—that is, one that can evolve through the generations but should never be modified lightly.

Living up to values is not easy, and this is where behaviors in the business environment come into question. A company that has pledged to value its people and manufacture its goods within its community may find that value challenged by some of its suppliers. A company that has a long-term commitment to its people may have to lay some of them off. If you state your values explicitly, the negative feelings that are inspired if you change course will be correspondingly greater, as people will feel doubly mistreated. The challenge facing the Ford family, and company, are a stark reminder of this. The family chairman, Bill Ford, explicitly embraced fuel-efficient vehicles years ago, but the company's pipeline and product mix did not express this. Recently it has become apparent that it would have been to his and the company's advantage if he had moved more quickly into this arena, but the company's legacy commitments to employee pensions and other costs—the company has since its inception paid well and offered its employees job security—made that difficult to do.

In a family in which values are explicit, conversations might emerge about how the family invests. Are their investments subject to their values? Do they apply to new family ventures or just the ones that the family has been involved in for generations? How is this decided? Who makes the decisions?

One family had a clear tradition of supporting the environment, but was also one of the largest local real estate developers. It turned out that some family members were working for community groups who were taking legal action against the downtown business association, which was headed by the patriarch of the family. This was very embarrassing and very public, as the media brought to light that one generation of the family appeared to be at odds with the next.

If you take them seriously, having clearly defined values sets the stage for difficult conversations about what the family does and how. In this family, many discussions about how they valued the environment led to a family value statement agreed to by all members of the family. This document spelled out how they would balance downtown development with environmental concerns. It enabled the younger group to feel their views were respected and allowed them to take their concerns into the community with the backing of the elders, who had great clout there. This agreement led to the family's leading an effort to consider how the city would develop in the future.

Values Are Just a Beginning

We can see from such stories that coming up with a values statement for a company, or a family, is not an end, but rather the start of a difficult path.

If you, as an enterprising family, have a public values credo—either a credo dealing with family values to be shared with your family or a credo your family developed for the company and shared with the community—you will be held to it. And because different people will see the values differently, an enterprising family with articulated values must, from time to time, invite members of the family and company into a conversation about how effectively they are embodying these values in their actions. This difficult but essential dialogue can lead to conflict as well as consensus, and the family must be prepared to evaluate the importance of these values in the current world and to their generation.

These conversations make several things clear and highlight the importance of considering various issues relating to values. First, a value statement cannot be just a few vague words. It may begin with a short statement, but to ensure the values are actualized, the people involved, whether family members only or a combination of family members and people from the company, need to specify what the values actually mean in action. They might shorten the list of core values to a group of about five, and then elaborate on the meaning of each one for the family, the employees, and the business. For each value, they might define how people can act on it and in what situations it would be relevant. If it is easy, and there aren't continual tests that challenge that value, it probably isn't worth stating. It is not easy to respect people, invite collaboration, respect the environment, promote quality, or deal ethically in a cutthroat marketplace, as many companies are learning. The bar is changing, and a values-based family must deal forthrightly with external changes.

A good exercise that companies and families can use is to think of tough issues that challenge a particular value and then have a discussion of how the value can be maintained in the face of such challenges. Some family-held companies collect case studies of such challenges. One company gives an award each year to a person who upholds the family values in the face of unpopularity. One family holding company looks at each acquisition not just through a financial lens, but through a "does this venture fit our family values" lens. Another family in its annual report on its family holdings includes a report on the family values and how the company is upholding them.

The rewards of all these efforts are great: The family enterprise is respecting something deep and important; family members and employees get satisfaction from and take pride in such endeavors; and the family and its company garner increased respect from the community.

Stick to It

The challenge is to take this work seriously—not to simply hold a half-day workshop and come up with a values statement that does nothing more than gather dust on the wall. The values that you define must be used as a yardstick for evaluation, as a basis for dialogue about what is right, and to help the family company respond to new realities without sacrificing what was special and important in the past.

This is a challenge for each enterprising family as it begins the transition between generations. Before defining new leadership and direction, the family—and then the whole company—should initiate a process for identifying and clarifying core values and determining how the family and its enterprise can work to make them more real and vital. This process can energize an enterprising family and its business to reconcile innovation and development with a set of underlying principles that have stood the test of generations.

2.5

Sustaining Connection Through a Family Council

A family council is different from a family board. The council, made up of family members only, is the voice of the family, helping it define, plan, carry out, and manage the activities that keep the family aligned and connected. It also works to guarantee that individuals can develop their own personal skills so they can lead satisfying lives. It meets regularly and helps the entire family act together to achieve its nonbusiness goals. The council is responsible for the "business of the family," while the board is responsible for the "business of the wealth." The family council is usually the entity that creates, monitors, and implements the family constitution.

Effective enterprising families understand that their long-term success is based as much on the health of their relationships as on the performance of their assets. As a result, they *invest in communication.* Communication is about more than information. It is about valuing and supporting the human connection of family members—knowing each other and caring about each other deeply. Families want communication that is two-way, personal, and direct. Therefore, the successful family creates activities and events for family members to get together to *learn about each other and dialogue frankly and openly.* By talking with each other, family members find out about far-flung and positive activities of their family and discover ways to become involved in them. In addition, powerful enterprising families often intentionally invest in developing "soft skills" of effective communication.

Open communication has several elements.

- Sharing timely **information** about their investments. As shareholders, family members want not only "the numbers" but also an understanding of what is going on with issues they care about—for instance, how the business is faring in the community, the outcome of key decisions, and new events that may be surfacing.

- Sharing personal experiences to develop the **emotional connection** that comes from knowing each other as people and keeping up-to-date regarding family events, changes, and the aspirations of other family members.

- Sharing **feelings, issues, and concerns** that arise through family interaction. Family communication often seems designed to avoid or not face up to and resolve differences that come up. These can have to do with financial decisions, family employment, inheritance, administration of a trust, sale of assets, or other areas in which one family member benefits or makes a decision that affects another.

Families that invest time and energy in deliberate communication about important ownership issues significantly increase family members' support and commitment to the family's collective actions. When family members feel their voices are being heard, they are much more likely to support the direction chosen by the group, regardless of whether that direction is one they would have chosen. In other words, as long as an individual feels the family listened to her concerns, a shareholder will "hop on board" a project even if its direction does not express her own opinion. A family communication process can lead to a more unified shareholder team. This in turn lowers shareholders' perception of the risk associated with holding onto the family stock. However, if shareholders are denied information and input, they tend to become suspicious, which drives up their perceptions of risk. By this point, if their fears are not addressed they may opt out of the business. Something as simple as initiating a family meeting can dramatically increase the sense of unity in the family system, affecting the entire system positively.

If the family has several branches living in different places, maintaining family identity can become a significant challenge. But such families devise methods for keeping in touch. Several families have created family websites containing information on investments, legal agreements, and other financial data. A website can also be a vehicle for sustaining informal relationships. For example, one very large family's website has a page for each family member on which he or she can share his interests, personal values, and commitments, as well as information about what he is doing. He can post requests for information or notices about upcoming activities that other family members might want to be involved in. Other families have annual newsletters, an extension of the family holiday letter. One family, active in philanthropy, has a family journal, which is printed before the annual family retreat and in which each family member presents her philanthropic endeavors and highlights the work she has done over the year in the community. A family can also make use of the enormous variety of newer technologies available on the Internet—such as blogs, wikis, and closed networks. These are somewhat similar to websites, but allow for two-way communication, so members can comment on articles or videos someone else has posted, present questions, and host family discussions. Some families are working collaboratively on projects through these new venues. In addition, they can be set up to be private, so that only family members have access.

The Tasks of the Family Council

The family council is a formal organization through which family members—either all family members, or when the family is larger, representatives of each branch of the family—can deal with issues concerning personal relationships, the family's assets, and its role in the community. The council's goal is to keep the "business of the family" where it belongs—in the family—so that it does not spill over into financial or business realms. In addition, the family council guarantees that all family members are kept informed, and kept involved; it assures them of having regular meetings with established procedures for sharing information and reaching decisions on key issues.

In the absence of a family council, the family patriarch or business leader, assuming that his power generalizes to all family decisions having to do with the business, will often reach major decisions on key issues without adequate input from other family members and without having shared with the family critical information on the issues at play. Frustration, resentment, and discontent can set in among those family members who are not part of the inner circle on whom the patriarch relies for advice or whom he consults before making such decisions.

Families often discuss topics of mutual concern or try to settle their issues informally, or with one person making a decision. But many issues are of concern to everyone and demand an open forum, either the family council or a full-family assembly (in small families, the family assembly and family council may be the same entity). Such issues include the following:

- How the family supports the growth, education, and development of individual family members
- How the family conducts philanthropy and is active in the community
- How family members can take roles in the family's business and financial activities
- How the family passes wealth on to the next generations
- How the family resolves conflicts between siblings or family branches

As we have seen, as the value of family assets grows or is passed to the next generation, issues arise about inheritance, fairness to different family members, and family members' differing expectations. Family councils provide a model of family collaboration in which such issues can be raised in a safe and confidential environment. Families that use a council are more able to keep family issues from affecting their business in a negative way. When family members are personally in touch with each other, they are less likely to feel the need to deal through intermediaries like lawyers and courts.

The council is the voice of the family. Its first task is to define the values that the family stands for and by creating a family constitution, to guarantee that those values will be communicated to each generation. Then, it determines the rules and policies the family will follow to achieve its values. For example, the council may craft a family employment policy or the terms and rules for being a member of the board of directors.

The council's membership grows and evolves with the family. It might start as a council of siblings, meeting with the family matriarch and patriarch to look at issues of succession into the second generation. As siblings marry, spouses may be invited to join. When numbers go above a dozen, which most always will happen in the third generation, if not the second, the viability of an all-family membership is called into question. At that point it has to become representative.

The council does much more than set and enforce rules. At these meetings, the family defines the way in which it values all its assets—the tangible ones and the intangibles—and supports the growth and development of its human capital. Within the council, the family can settle its internal conflicts and make decisions about its investments and future. These personal—rather than strategic—decisions are more appropriately made by the family than by the board of the holding company, family office, or foundation. Some decisions that are not collective decisions—like the estate plan—still may be fruitfully discussed by the family at the council even if the older generation makes the final determination.

The council should operate according to a **charter** that defines its purpose, its method of operation, and its decision-making authority, clearly specifying areas on which it will focus. The charter also defines the council's powers, its membership, the way in which its leader will be selected, procedures for how decisions will be made and who will make them, and how it will interact with the CEO of the business.

The boards of directors (of the business, holding company, family office, and foundation) have a direct relationship to the council. As the *voice of family shareholders*, those members of the council who are owners can determine the makeup of the boards, specifying who is on each, the length of their terms, and other elements reflected in the various agreements and values of the family. As the *voice of the family*, the council suggests or elects a set number of family members to each board. (As a family grows only a few of its members can be on a board.) It also communicates with the boards and receives briefings from them about various assets.

Many choices must be made regarding the form and operation of the council. Does a council have all family owners meet in a large "town meeting"? Do individual family branches form their own councils? Does the council create an executive or steering committee to represent all the owners, a sort of "family board"? Multigenerational enterprising families have created all manner of family councils, including those using each of these forms, and they all seem to fulfill the goal the family requires from such a body: They provide the family with a formal method to give voice to the family-oriented concerns of shareholders and a process to mediate the complex preferences and cross-currents of such families while ensuring effective continuity and profitability of the core businesses.

The family can create several **task forces** across branches under the family council umbrella. They might include a group focusing on family education, business development, or planning and running the annual family assembly. They might create a junior council that offers younger members a chance to take on family leadership. They can have a communication group that develops a website or private blogging and discussion network for the family. Some families have created a council of elders charged with sustaining the family legacy and mediating family disputes. There may be a group representing the family in a community project or initiative, among many other possibilities.

Operating the Family Council

For second-generation families, the family meeting is small and intense. Because of the potential for conflict when an issue like inheritance or sale of assets is involved, some family members want to limit or even avoid such meetings. Although the family has issues and concerns they want to share, the fear of managing conflicts or disagreements makes it hard to convene the meeting without professional help. Having a council means that family members know there is a proper place to raise issues with a safe and clear path toward resolving them.

The composition of the council raises questions for families. Often the council will include family members who are not owners but who are still interested in the business, for example, spouses or members who have sold their shares. Some include in-laws, with the goal of having the spouses feel connected to the family. However, some family council sessions may include only blood-family members. Young family members may also be encouraged to attend when they become interested, in their teen years, say, for the same reasons and as a training ground for the day when they may become shareholders. The family council, unlike a board, should err on the side of inclusiveness. But each family must decide the question of inclusion for itself.

Council activities are set by the family. Many families hire a consultant or facilitator to work with them, but if there are more than a handful of people in the family, they should also name a steering committee of a few members to set up the council. This committee should represent all the generations and roles in the family, not just the business elders. The steering committee will then set a date, design an agenda, contact family members, and set up a family meeting or retreat to define and organize the council.

The family council is not a business entity, though it may deal with business issues. Its primary function is communication and dialogue, not voting and making decisions. Its activities, therefore, will focus on broad issues, such as the mission and purpose of the family and its wealth, as well as personal issues, such as the support of the personal development of each family member. The best councils meet annually for more than one day, with time for family fun activities. They have formal work sessions, sometimes for half the day, and recreational activities for the remainder.

The style of the meeting is important. Having everyone sit in a circle around a flip chart on which someone can record members' main ideas and thoughts is a preferred format. The facilitator (whether a consultant or designated family member) is in the front and makes sure that everyone has a chance to contribute and that the discussion stays focused. Because one or two family members—generally the family leaders—may tend to monopolize discussion, it is especially important that the facilitator sees that everyone is able to talk. Specific devices, such as not interrupting a person until she is finished, going around the room and having each person talk, and giving one person the floor to make a personal presentation, can help equalize communication.

The Big Task

Generally, a family council begins with one **Big Task**. It may be drafting the family mission and constitution, creating a set of guidelines for family involvement in its wealth-management activities, or determining whether the family wants to remain together as a business entity. This Big Task is the rationale for getting together and gives the family a chance to define itself.

There are other potential Big Tasks for a family council. One is to build the family's awareness of their wealth-creating activities. The council may create a family foundation or establish community and philanthropic activities family members may engage in together. They may articulate values that guide investments and a set of criteria that potential investments must satisfy. The council may also set rules and mediate issues having to do with family employment and participation in various business and financial activities. For example, many family councils, not boards of directors, create family employment policies that outline who in the family can work in a family-controlled venture, the required qualifications, and the methods by which family employees are selected, compensated, and evaluated.

Another Big Task for the family council is supporting the personal and professional development of individuals. The council offers a place for family members to talk about their passions and receive support for pursuing them. Some families, for instance, fund social ventures or educational pursuits guided by family members.

The council must attend to follow-up and next steps. People may have a great experience in the meeting, agree to do things, and then forget about them. A council must follow through on its decisions, and its members must be accountable and responsible to each other. The facilitator or the steering committee must keep track of what people agree to do—action steps—and set up the next meeting. Generally, they require some form of between-meeting communication. Also it helps to set the time for the next meeting at the end of each meeting.

Family Retreats and Reunions

Families come together for many reasons. If they don't, they cannot develop a sense of identity as a single unit. An annual, or semiannual "gathering of the clan"—at a resort, with name tags, interest groups, and of course, fun activities—is one critical way to build a sense of shared identity. These family reunions are primarily social affairs, but an effective family sets aside time for the family council, educational activities, and consideration of major choices facing the family. For example, the 100+ family shareholders of a large, diversified ranch meet every summer on the ranch for an event that includes educational events, communication about family assets and activities, election of family leaders, and many social events. Family retreats often include a family shareholders meeting at which the financial activities of the family are reviewed and appropriate decisions are made. This family assembly is similar to the annual meeting of a public corporation.

2.6

A Good Board Can Save the Business— and the Family—from Itself

An advisory board or a board of directors is necessary for every corporation, but in the case of a family business or a public company controlled by a family, the board has the additional challenge of helping the family manage its relationship to the business, limiting the family's influence to appropriate activities, and ensuring it does not cross the line into unhealthy or legally questionable activities. A board can be a resource helping the family with regular issues like family employment and succession. As the family grows through generations and as the business grows in size and complexity, the board emerges as a key resource in helping the business grow and separate itself from the family.

Irwin Jacobs, a visionary engineer who created the internal workings for many of today's cell phone networks, founded Qualcomm in 1985. It has since grown to be a public company with $5.7 billion in annual revenue. Irwin's equally brilliant son, Paul, now 42, joined the company in 1990, after earning his Ph.D. in robotics with the clear expectation of becoming his father's successor. After a career in various entities within the company, he was named by the board as CEO.

Sounds like a familiar family-business succession path, without much suspense as to the outcome. But the family owns only 3 percent of the company, and it was the board, not Irwin, who appointed Paul. Eyebrows can still be raised, as an image of the board as "friends of Irwin" comes to mind. But in an era of increased focus on the independence of corporate boards, the choice of Paul can be considered an informed one. Of course the board took into account the continuity of passing from father to son, but they also spent years overseeing Paul's performance and looked at other candidates. It cannot be considered a rubber stamp, and the board will now carefully monitor his performance.

A few years ago, at a similar family company—Motorola—the board reluctantly decided to remove third-generation heir Chris Galvin from the leadership

73

after some severe business reversals and gave the reins to Ed Zander, a talented Silicon Valley executive. While both boards were keenly aware and respectful of the respective family's heritage and leadership of the company, it appears they acted judiciously and came between the family and the business to do what was right for the company.

Such behavior should be expected in publicly held family businesses, with independent directors exercising oversight over the wishes of family members. But what is the role of the board of directors at a closely held family business, where there is no requirement that there be outside directors? Increasingly, an independent board is being seen as a resource for a family, not as a burden. A good board can help the family let go of residual bad habits that became entrenched when family needs took precedence over business realities. Dispensing with these habits will allow the company to grow and develop.

The emergence of a board can be viewed as a key developmental stage of a family business, but as the second generation of a business approaches or as a business grows and thrives, the family owners may not see the need for a board. Since they have all the control; why do they need one? Why should they want someone looking over their shoulders? They are doing just fine.

Why Establish a Board?

There are several reasons to think about creating a board when the business is successful. First, differences emerge within the family. There may not be a single potential successor, but rather more than one sibling or cousin and even some nonfamily candidates. Family politics can turn their attention inward—to infighting—and take their eyes off the business and its environment.

Second, every management team develops blind spots and bad habits. The tenure of a CEO is usually shorter than the CEO would like. The founder may not be interested in considering succession in his lifetime, and the next generation certainly can't bring up this issue without seeming disloyal. Or the next-generation family managers may not be able or willing to do their jobs effectively, and nobody within the company is willing to give them feedback. A culture of mediocrity or self-satisfaction may mask business challenges.

A board consisting of the family members most attuned to the business environment, with several independent, nonfamily members, can become "the voice of the business" and challenge the family—in a tactful and respectful way that can achieve positive results. A board has the potential of gently stepping in between the family and the business, between family members, and between generations to mediate difficulties that would otherwise not be addressed. A good board, with wise independent members, may form a "neutral zone" in which family members can face their differences head-on, look at challenges, and make difficult decisions.

A family-business board has several functions, none of which are carried out easily by the family alone. A board asks the business leaders to stand back and define and clarify their strategy and reflect on major choice points. It looks at financial results, asks probing questions, and challenges thinking. As we saw above, it makes selections of key leaders, holds them accountable, and defines their compensation. In most family businesses, these are very contentious areas. And finally, there are informal things board members can do. They can mentor young family members as they move into leadership and even sometimes counsel them out. They can talk to dissident family members and help them understand the limits of their power as family owners or the wisdom of their policies. They can mediate conflicts between different family factions. Only a board that has the requisite gravitas and standing with the family can do this.

The first person who must accept the need is the founder-owner-leader who wonders why he or she should give up total control. The way to convince this person is to iterate that although the board can challenge the company and the family, in fact, the board is appointed by the family. If there is a crisis and the family owners think a board member is not being effective, they can remove that director. So when planning to install a board, the founder-owner-leader is not losing formal control—but rather gaining good counsel.

The devil is in the details, and even when a family, including the most-senior owner or leader, sees the virtue of having such an entity, they tend to find it hard to set up. In its first iteration, the board may consist of the family managers. They may even include a family member who doesn't formally work in the business—say, the spouse of the founder—but who is deeply engaged in business decisions.

After the family has worked with this family-only board for a time and has become comfortable with the relationship, the next issue is how to initiate the shift from the family-only, or rubber-stamp, board. A first step is to look for potential independent members, usually elders in the community who have run their own family business or are prominent in the industry. While family advisers sometimes are thought of as potential board members, it may be best that they remain advisers. After all, the family already purchases their advice, so it would be redundant to make them directors. A good board for a large family business should have a narrow majority of nonfamily directors.

A related issue is that of family representation. The family may be used to having most, if not all, of its family owners on the board. Over time and as a family grows, as we noted earlier, this can become unwieldy. Some family members, though owners, just don't take the time or have the capability to be directors. The family should transition to a process by which the family selects as its board members a group of family members who represent the entire family.

The family board members, sometimes along with the independent members, should then schedule periodic—maybe yearly—joint meetings with the family owners, to hear their concerns and share information. These are much like a public company's annual shareholders meeting, but hopefully more informative, open, and collaborative.

Just the First Step

Having a good board is just a first step toward using it wisely. Board meetings should be frequent enough that the directors can keep their eyes on relevant changes, but not so frequent that they become quasi-managers. Sometimes a family-business board can become overinvolved and not allow the management team enough autonomy. Meetings can be quarterly, or twice a year, in most cases, unless there is a major crisis or transition.

Recent writings on boards have noted that the mere presence of a board doesn't do much for a company. The board must be a forum for debate and exchange about relevant issues. The board members have to arrange to spend some nonmeeting time with the company leaders and become informed in key areas. The meetings have to be scheduled so that the family leaders have time to assemble the data needed for a meeting and get it to the board members in time for them to look at it. The meetings themselves must be organized in such a way that there is time on the agenda for the members to talk about issues, rather than simply listening to a lecture by the family leader. The exercise of gathering data and presenting a case to the board is a deep learning experience for young family executives.

A good board is a priceless source of added value for a family company as it grows and develops. It serves as a buffer to help the family—who may otherwise avoid the most difficult issues—address what is important. It brings in business knowledge from experienced people who could not be hired as consultants. It helps the family leader see his or her blind spots and begin to make plans for the next generation. Although a family business can succeed without such a resource, as a business faces the dual challenges of separating from the family and thriving in a complex business environment, developing a board of directors can spell the difference between success and failure. It becomes an open window, bringing fresh air into the family enterprise.

2.7

The Independent Family Board

Many family enterprises miss the opportunity to develop an advisory board or a board of directors simply because they misunderstand how it can be a resource for them. Any family enterprise has a need for a sounding board or a senior group who can offer their wisdom to the family at times of crisis and challenge. The board can be a check and balance over pitfalls and miscalculations by the family leaders, especially in areas in which family issues intrude into business decisions. This selection presents the nature of the board of a family enterprise—how it is constituted and how it works for the support of the family leadership as a governance body.

This selection was written with Sam Davis of Relative Solutions.

These are challenging times for family businesses. Large publicly held but family-controlled businesses have been in the news, for example, as the Busch, Wrigley, and Bancroft families sell their century-old businesses. Other long-standing and successful privately owned family businesses are under the gun. Some are challenged by the current economic slowdown and may have to consider a sale or major transition they had never before contemplated. To make the best decisions, family businesses of any size need to have a reflective capability, a level of expertise, and access to information that allow them to make the best choice from what may be an array of options within limited timeframes and with incomplete information. The governing boards of these family businesses are a resource that must be mobilized to make decisions about purpose, leadership, strategy, and future ownership while considering the needs of various constituencies, including owners, managers, and the community.

Yet families are slow to realize this and to use them in this way. A 2007 study of nearly 800 family-business leaders by Laird Norton Tyree, found that while three-quarters of the businesses had a board, fewer than half had nonfamily members on them. If you also discount the presence of close family advisers, only about 37 percent of these businesses have a nonfamily presence on the board.

In closely held family businesses, directors are appointed at the discretion of the family owners but expected to consider the broader needs of the business and balance them with the family's desires. When a family business is publicly held, the family may retain control by having special voting shares that enable them to select the majority of directors, who, although independent, are expected to reflect the desires of the family. Although the directors represent the family, they are also held to standards of fiduciary responsibility, which means that they have to act in the best interests of the business. This can result in a delicate balancing act—in situations, for example, in which the family is unrealistic or wants something done that is not appropriate. If independent directors had challenged earlier the practices of the family in a company like Adelphia, they might have reined in their excesses.

This selection considers one central element of board governance: the presence and role of independent directors, those who are not family members, owners, managers, friends, or paid advisers, who bring a higher level of expertise and experience to the tough choices. Outside directors can challenge the family to look at ways that they might balance their long-term financial interests with competing short-term interests. We explore ways in which an independent board can be formed in a founder-dominated family business and can act as a resource to help the family balance its own needs with those of a growing business.

The Need for Outside Counsel in a Growing Family Business

As a family progresses through generations, it will contain more owners (and potential owners in the next generation) who have diverging interests and concerns, and because of this, it needs to take the governance of its family enterprise more seriously. The appointment of independent, nonfamily members to a family board can be seen as a marker that the family has begun to place the needs of the business ahead of family patronage.

Most family businesses start with the dream of a founder, who acts as owner-manager and sole authority. As the business succeeds, it initially becomes more and more of an extension of the family, but under the control of the founder, who acts as a benevolent despot. If the business provides wealth to the family and employment to many, nobody will fault the founder's leadership. But at some time the needs of the family and those of the business will diverge, and the founder may not be able to make the necessary changes. The business, for example, may become burdened by family members who expect salaries or distributions, which may inhibit the ability of the business to invest in itself.

A business should first look to its key executives to provide new ideas for innovation and change. In a family business, these executives often include family members, relatives of the founder, and members of the next generation. The implicit message for them may be not to rock the boat, to please "Dad" or "Uncle Jim," who has provided so much for family members. But family members may be selected to fit the needs of the family, without thought to their competence or ability to do what the business needs. Nonfamily members also may be recruited for their ability to go along with the owner. So over time, the business may stagnate, as family and nonfamily members alike share their devotion to the ways of the founder.

When new external conditions arise, a crisis like the sudden death of the leader or loss of a key customer, or the business simply needs to reorganize to cope with the challenges of its successful growth, the family founder has too often failed to make room for new ideas or changes in behavior. Family members, especially the members of the next generation, often have the lowest credibility. Even if they have been to elite business schools or developed impressive technical or financial skills, they are always seen through the lens of their parents—as children who need guidance and direction—and thus have the least credibility in the leader's eyes.

Who can successfully challenge this state of affairs? The inability to change and adapt has become part of the corporate and family culture because the family leader is convinced that the way he has always run the business is the only way. The leader's myopia may lead a formerly successful family business to flounder at the point of generational transition or at the point at which growth or market shifts pose new challenges to the business.

But some businesses are able to adapt, change, and transform themselves. Some family leaders are able to listen to other views, and grow and learn from them. They select key employees who have skills and train family members to offer their new ideas. Others (possibly a majority) inflate the confidence founded in their past success, making it difficult to regard the ideas of others as worth exploring. The ability of the leader-founder to find peers he or she is able to listen to, who can challenge ideas and help the business move in new directions is a critical success factor as a family business moves from the founder-dominated to the professional-management stage of development.

The governing board is an important resource that can help the family business change and adapt. The board can represent the family shareholders in an objective manner and serve as a check and balance on the power of the majority owners, who may include the family patriarch and long-time family shareholders. Boards are expected to look over the shoulders of family management and represent all the shareholders. In a family business, the board has an additional role: to ensure that the family's voice is represented. This can mean educating the family to financial or market realities—like the value of the business or the amount of money that can be taken out of it—and challenging them when they expect the business to do the bidding of the family. Too often, the family has unrealistic expectations or ideas of what the business can provide them. The board's role is to ensure that the family expectations and the needs of the business are balanced in a manner that will sustain the business and satisfy the family's long-term financial interests.

The idea behind bringing in independent directors is to offer this expertise to the family owners and to make sure they will be able to "hear" it by including directors who will appreciate the special needs of the enterprising family. While the family owners have the right to make decisions, sometimes a large business faces legal or management responsibilities that require expertise in specific areas. In this case, the board (which often is no more than the family owners and one or two advisers or relatives) can bring in a nonfamily, nonmanager adviser as a director because of his or her skill or knowledge. Such independent advisers offer their special expertise to the business because they respect the business, its owners, or what the family enterprise does, and because they want to serve family business in general.

While this seems like a clear benefit, the act of opening up operations, finances, and family relationships to an outsider is a giant step for a family and for a business leader, who is used to keeping his own counsel and is used to success. The owner has to find people he respects and trusts, but who are not so "respectful" that they will not tell him the truth. The process of bringing them on must include clear and deep discussions that acknowledge the owner and family's concerns about letting someone in and the difficulties involved in changing their ways. A sensitive candidate will gently but firmly help the family step up to this new level of openness.

In times of calm, the board can seem like a rubber stamp, but when there is a crisis, they have to step up to—or even take over—management. They also need to anticipate crises and help the business prepare for them before they happen. Yet, too often boards get lulled by the steady state and do not work diligently to anticipate challenges in a way that would allow them to prevent crises. As a result, they are not prepared for critical situations when they occur. The enterprise has no policies or procedures to deal with events such as the need for capital, leadership succession, or sudden market changes, all of which are hitting family businesses today.

Too many boards of family-owned companies either are pro forma exercises in oversight or carry out their oversight functions in a perfunctory manner that adds no value to the company. Even if the directors have experience, knowledge, or contacts, often they are not in a position to make the best use of these. But if the board is a creative force, it has the potential to help a company "wake up" to the need for change, bring in resources and wisdom that did not exist within the company, and discover and act on possibilities that management are not aware of. Furthermore, it can do all of this without the leadership team feeling diminished, undermined, or put down.

The Role of the Board in Family Businesses

The board of a family enterprise is responsible for adding value to the business in three ways:

- Overseeing the leadership, operations, and finances
- Providing strategic direction by anticipating the need for change and identifying new opportunities
- Mediating between the needs of family shareholders and the business

The board helps the family deal with leadership succession and strategic initiatives, and it must help the business remain focused on the external environment and be open to innovating and investing in new opportunities. We can view the board as a resource helping the business to face short- and long-term internal and external challenges that can be represented as follows:

	Internal Focus	External Focus
Short Term	Selection and oversight of the executive	• Generation of revenue • Customer service
Long Term	• Leadership succession • Mediating shareholder differences	• Strategic planning • Sustaining the business & generating new business opportunities

The Board's Long and Short Term Challenges

Both executives and owners need objective advice and support in these areas. From time to time there are family members who share ownership and who may want the business to do things for the family that can undermine the business itself, such as hiring family members or providing dividends. Independent board members can act as a mediating or restraining force on unrealistic family requests.

A board helps management see the challenges ahead more clearly and prepares the company to respond more quickly. Ideally, it acts as a partner to an already committed management team, providing support, encouragement, and resources to make more than just cosmetic changes. The board may support management in doing the right thing by not taking a limited or "band-aid" approach at the expense of long-term strategies. The oversight role of an effective board leads from evaluating current data to exploring immediate and longer-term strategic issues that the current leadership may not have even considered. For example, the board can help anticipate technical innovations and help a company manage its growth by developing its infrastructure or management skills.

Becoming an Independent Board

There are several guidelines to select and reward independent directors. Independent directors are key to ensuring objectivity and innovation in a family enterprise. In the United States, Sarbanes-Oxley mandates the appointment of independent board members for public companies. Although not bound by law to adhere to Sarbox, family enterprises have the same need as public companies for independent advice. An effective board adds relevant experience and knowledge to the company. These directors can provide resources and wisdom that the company cannot afford to hire internally. Good directors are selected for the specific capabilities and experience needed by the company. They may be retired corporate leaders from the same industry, academics, professionals with specific expertise, or executives from other family enterprises. In addition to seeking specific capabilities, a family should look for the willingness of an independent director to understand the family.

Like the boards of public and nonprofit corporations, boards of family enterprises are best served by board members whose talents and experience match the needs of the family enterprise. To recruit the best possible board members, the family needs to assess the capabilities of its current board against the needs of the business to identify those capabilities and experience that would most benefit the family enterprise. With a defined set of criteria, the family can cast its nets in a systematic manner designed to attract the most-qualified board candidates. They should look at not just where the business is now, but also at where it wants to be. For example, a manufacturing company that needed to find markets around the world, sought a director who had experience in a global consumer manufacturing company.

Why would a skilled director want to serve in such a role for a family business? Families have found that they should look beyond their personal network of friends and advisers. In the community are people who have worked for large companies and family businesses and who are either retired or who have moved on to lifestyles that allow them to take time to advise families. If they have come from a family business themselves, they sometimes really understand the importance of such an endeavor, empathize with its goals, and feel called upon to help other families. Or after leaving their own business, they may want an opportunity to use their skills in a creatively challenging environment.

Recruiting independent directors is serious business that must be undertaken systematically. Executive search firms are proficient at performing board searches, but few understand the unique requirements of family enterprises. Whether the family retains a search firm or undertakes its search using internal resources, the first step is to determine the needs of the company and the skills and experience required of prospective directors. The preferred method of searching for candidates is to cast one's net wide, seeking candidates from friends, advisers, colleagues, and the community. Very often the best candidates are people not known by the owners, except maybe by reputation. Finding a person whose expertise fits the needs of the business and who is willing to serve entails a great deal of conversation. Because of the range of skills needed and the elaborateness of the search process, the family may find it advantageous to pursue two or more viable candidates and consider inviting two to join.

The demands on directors are growing in this era in response to the criticism of the lax oversight of earlier times, and some directors are reluctant to join a board because of increased financial and legal liability. Even so, some potential directors may want to serve as a resource for the family. For this reason, some family businesses have found that they can create a board of advisers, or advisory board, whose members serve without this legal liability. Some practitioners in this field would argue that without the authority inherent in a director's role, such advisers cannot really challenge the family owners. In practice, if the directors are significant players, who have an authoritative presence and take their position seriously, this will not be a concern. If it is, however, such advisers have the option of resigning if they do not think their advice is being respected by family management and shareholders.

Families should resist the temptation to bring their professional advisers or family friends onto their boards as outside directors. Attorneys, accountants, or investment advisers who are being compensated for providing services to the family or the family enterprise can hardly be expected to be "independent" board members. Such professionals are more likely to have conflicts of interest than they are to be able to act as independent members of a board. The same can be said of family friends whose loyalties will always be with the individual family members with whom they have a bond. In each case, board members do not satisfy the criteria of true independence.

It is good practice for a family business to eventually have a board of directors or advisory board on which independent directors constitute a majority. However, owners and families may find it hard to cede control until they have experienced the benefits of independent directors over a long period of time. In fact, the by-laws of the family enterprise may ensure family control even if there are a majority of independent directors on the board by providing for the removal of directors if the shareholders believe their interests are not being adequately served. Thus, the family enterprise can enjoy the benefit of having objective outsiders control the board without risking the unwanted loss of ownership control.

Families bringing on independent directors for the first time should begin with at least two directors at once. Then, over time, the entire board can consider whether bringing on more independent directors is desirable. A good board of a growing family business will be served best by a relatively small board of six through nine members. A trio of independent directors would be a good starting point for a midsize family business. As the family becomes more comfortable with the value added by independent directors, additional nonfamily directors can be added, thus changing the balance over time.

Few, if any, qualified professionals join the boards of family enterprises to enhance their financial standing. Still, those likely to make the best board members are experienced business people and professionals whose time is worth money. The work of a board member involves committee meetings as well as board meetings. If an individual contributes time and takes on the legal and financial responsibilities of a board member, he or she should be compensated. The question is, What level of compensation is appropriate? Unlike those of public corporations, board members of family enterprises receive no stock or other corporate benefits. Instead, board members of family enterprises are generally compensated at a modest daily rate, lower than the market rate for their position or experience but enough to acknowledge the seriousness of their contributions.

The Board and the Family Owners

One of the unique elements of being an independent director for a family business is the need to be in touch with the family shareholders. Often the family elects several family members to the board, but independent directors have a special role. They do not represent any one family branch, generation, or constituency. Rather, their role is to listen to what the family wants and help them balance what they want with what is realistic. A family may "want" a certain rate of return, but sometimes the independent director must explain that the company "needs" the money for other purposes.

As well as getting to know key executives, the directors should be free to get to know family members who envision a future management role in the business. While it is hard for a father to mentor his children or other relatives, the outside director who has no operational role may be able to help. A good independent director may become a sort of Dutch uncle to the family and its business.

The board often represents many family shareholders, some of whom may be very sophisticated, while others are concerned only with their own immediate income. The family may also feel pressured to approve leadership by family members when they are not really capable of doing the job. One of the biggest challenges for large multigenerational families is to provide for effective communication between board members and family shareholders. In most cases, family shareholders elect board members but have no process in position for communicating with the shareholders between annual shareholder meetings. This leaves board members with the unenviable task of having to predict what family shareholders would want to do. The role of an outside board member is easier if family shareholders provide direction through established guidelines and open communications.

The family shareholders often meet as a group to determine and articulate what they need from the company. They may have codified these in the form of a **shareholders position paper** that defines the values, expectations, and rules for governance within the family. This paper both may set forth values they want the company to embody and clarify policies and practices such as how family directors are selected (for example, by branch or by at-large election). While this statement can guide the board on general policy, it is also important that the independent directors meet with the family shareholders informally on a regular basis. Many families have dinners or special meetings with the board and the family members.

When a major transition in the nature of the business or of its family ownership is planned, the board and family shareholders must work closely together. For example, in the recent sale of *The Wall Street Journal*, the Bancroft family's board at first resisted the efforts of News Corp. to buy the company. But then, News Corp. family chairman Rupert Murdock met directly with family shareholders and assured them that their values would be respected. At the same time, he made his case for the sale. While the board makes decisions for the business, every company has situations that demand direct shareholder votes.

As family businesses grow, family owners may have voting control but lack the objectivity and expertise to give their business the strategic direction it requires. It is especially important that a family look for ways to add these into the mix that is responsible for the oversight of its enterprise. This is especially true in today's rapidly changing global markets, and in the face of proliferating threats presented by external factors beyond control of the family enterprise. Independent directors can act as an open window, offering the family and management the financial acumen, imagination, and courage to look strategically at their business practices and the challenges of their markets. While there is no guarantee that naming independent directors will bring wisdom to the business, their addition to a family business signals that the family is serious about making business decisions based on sound principles and objective data. An independent board can help the family owners get beyond the idiosyncratic personalities and practices of the founder or majority owner and the related family dynamics that may impede successful business management. If a family business hopes to succeed today, it needs all the help it can get. Independent directors are one resource that business-owning families should pursue.

 **Part Three**

Building Communication
and Resolving Family Conflict

Before there was a business, there was a family. While they may become business partners, they are first parents and children, siblings and cousins and in-laws. Whatever happens in the family creates waves that influence their working relations. In addition, some family members work in the business, and others do not. Some own more or less of the assets and have more or less say in how they are managed. Because the individuals are also a family, their relationships with each other are deeply affected by their personal history. In order to create governance, manage the business through transition and crisis, and achieve the goals of the family enterprise, a family must deal with their reality as a family. This section of the book deals with how a family can develop effective communication and positively face and resolve the inevitable conflicts that arise between family members when their roles as family members and business partners collide. These occur in different ways in different families, but they always surface at some point. A successful enduring family enterprise has mechanisms to face them openly and resolve them.

Common elements arise in the family dynamics of enterprising families. First are relationships to the parents. A young person must understand the importance of developing a working relationship with a parent, which is quite a challenge. A successful parent–child *working* relationship must progress beyond a parent–child *family* relationship to a mentoring or partnership relationship between two adults. Not an easy task.

Second, families must deal with the elements of gender and birth order in their working relationships and succession. Each family has a family hierarchy of age: The oldest has certain privileges and is first on the scene, and younger siblings will always be aware of this when they work together. What happens when a younger sibling is more competent or becomes the leader in the family? How does he or she face the older siblings? As family members marry, their spouses may become involved with the business, and, the relationships with in-laws can also be working relationships. In each case, family members need to navigate both a family reality and a business or financial relationship. The potential for conflict is quite high, as is the potential for disaster. The following selections examine the influence of these relationships on the family enterprise and offer suggestions for resolving the conflicts between work and family. They examine the dynamics that arise as an enterprising family embarks on the journey of working together and explore some of the pathways a family may adopt to manage the complex relationships they share as owners, business partners, and family members.

Two core principles should be observed by the family: 1) openness and transparency, and 2) collaboration to resolve differences. Too many families maintain secrecy, or even denial, about things that matter. But not talking about difficult or troublesome issues doesn't make them go away. Instead they brew below the surface. And sure enough, the longer the family refuses to talk about them, the worse they get, until they erupt in a hurtful emotional outburst that leaves scars on everyone. Because money is involved, emotional conflicts can be accompanied by lawsuits and may involve many outside institutions, resulting in the family's dirty linen being splashed all over the media. As we will see, this all can be avoided if the family faces its conflicts when they are small and manageable, using practices for sharing information that are presented in this section. When the information is brought into the light of day, very often it becomes clear that the conflict was based on a misunderstanding.

If not, the second principle comes into play: collaboration to resolve the issues. This means that the family members have a genuine commitment to engaging with each other to work together toward finding a solution all parties can live with. This is best done not in the courtroom, but by bringing the family members together so they can try to understand the deeper nature of the conflict and then figure out a way to resolve it. This section of the book presents some of the ways that successful enterprising families build communication and deal directly with conflicts and differences before they harm the family, and perhaps even the business.

3.1

Conflict, Emotions, and Family Dynamics

This selection introduces some of the reasons family emotions lead to escalating conflicts in the business arena. It suggests ways enterprising families can both understand how this happens and begin to find more-positive ways to engage each other in areas where they differ.

In many enterprising families, conflict seems to go along with the territory. Family feuds are a staple of articles in the business press, which abounds with stories of terminated relatives and siblings' public battles for control. These clashes can even erupt in violence, as occurred when one member of the fractious Gucci family, renowned for its fashion design, got into a fistfight with another at a board meeting after being fired by his uncle. The Ambani brothers, Mukesh and Anil, of India, from one of the world's wealthiest families, have been fighting since their father, founder of Reliance Industries, died in 2002. Their mother, whom many say is only person they both respect, split the Reliance empire up between the two in an unsuccessful effort to quell the tension. In September 2008, the government of India, fearing they would withhold a major portion of the country's oil supply from users, intervened in one of their most contentious struggles. Exactly a year later, the two famously embattled brothers are at it again, locked in a new dispute over the ownership of oil and allegations of libel. Quieter business conflicts can also damage family relationships. Cousins in one branch of the DuPont family of Delaware were estranged for many years when they thought a cousin had unfairly used his leadership position in the family's chemical business to refinance the company for the benefit of his branch. We all have read reports of sibling rivalries erupting into business disputes when one brother or sister disagrees with another or one is promoted over the other.

Since conflict is so common, families in business should learn the best methods for resolving differences before they boil over. Yet too often, family members feel that they are helpless to resolve them or that their anger or hurt leaves them no choice but to react as they are. Other families just deny or avoid conflict, carrying their hurt feelings and resentments along with them to family meetings and into endless disagreements. Many business difficulties originate with issues in the family. The business or financial adviser who tries to deal only with the business dimension may find that things just don't get resolved.

The frequency and severity of conflict in a family business stem from the fact that family companies constitute a unique form of business. Family members, who have a biological and personal history, try to transfer the good elements of their personal relationship to their relatives who are business partners and colleagues. But family systems theory suggests that the journey from household to office suite is fraught with pitfalls.

The Family as a System

Psychiatrist Murray Bowen and other family systems theorists have postulated that a family can best be understood as a single integrated whole, not as a group of separate and autonomous individuals. The family, in other words, is a *system*—much like fish in an aquarium or attorneys in a law firm. The system has its own rules and recurring patterns of behavior. Like the fish in the aquarium, which don't seem to contemplate the water that surrounds them, the family is usually the last to recognize and understand the system in which it lives.

A system has clearly defined boundaries and rules of membership. Many families are very closed systems, isolated from the rest of the world. A tightly bound enterprising family will try to keep financial and other information secret, which may cause difficulties for employees. They may not trust nonfamily members, even those who marry into the family.

A system tends to have an informal set of rules or procedures regarding how its members function and interact. Examples of such rules may be, "We don't say anything negative to each other" or "Family members are all expected to be perfect." The system resists change and thwarts efforts to impose change. The emotional reality of the family's early years remains, even as the children become adults. So not only do many business troubles have their roots in family issues, but many family conflicts simply repeat early patterns.

Many of us grew up with an unrealistic expectation of what we should receive from our parents. A son may expect to inherit or share ownership of the family business even though his older brother worked for many years in the company with the expectation that some day it would be his alone. When the younger son enters the business, a clash is inevitable. These expectations become magnified in a family business in which it is anticipated that large amounts of cash and other assets will be equitably distributed at some point.

The system has a hierarchy, with unwritten and often unspoken roles and tasks. If you are the big sister, or little brother, you have a role. You are the funny one, the smart one, or the carefree one. When you work in the business, although your role may demand different behaviors, you may find it hard to be seen differently. The family hierarchy often gets transferred to the business. It is hard for an older brother to take orders from his kid brother.

The separation of the family business from the family system is often not complete, and the two may overlap. The family business is an extension of the family system and its rules and patterns. If the family's pattern of functioning supports sound business practices, there is no problem. But when the family pattern is antithetical to prudent business management, the family-operated business is in danger. If everyone feels entitled to take out lots of money or receive generous perks, financial difficulties are likely to spring up.

Problems develop when a pattern is transferred from a family into the business. For example, one group of siblings extended the pattern of taking care of their younger brother, the baby in the family, when he entered their company. His older brothers "looked out for him" by not giving him real responsibilities and not expecting very much from him. He continued his part of the pattern by being an irresponsible clown, acting like a child. This family pattern had damaging effects on the business.

In times of crisis, relatives in business together can behave in ways shockingly similar to the ways they acted when they were little. When a family finds itself in trouble, its members rarely look to themselves as a unit to find the remedy. The family blames either one individual who exhibits behavior that goes against the family's rules—which may or may not conform to society's rules—or an outside agency, such as the tax system or their adviser. Though this may prove to be an effective way to keep relatives from seeing their own role in the problem, it is not an effective way to remedy family problems.

Enterprising families also tend to incorporate triangulation into their business relationships. Triangles occur when there is so much tension or such a strong difference between two parties that one of them seeks out a third party and tells that person about the problem. That third party then turns or goes to the other individual and berates him or her or meddles with the tension.

For example, if members of the next generation habitually complain to their mother when they are upset with their father, the pattern may continue even if Dad is the CEO, brother and sister are division managers, and Mom is not involved in the business. When they are upset at Dad, the young managers may talk to Mom, who in turn berates Dad in private for his alleged insensitivity. This violates the boundary between the family and business and shifts a business disagreement to the family. This triangle ends up leaving Dad more disconnected from his kids and gives Mom a role as a business mediator that is not helpful to the business. In a healthy situation, when the third party is told of the problem, that person will suggest that the individual go back to the person with whom a conflict exists and work it out.

Many family disagreements tend to revolve around the issue of fairness. Because good parents love all their children equally, childhood fosters an expectation of being treated equally in the family setting, which is perceived as being treated "fairly." Since parental attention and rewards were a precious commodity when the children were young, intricate rules were established within each family to ensure "proper" allocation. If any family member sees the business as violating these usually unspoken expectations, conflict can arise. Yet a CEO is likely to have different plans for each of her children in terms of their positions in the company, salaries, and ownership shares.

If the family does not know how to bring these differences to the surface and accept them, conflict can build and escalate over time. As it builds, people get more estranged, and minor issues are apt to trigger venomous responses. With all these difficulties arising in families, it is no wonder that conflict is often recurrent and potentially poisonous.

Family and Business Systems

Systems theory teaches that all aspects of a system (subsystems) are interdependent. Anything that affects one part of the system also affects the others. Therefore, in a family business, business problems can't be addressed by looking at the business or its finances alone; their resolution involves the family. Because the family has formed the company, many of its problems stem from the ways in which it is modeled on the family.

The family and the business, while including many of the same people, are vastly different worlds. Each has its own priorities, goals, and expectations. They are two different systems, with different—yet interlocking—purposes. One system involves emotional acceptance, the other rationality and results. Difficulties arise because it's hard to learn how to shift the relationship when family members move between the two systems. But despite the difficulties, the rules, expectations, and behavior must shift somewhat as one moves from family to business. Together, these two interlocking systems become a third system, the *family-business system*.

The family system's specific needs and energies are sometimes at odds with those of the business system. For example, the family system seeks to preserve harmony and minimize change, whereas the business system sometimes *requires* conflict and change. The goals of the systems are very different. The family must develop and nurture its members; the business needs to generate profits and operate effectively in a competitive environment. Many family-business dilemmas arise when family needs or priorities overwhelm the business's needs. Problems inevitably erupt when a family member expects people in the business realm to operate by the same rules they use in the family realm. If you deal with one system to the exclusion of the other, you are not going to achieve a long-term, lasting solution to your family-business problems. The goal is for the family to learn to make good business decisions that also sustain family harmony.

The term *stakeholder*, a takeoff on the term *stockholder*, is used to convey the point that people who don't own stock in the company often have as much stake in business outcomes and are as personally and emotionally invested as those who own stock. These stakeholders are members of various constituent groups in the family-business system. Their roles are based on their positions in the family and the business. A typical list would include the following:

- Family members who work in the business and own stock
- Family members who don't work in the business but own stock
- Family members who work in the business but don't own stock
- Family members who don't work in the business and don't own stock but have a stake in maintaining amicable relationships in the extended family
- Key nonfamily managers, who may or may not own stock
- Spouses and children of the people in the above groups

The best long-term solutions to family-business dilemmas are developed when stakeholders are aware of the differing ownership, family, and business roles and learn to integrate and balance them. Passive shareholders, for example, may prefer to receive dividends or not take risks that may endanger their equity, whereas those family members who work in the business often want to invest profits for the future. Such conflict has paralyzed many family businesses. In cases like this, expectations must be shared and the rules must be balanced so members of each group feel their concerns are taken into account.

Two basic paths to resolving conflicts can be implemented. The first path is **structural clarity**. This involves clarifying agreements and creating formal procedures to resolve issues that may arise. Taking the time to develop a clear set of rules about ownership transfer or unambiguous guidelines for employment can go a long way toward preventing future flare-ups. With clear agreements, family members as they grow up know what they can expect and where they stand. The family business is not a mystery to them.

The second path is to **communicate openly and directly.** This means approaching the person or people you disagree with to discuss your differences of opinion, differing expectations, or hurt feelings. It does not mean that every issue is legitimate or that each person has an equal vote in determining a course of action. But, for example, if a father is disappointed with his son's performance, isn't it better for him to discuss the deficiencies and ways to correct them than to send a letter of termination without warning? Such failure to communicate has ignited many long and destructive family feuds and lawsuits.

In bringing problems to the table, family members have found it is helpful to focus on the separation of roles and interests (i.e., what we do as family members as opposed to what we do as business owners and managers). Another strategy is to determine "who owns the problem."

For example, if a daughter would like to leave the business but feels obligated to stay, is it a personal problem or a business problem? Initially, it is a personal problem to be addressed by that person alone, although she may need the help of a psychotherapist, career counselor, or other professional to resolve her internal conflict. If she ultimately decides to leave, it may become a business issue, requiring the family to address the conflict in terms of the succession needs of the company. If her father expresses disappointment or hurt or tries to put a "guilt trip" on the daughter, it may become a family conflict. In such cases, father and daughter may need to discuss their expectations of one another, hopes for the future, and other matters.

Family-business conflict resolution is not a one-time event; it is a process that requires family members to develop sensitivity, learn effective communication techniques, and remain continually alert for hints at underlying issues. When a family comes together to resolve their differences, with each relative stating his or her own interests and needs, it is helpful for everyone to step back and assess what is best for the system as a whole.

3.2

Openness and Transparency: Informing Family Stakeholders

One would think information would flow freely and openly in a family, but in fact many families are plagued by areas in which information is not shared. This is especially true in relation to family money. Family members who are in control often have reasons not to tell other family members about their investments or the business entities in which they are partners. This can lead to nonproductive conflict that can escalate because of distrust and fears about what is not shared.

The very private Pritzker family of Chicago, who owns one of the largest and most-respected family-held fortunes in the United States, has been hit with lawsuits by family members from two family branches. At the death of patriarch Jay in 1999, control of the family wealth—which included ownership of Hyatt Hotels and the Marmon Group, a holding company with many individual corporations that are owned by a network of nearly a thousand family trusts—went to a team consisting of Jay's son Tom and two of Tom's cousins, Penny and Nicholas, who had been designated and in place before his death. By all accounts, they are competent and dedicated to the family mission of preserving the family's wealth for future generations.

In a letter to family members presented at a family meeting before his death, Jay expressed his wish that the family maintain the trusts and keep the fortune together, under the leadership of the three fourth-generation successors. The sudden eruption of lawsuits and family strife within a family known for a deep dedication to family, a frugal and philanthropic lifestyle, and tough but fair business practices in buying and selling businesses was a shock and seems nearly certain to mean that contrary to Jay's and other family members' wishes, their wealth will be sold and divided among the 50-plus fourth-generation heirs.

From the public record (I know none of the principals personally), we can learn something of what happened to precipitate this within the family. Its roots seem to lie in the personal relationships between Jay, his brother and partner Robert, and their children. Jay and Robert were partners for life, living and breathing business and making deals. While committed to family, the brothers seem to have communicated to their heirs that the only way to be respected within the family was to join the business.

Although the family has supported the ventures of many family members, the competitive ethic left family members who failed to be dealmakers feeling less valued, even disparaged. The family would support their ventures, but did not make them feel valued or give them the sense it was OK to create a life in other areas than business. Jay's son Tom has a deep interest in Buddhist culture but was persuaded by his father to enter the family's business. We can only speculate what a dilemma it must have been for him to choose between these two forms of livelihood. He has been very successful as one of the leaders of the family's business ventures, working with his father when he was alive.

His brothers, it appears, either did not choose a career in business or did not do well in it. While they were supported financially, it appears that tensions rose as the brothers felt increasingly devalued, disrespected, and even shut off from the center of the family. This experience was shared by Robert's children and other cousins. An added complication is that two of Robert's children, by a wife from whom he had had an acrimonious divorce, seemed to be treated differently from other members of their family generation in terms of inheritance.

Like many families, the Pritzkers have a very paternalistic style of operation. The family leaders, who manage the businesses owned by the trusts, do not include other family members in any aspect of what they do. Although family members are very comfortable and never have to worry about money, most are not involved in the business or financial side of the family in any way. They are told almost nothing of what they own, what is being done, how, or why. They are "owners" of the family's wealth but only as beneficiaries of trusts, with no rights to any say in the finances. So their experience of being part of the family is that of children who are taken care of and even indulged, rather than adult contributors to a serious and consequential venture.

Lack of communication and knowledge, in an emotional field of rivalry and jealousy, inflames passions. Already feeling devalued, ignored, and neglected, family members learned that the trio who ran the business were paid unusually large salaries and fees for their work. The family owners had no idea what the rationale was for these payments, but they appeared to be unfair, as have the salaries and perks of CEOs in other enterprises that have been questioned by shareholders.

The whole story is shrouded in secrecy, but there appears to be an agreement by the controlling heirs to break up the family wealth over the next ten years. As in other family lawsuits, individual family members do not see the offer of substantial payouts as a resolution of the conflict, but rather as another insult.

What are some of the lessons that other families might learn from the imminent dissolution of this great fortune? First, there seems to be a failure of balanced attention to the shareholders. The focus of the family leadership had been to reward and value the family's work of wealth creation rather than develop the family as a community that supported the values of the family. Simply put, there were no roles for family members to serve the family if they were not in the business, and only a few could find a fit there.

Related to this was a lack of appreciation of the role of two-way exchange within the family. It was reported that when Jay presented his wishes to the 50 or so members of the fourth generation at the brief family meeting in which he read his letter regarding succession and the family trusts, there was very little discussion of this very thoughtful and deeply felt work. What might have been going on here? Was there nothing to say about it? I suspect the tone of the meeting did not invite exchange and that family members had profoundly emotional responses, many feelings and concerns, as well as many questions, but thought that the norms of the family were such that the sort of exchange that would allow them to voice these was not welcome. In many enterprising families, asking a question or expressing a feeling or a different view is seen as a challenge to or lack of respect for the patriarch. Families need to work hard if they are to overcome this norm and open themselves to input from all family members. My experience working for many families leads me to believe that a great opportunity was missed for exchange around this document and in the aftermath of its presentation.

Another enterprising family at a similar crossroads began to consider succession in the same way, with an address from the patriarch. But that was just the beginning of a yearlong process. While not questioning the right of the patriarch to set the terms of inheritance, the family had many small meetings—and a great deal of often-heated discussion—to help make the next generation capable and prepare them to take on the burden of the patriarch's wishes.

The family tradition of keeping information closely held seems to make the differences worse, as imagined deeds are added to real difference. As part of its work as a family, the Pritzkers could have come together to celebrate and share with each other what they were doing in their many ventures. While not legally required to do so, they might also have taught family members about their ventures, inviting them to learn more and understand their complexity. They might even have solicited opinions and input about what they were doing without giving up the fiduciary role they had as trustees and executives. It is hard to think that if family members felt valued and included, they would feel the same resentment against the business members of the family.

When family members in one's own generation are elevated to a position of family leadership, they necessarily become somewhat separated from their generational peers. They have a special role in the family and the community. They take on an obligation not just to be successful in their stewardship of the family's wealth, but in relation to the other members of their generation. I suspect that the three family leaders did not see their role as including informing and leading the other members of their generation. They saw their succession only in business terms.

At the time of succession, the family also might have established clear family policies governing employment, compensation, distribution, and exit from their ventures. Since the family had several branches, some of which had no active members in the family's ventures, such policies were especially important. How does a family member enter the business, and what is expected of a family manager? How are family managers compensated? What sort of payouts and income can a family member expect from ownership? How does the family support the individual ventures of family members? What are the values that underlie the way the family does business? The lawsuits reflect differences and feelings about all these areas. How different would it have been if the older generation had made these policies clear and explicit as they were planning the succession process?

In every family with a trust and a unified fortune, some family heirs will feel that despite the wealth they have in paper, they do not in fact have the means to pursue their own destinies. Some individual family members would prefer to be the captain of a smaller ship than a passenger on a luxury liner. They want an option to exit from some or all of their vast holdings, to be able to fund their own lives, charities, or ventures. Many family lawsuits arise because family owners feel they are imprisoned in the family web rather than colleagues who have freely chosen to associate. Every shared family venture should find ways to allow those who do not feel comfortable in the family business to break free of it but remain a member of the family.

These reflections are not meant to be critical or presume to second-guess the struggles of a great and good family. Rather, as we hear of the struggle of a family, we can use their experience to consider some wisdom that we can in turn apply to our own families, as we take on the task of moving from one generation to the next.

Keys to Success: Sustaining Unity Among Family Shareholders

- Treat family shareholders as adults, rather than as dependent children
- Every family member should receive the support and encouragement of the family and its resources for his or her full development as a productive individual
- Leaders must be transparent about what they are doing and why
- Policies about payouts, exit, and compensation should be clear and agreed upon
- Shareholders should have opportunities for two-way exchange with family and nonfamily operating executives in ventures

3.3

Clear Boundaries Make All the Difference for Family Business

When family members are in business together, they will have to cross the boundary between their family and business relationships many times a day. The major challenges that come up in a family enterprise have to do with the skill with which family members navigate across their roles and responsibilities as owners, coworkers, and family members.

The American poet Robert Frost said, "Good fences make good neighbors." Some family members may be involved in both ownership and management of the family business, while others may only have one of these roles. To navigate effectively between family membership, ownership, and management roles, it is necessary for a family enterprise to create clear differentiation and boundaries between them. A boundary is defined as "the point where something ends and something else begins."

Think of a family—say two parents and their adult son—having a meal together. Their relationship is informal and playful, with the conversation ranging over many aspects of life. Then, consider what changes occur when they act together as three one-third owners of a business, looking after the health of the business and the effectiveness of its management. In that role, they are not primarily father, mother, and son, but become three partners, with a shared interest. To add to the complexity, what if the son is the CEO of the business, and the parents, though owners, have recently left active management of the company they founded. Can the parents tell their son what to do? The parents' emotional investment in the future of the company, and their relationship with their son—whom they still see as a young man, very unsure of himself—will certainly come into play. The challenge is to make sure emotions don't lead people to become involved in ways that confuse employees, undercut decisions, and stifle necessary innovation.

I recently worked with such a family. When they talked, they were not sure which role they were speaking from. The parents tried to be good parents, while the son was trying to be a CEO and also to please his parents. As business founders, the parents felt free to come to the business and tell employees what to do and make suggestions. The employees weren't sure how to respond to them. This is a classic example of how a family business can be confused, even paralyzed, by boundary confusion.

The learning process for this trio focused on creating appropriate boundaries and having the discipline to maintain them. When the family members had a conversation, they had to define whether they were acting as owners, parents and adult children, or managers. For each role they had to clearly define what they could and could not do. In fact, only the son was a *manager*. The son had to have full authority to act as CEO without being overruled by the other owners. But the owners group could ask the CEO to leave, or hold him accountable for results. When they did this, they were acting as *owners*. And the parents had to see their son not as a child needing guidance, but as an adult manager and peer owner of their business. Of course, as parents, they could decide to leave their two-thirds interest to their son, or to someone else.

To help define clearly the boundaries and roles, together with the family, I created a **Code of Conduct** for the trio as a board of directors. It contained explicit rules spelling out the areas in which the son had the authority to act as CEO and those that required him to consult his board. There were also limits to what board members could do—e.g., they could not talk to employees without informing their son and would not overrule or question his decisions to employees. The goal of a good family–business boundary is that it clearly defines the family members' roles, expectations, authority, and behavior. Although it is easy to say that family considerations should not influence the business, ensuring that requires the creation of clear and explicit boundaries.

Probably the major source of difficulty in a family business comes from the many aspects of relationships that cross system boundaries. When people are in such dual or triple relationships, they have to ask themselves if what they want to do, or are about to do, is appropriate for the role in which they are acting. Can a mother come to her CEO son and ask or tell him that he should hire his cousin who needs a job? I saw a business in which the mother actually gave her nephew a job without telling her CEO son. Imagine the consequences if the nephew is a failure, or the message that employees get when he shows up to work one day, clueless about what to do, or when the CEO son sees him at work without having hired him.

Good boundaries are needed in other areas as well. Family members routinely have business discussions at family dinners, leading the family members not in the business to feel left out. To maintain boundaries, many families create specific times when there are to be no business conversations. A boundary also exists between parents and their children. Certain things that the parents feel and do are private, and should not be shared. A family faces boundary confusion if a father talks to a son or daughter about issues in his marriage, or if one sibling goes to her mother whenever she disagrees with something her sister and business partner does.

In an enterprising family, members may be together even more than in other families, and this can lead to knowing too much about each others' lives. A young adult in a family business often feels pressure to socialize all the time with the whole family. A daughter-manager may have married a man who respects and likes the family, but who wants to create his own family with her. The boundary issue for the young nuclear family is how to create a boundary of privacy so that they do not feel obligated to do everything with the family. For example, they may want to take a cruise for the holidays, rather than go to the family retreat to ski. The parents may take the efforts of their child to create a boundary as an affront to the family. Tension ensues. Part of growing up and becoming independent is creating one's own identity and not feeling like a junior part of one's original family. This is made more difficult in an enterprising family in which the generations are business partners.

Another kind of boundary is between the family-owners, their employees, and the community. As young people grow up and become privy to the family's business information, they must learn what can and cannot be shared with employees, friends, and the community at large. They learn that they may share intimate details of their lives, business, and finances within the family but that such information is not to be shared outside the family except with the appropriate advisers. They learn the boundary of privacy.

It is always a temptation to bring long-time employees, who are also friends, into the issues of the family. In one case, a brother talked with his brother, who was also his co-CEO, about the time schedule for a new product in development. Not satisfied with the timetable, without his brother's knowledge the brother went to a key employee who was in charge of the area in question with his brother, and asked for the employee's assessment. A type of communication breakdown known as a triangle was created. As we saw earlier in "Conflict, Emotions, and Family Dynamics," in a triangle an issue between two people—in this case the co-CEO brothers—is transferred to another relationship in which there is less conflict. As a result of one person's confiding in a third person, the two people directly involved become more distant. Good business boundaries are often violated in family enterprises because of triangles.

In another case, a CEO son and his brother-in-law, who was a manager in one of the family businesses, had an argument. The brother-in-law resigned and walked out. He went home and told his wife, the CEO's younger sister, that her brother had fired him. She in turn called her mother, who talked to her husband about what their son was doing to his sister. Just three hours later, the son got a call from his irate father, the chairman and majority owner, telling him that he had better do something about this.

Every family is full of humorous and aggravating stories of boundary violation. They are also inevitable in a family business. So what can an enterprising family do to create useful boundaries reflecting that they are both family members and business partners? First, they can recognize that such boundaries exist, and that as a family member one's role changes in different situations. Asking one another if you are talking as a family member or as a colleague may help clarify what is going on. Second, as families grow and new generations move into the business, a family can create an explicit statement of ownership and management rules for family members. Clarifying these rules helps people understand what behavior is appropriate in each role. Finally, and most difficult, family members can learn to see their relatives through different lenses in different roles, and to separate family-based feelings (rivalry, jealousy, competition) from those more appropriate to their business and ownership roles.

The irony of Frost's statement is that boundaries are often thought to separate things, rather than link them. However, while clear and proper boundaries do separate, in so doing, they allow individuals to grow and thrive, decisions to be made fairly and appropriately, and people to understand who they are and where they stand when they are together.

3.4

Repairing Short Circuits in the Family-Communication Process

While a business needs openness and clear communication to thrive, in a family, relations are often characterized by denial/avoidance, a tendency to keep issues secret from each other, and distrust. These patterns evolve because people want to achieve short-term harmony or hold on to personal power, but in the end, the instigator's improvisations often backfire and lead to greater difficulty down the line.

The leadership group of a family business enjoys a much longer tenure in office than their counterparts in public companies, and therefore they have a wider time frame—often a lifetime—to steward the business through challenges and opportunities. Longevity offers many opportunities to develop greater wisdom and patience and to take initiatives that may not pay off for decades. However, the downside of family-business leadership is the tendency to narrow one's openness to new information and change as time passes.

While the business leader should be alert to threats arising in the external business landscape, more often the decline of a family business takes root from within. In my work with business leaders, I have found that their confidence, success, and power to govern the family and its resources can lead to bad habits in communication that can in fact set this decline in motion.

The world of business is a deep and omnipresent backdrop to the life of the enterprising family. Their identity is molded by it. Success is often defined in terms of it. And the shifts of fortune of the business and the family members who work within it are the subject of endless dinner table and late-night conversations. Like a royal family, the family who shares a business can be the source of endless politicking and intrigue, as various family branches seek to further their fortunes and gain power and access.

Although some families can thrive despite—or because of—the Darwinian competition of such a feudal climate, the family must develop certain qualities as a whole system. These include ways of communicating—such as facing issues and resolving them—that can be characterized as direct, open, and collaborative.

Here I focus on ways that family leaders inhibit communication within the family and how to reverse these tendencies. There are several common ways that a leader, or indeed any family member, can shut down communication in a family business: avoidance/denial, secrecy, and distrust. Each of these is set in motion by a danger or threat, which is then compounded and escalated by the ensuing lack of communication.

Let us take a common example of the first issue, **denial/avoidance**. A young son enters the business in a responsible position and begins to get into trouble. He promotes the fortunes of his friends and cronies, disparages women employees, and ignores important aspects of his job. If he were a regular employee, sooner or later someone would wonder, "How did he ever get into this job in the first place?" and his patron or protector would be called to account.

But if he is the boss's son or cousin, another dynamic ensures. People protect him, make excuses for him, work around him, or simply do not share the truth with the family leader. This is misplaced loyalty, but is often fostered by the family leader. Denial/avoidance arises when the parent does not want to hear that his or her relative is less than stellar or has a problem—or when the parent becomes aware of the problem, but the family relationship makes it difficult to confront or challenge the offender.

This leads to a negative communication cycle, or a lack-of-communication cycle. The young person does not get confronted or is not given feedback, and his behavior is never challenged. He has no incentive to shape up. Other people are demoralized and avoid him, isolating him further. In addition, others see in him a chance to curry favor and move up without producing results.

The negative consequences multiply, on the family, the individuals involved, and the business. Examples of the cost of avoidance can be seen in families in which a drug or alcohol problem gets worse and worse, illegal actions are initiated, staff members desert en masse, or the efforts of helpful or positive family members to contribute are blocked, and they move away from the family.

A second communication short circuit is **secrecy**. This behavior has more-complex roots. A business leader has a responsibility to keep counsel and limit sensitive business information to those who need to know. Most family businesses are privately held and maintaining business secrecy provides a competitive advantage. Secrecy is also comfortable for the leader, because he or she does not have to account for difficulties or discrepancies. The leader shares his or her figures and plans with only a small coterie of people who are characterized by their acceptance and willingness to cheer on the leader.

Family owners (current and future), young people emerging in the family with skills and capabilities, and different branches of the family are left out of the loop. Lack of information and contact with the business causes a vacuum in which rumors and misinformation replace fact. Well-intentioned actions by the family leader may be viewed by others as damaging or irresponsible. Checks and balances on perks that flow to leader-managers do not exist, and family members may feel that the managers are being unfairly rewarded. Young people of talent may feel there is no place for them unless they are willing to become one of the sycophants giving good news to the leader.

Most ominously, the leader is cut off from information that can challenge poor judgment and avoid decline and erosion of the business. In a public company, the board, especially with a majority of independent directors, can challenge and even remove the leader if necessary. But in a closed family business, there is no one to make sure the leader has not succumbed to arrogance or ignorance in stewarding the business. Secrecy coalesces power in the leader and makes it less likely that new ideas, new directions, and positive challenges and innovation will take place.

The third communication cut-off is **distrust**. It works in this way: A family adviser says or does something with which the leader is uncomfortable. For example, an accountant challenges the use of the business jet for personal expenses. The leader, not accustomed to being overruled, is embarrassed or hurt. In response, he or she begins to withhold information and to confide in others that the adviser costs too much or is not being helpful. Distrust is a process of shooting the messenger rather than looking at the message.

In a family, since the messenger can't be sent packing, distrust leads to all sorts of barriers. Instead of working directly on an uncomfortable issue like succession or financial accounting, two proud family members, representing different branches, will begin to question each other's integrity and motivation. They will stop talking with each other, and instead, begin to recruit other relatives to one camp or the other. People will feel they have to choose sides, and the sides will become more and more polarized. This cycle leads to splits in which family wealth is divided; family members go out on their own; and a business is sold. This is not necessarily bad in the long term for the business, but the negative consequences for the family usually linger.

Repairing Communication

Denial/avoidance, secrecy, and distrust all erode family communication with negative results for the family and the business. If you are a family leader, or any family member, there are steps you can take to repair these breaches and establish greater positive connections in your family. These actions begin with yourself: Any family member, by virtue of his or her membership in this club, can initiate actions to reverse this negative trio.

You can **directly address an issue.** In the case of a family member whose problems are denied or avoided, you can challenge the family member or the family leader directly. You can assemble information that challenges or confronts the issue with evidence. This sort of challenge is very sensitive, because your own motivations and intentions may become suspect. The cycle of avoidance can only be broken if the people who carry an issue deal with it directly. So getting a number of family members to talk about the issue will not lead to resolution unless the parties who created the problem are included in the conversations. One aspect of the avoidance cycle is that everyone talks about an issue, but the people who are directly involved are not in the loop.

The key to making a challenge to an avoided issue is your own personal stance when you make it. If you are seen as self-dealing, negative, or hostile or if it seems as if you are attacking another family member, you will not make much headway. The positing of a challenge to a family should be made with the intention of a positive outcome. You want the family member to get help or succeed. You are concerned about the morale of nonfamily employees, and you want the business to succeed. You can raise the issue to those involved and then ask that they work it out.

Second, you can promote the airing of information in a **family forum**—a family council or meeting of key or all family members. The cycle of secrecy ends when there is a family meeting in which you can raise a concern without having your motives questioned and during which information and divergent perspectives can be shared. Those family members who are owners are entitled to information about the business, but they are required to keep it confidential, and certain aspects of operations, such as details about pending decisions, are out of bounds. If a family has an opportunity for informal exchange about key business issues, in an advisory, non–decision-making capacity, some short circuits can be overcome.

Limiting information and communication can drain the energy from a formerly hardy and strong family system. As a family leader, or family member or adviser, you must take steps to open up the system to a higher level of communication that addresses key issues.

Third, you can initiate a process of **checks and balances** on family behavior and decisions. In a business, this means naming independent board members to the business board or developing family advisers who will work with the family to review information and deal with areas of potential conflict of interest within the family. In this scenario, some types of decision or areas of operation are regularly reviewed by independent advisers and family members.

3.5

Moving Beyond Emotional Reactions to Effective Family Communication

Hurt, anger, disappointment, jealousy are deep and violent emotions quite common in a family. When the family is also a business unit, the emotional reactivity so common in families can escalate conflicts and make them difficult to resolve. The tool of Appreciative Inquiry, focusing on what is good and positive and building upon that foundation, can help family members shift from blame and negativity to positive responses to emotion-laced differences.

A while ago, I was locked up in family vacation house facilitating a retreat with two generations of a business family—two parents, their four adult children, and two spouses. Three of the siblings and a spouse worked in their successful business. Absent physically, but very much present, was the matriarch, the eldest of three generations, who had founded the business and ran it successfully for 30 years. The challenges were deep: The matriarch had sold the business several years before but continued to come into work every day as if the sale had never taken place. Two siblings who worked closely together had very different visions of what was to be done. The parents felt caught in the middle of the two generations. Everyone felt there was difficulty communicating in the family, with the result that nothing ever improved, causing more and more distress to all parties.

What constituted poor communication in this family? It was clear from the moment they began to talk: Each person would complain about the behavior of the others: "Mom, you call us up every day and tell us what to do." "You hire all your friends to work there." "You takeoff time every day to go home to your son." "You keep changing the pricing of items, and we never know what you are selling things for." The litany went on. The person accused would argue back with other accusations. It became clear that each person had come to the retreat with the idea that he or she would berate someone else into submitting to her view but also with the knowledge that this wasn't likely to happen.

One could argue this was progress; before the family meeting, people had made the accusations to a third party—a form of communication called triangling (discussed earlier in "Conflict, Emotions, and Family Dynamics" and "Clear Boundaries Make All the Difference for Family Business") in which a person who has a conflict with another, rather than approaching that person directly, deals with his or her feelings by talking to a third person, who is then caught in the middle. At the end of every day, the phone lines would light up as everyone involved complained about everyone else to a third person. But the issues were never talked about directly or face to face.

Confronted with this, what was I, as the facilitator of this family meeting, to do? I could of course instruct the family members in how to talk with each other and ask them to try to talk with each other differently, practicing good communication skills. But I needed to get their attention and most of all, to shift the tone from one of blame and recrimination to one that would keep a keen focus on the business.

I used a tool that has had a marked impact on many types of organizations—from large corporations to nonprofits and communities. While it is deceptively simple, it has a powerful effect on a group. The process, called Appreciative Inquiry, developed by David Cooperrider and Diana Whitney, posits that change can best occur in a system not by focusing on solving problems or finding who is responsible for them and fixing each one, but by shifting the focus to what the system (group, organization, family, or community) is doing well and building on those activities.

I stopped the bickering, and asked people to step back and take a few minutes to talk about what went well in the business. The tone changed markedly, and people even had some nice things to say to each other. They talked about each person's skills and the long history of the business through three generations. They recalled successes and achievements and recognized their grandmother's wisdom. The tone of the group softened as they looked at their common heritage.

Then I framed a question, How can we develop what we have that works well and prepare the business to succeed in the new millennium? I asked each one to make positive statements about what they would like to see and instructed them not to say what was wrong with someone or something. After a while, they caught on and began talking about how to make things better.

The Appreciative attitude is one that you can take into any meeting. Focus the discussion not on what is wrong or who is to blame, but on the future, what you want to achieve and how you can do it. Rather than trying to fix the negative, build on the positive. Critics suggest that this practice glosses over and avoids facing real difficulties, and sometimes that can be so. But the experience that I have had with warring families is that the search for someone to blame and discussions in which people talk about what is wrong with each other just lead each person to turn off from the rest of the family.

This attitude can help pairs of people in a family communicate better. Consider an exchange between two family members with a long history of disagreement. One of them begins; the other gets upset; and an emotional trigger is pulled. The person listening reacts, interrupts, and the heat rises. Family members have spent years learning each other's emotional triggers and get stuck in exchanges that are simply emotional reactivity. To build communication, you must help people step back from their immediate emotional responses to each other.

There are several ways to do this. One very simple technique is to just allow each person in the family to talk without interruption. Think about what a change this can be in a family. People who are used to interrupting, arguing, blaming, and never listening to each other now have to step back and listen. They listen not just to the *other person*, but to *their own emotional responses*. Sometimes, they can learn to watch their emotional response and ask themselves why they are so upset at what their sibling or parent is doing. They also learn that even if they are upset at what someone else is saying, they don't necessarily have to get angry or fight back.

Another way to begin to move from conflict to understanding is to help family members understand that the effect that someone's behavior has on others is not always what was intended. One person's intention and the effect of what he or she does may be quite different. Not saying hello to your brother in the morning does not mean you are angry or don't like him. There are many reasons for this behavior. If your brother assumes that he was intentionally snubbed and then adds his own assumptions about what you were thinking, emotions begin to escalate. You can resolve a problem before it starts by checking with the other person to find out what he or she was thinking and feeling. Looking at this situation, you can begin to see how communication becomes more difficult when one family member reacts and assumes the other's intentions, without making sure they are correct.

One can consider a family to be an emotional system, in which people react to each other in ways that have developed over the years and find it hard to step back and see that people have grown, matured, and changed and are often very different than they were in earlier stages of life. In order to build working relationships as adults, each family member must get beyond emotional patterns formed in childhood. Feelings about ways that parents treat their offspring differently, favor one or another, or make promises that are not fulfilled, must be overcome. The personal hurt a person feels because of what took place in the family—or may still be a part of the family dynamics—makes it almost impossible to step out of one's own perspective and see things through the others' eyes.

This ability is part of what Daniel Goleman and his associates have called emotional intelligence, or EI. This quality is essential to effective family leadership and successful transition between generations. If more than one family member is to work in the business, and the family members are to develop good professional relationships with each other, the individuals must learn the skills of EI. Several such skills have been identified—including the ability to notice and understand one's feelings, the ability to listen to and hear the feelings of others, and the ability to moderate one's emotional impulses to consider the impact of one's actions on others.

These skills may be practiced in a family meeting. One can learn about one's own feelings by not allowing oneself to reactively blame others but rather by asking, "What is making me so upset with this other family member? What am I afraid of?" In this case, one's attention shifts from what one wants from the other to one's own reactions and their nature. In a family meeting, another way to slow down the emotional roller coaster is to ask an upset individual to explore and learn about his or her feelings. Like Appreciative Inquiry, this shifts attention and leads to a more reflective, open tone.

Another technique that helps family members improve their understanding of each other is to ask the person whose response has triggered an upset reaction to talk about his or her feelings and how he or she sees the situation. The upset person is asked to stop and listen and try to understand how the other feels. This sort of learning helps family members develop the emotional intelligence to learn how to work together.

It is hard enough staying connected as a family without adding the complexity of money, inheritance, and work relationships to the mix. To navigate these multiple layers of complexity, enterprising family members must work together to develop the skills of good communication using techniques like Appreciative Inquiry and emotional intelligence.

3.6

Preventing Family Feuds

One of the deadliest "natural" disasters that can befall a family business is a family feud. Tied together by blood and business, siblings or parents and children can find their connection boiling over to destructive conflict. While family conflict is healthy and inevitable, when it becomes a feud, the degree of hurt and anger makes resolution very difficult. Feuds often escalate out of control, leaving businesses wrecked, families estranged from each other, and "resolutions" that feel like defeats for all involved.

The Gucci brothers' feud is legendary, and represents a pattern of escalating sibling rivalry that is all too common.

Founder and proud father Guccio expected each of his three sons to take his place in the business. Oldest son Aldo, followed by Vasco, and, after a successful career as an actor, Rodolfo, all came on board. Each member of the volatile and highly competitive clan had different roles and lived in different places as the empire expanded in the 1950s and 60s. After the death of brother Vasco, Rodolfo and Aldo each held about half the shares of the family companies. They were fierce but contained rivals; each had different ideas about how to expand and about roles for their own sons.

Aldo's three sons entered the business, as did Rodolfo's only child, Maurizio. Resentment grew between Rodolfo and Aldo over Aldo's increasing control over the business in the United States, and Rodolfo's feeling of being slighted by his older brother. With Aldo and Rodolfo no longer having their middle brother to balance things, the situation boiled over. Aldo's son Paolo was openly critical of his elders, and he tried to go into business using his name to market his own Gucci line, raising deep family opposition. Control became very convoluted among several entities, and board meetings became family wars. Paolo was fired by Rodolfo, and as we mentioned earlier, a well-publicized physical fight erupted at a board meeting. Events escalated even higher as Aldo was convicted of tax evasion in New York and sent to jail. Control of the company shifted to Maurizio, before the empire was hobbled by the conflict and sold.

In the age of multiple marriages, stepsons and stepfamilies can also come to blows. Heir J. Seward Johnson's two sons, who inherited majority ownership of Johnson & Johnson, as we saw earlier, had a much publicized and costly lawsuit with their young stepmother who had been their father's companion for more than a decade before his death. Although the fight was about money, the feelings held by the children most likely had to do with not being recognized or respected by their father. Like most feuds, the resolution cost both sides considerable dignity and legal fees, and led to victory for no one.

Other feuds arise between family branches and can simmer for generations. In the DuPont family, one branch became deeply disaffected for more than a generation when they believed that family leader Pierre had cut them out of the lucrative sale and refinancing of the company. In the late nineteenth century, the Warburg banking family was composed of two equal family branches. By tradition, each branch was represented with one directorship in their bank. But one family branch had five charismatic sons and accounted for much of the family wealth before the devastation of the Second World War. Their cousin Siegmund was raised with the feeling that his branch had not received fair representation. As he rose to prominence after the war, he alternated between outfoxing and cooperating with his cousins for control of the scattered Warburg ventures.

It is hard to sustain harmony and avoid conflicts with any set of siblings, parents, and cousins. Families often dilute potential conflict by avoiding it, separating, and having little to do with each other. When a family has a vast business, however, the forces of connection make it imperative that they have effective conflict-resolution mechanisms. These should be both structural and personal.

The features of family feuds are familiar. A deep resentment grows among the parties, with each feeling the other has been taking advantage of them. There are hot families, like the Guccis, and cool ones, like the Warburgs. Their anger and mutual recrimination keeps them from feeling there is any possibility of resolution or fairness by direct negotiation. The other party is always to blame, producing a stalemate in any attempts at effective resolution. Winning the feud comes to mean making the other side lose.

While many feuds are about money and control, looking into the past, one can see that the seeds are often in family relationships—parents not having been respectful, loving, or present enough to their children, or a family feeling that one gender, child, or branch is favored. A feud begins when one family member believes that his or her role, share, or influence does not allow her to feel respected. Siegmund Warburg and Arthur DuPont both felt slighted by their families, and all the Johnson children felt neglected and deprived by their father over many years.

Principles for Preventing Family Feud

The best medicine for family feuds is prevention. Anyone observing a family feud can see that it hasn't sprung up overnight and isn't about business disagreements alone. When bringing siblings into the business, parents can minimize the possibility of destructive feuding by following four key principles.

Define family fairness and justice.

There is no deeper hurt than the feeling of a young boy or girl who believes he or she has been treated unjustly. Every family member has a sense of what is fair and just in a family, and as they grow, these concerns become more real and serious in their consequences. Families need to discuss fairness and expectations, especially in relation to the business. What can a male or female sibling expect, and what differences will there be for those who work in the business and those who do not? This is not done by fiat or decree, but must be done with open communication—including discussion of differences—among family members.

Respect each individual's growth and development.

Many feuds are the frustrated cries of siblings who think that the family has thwarted or frustrated their development. They are not encouraged or supported in their attempts to do something well, and have been brought up to see validation in terms of being given power or money, rather than in the satisfaction that comes from doing something on their own. Families who have a clear expectation of outside employment, and support for heirs who take up many forms of work, are less likely to fight over pieces of a smaller pie. Competent and confident people tend to feel less need to blame others and are more willing and able to compromise and see the other's perspective.

Create structural clarity.

If ownership or agreements are vague, they can be interpreted differently. In the Gucci case, the development of many entities with different shareholdings and unclear mechanisms of control created conditions for a fight. The presence of different numbers of siblings in different family branches means that a large family business must have clear structures to define how succession and other key decisions are made.

Include respected outside mediators.

Families are on better behavior when there are guests. A close family friend can often say things that father cannot. In a family business, the presence of respected elders on the board, and available to the family, can help mediate and reduce friction in succeeding generations. Feuds gain unnecessary heat when there is no outside presence to sit the principals down and cool things off. If the Guccis trusted any outsiders, they might have had someone who could have put their issues into perspective.

Moving Toward Family Reconciliation

But most families don't expect a feud to erupt or have mechanisms that blind them to the potential hurt that can be triggered many years later. Feuds can simmer for years, only to erupt when there is a death, a trauma, or a seemingly minor slight. If your family has had a rift, and there is a deep conflict that estranges two siblings or families, what can be done?

In a family feud, the hurt is so deep and the people on both sides of the issue so contentious and volatile that the conflict will not heal by itself. In desperation, the two parties build walls to separate themselves from each other. But even if the feelings seem buried, they don't go away. If the two feuding parties find themselves in the presence of each other, at a family wedding, say, or to sign legal papers, the conflict erupts as if the fight had taken place yesterday. The destructiveness of feuds stem from deep anger that cuts people off from positive feelings they also have for each other.

Healing in families comes about when one of the parties decides that he or she is losing too much by perpetuating the schism. In some instances another family member thinks that the discord has gone on enough and decides to try to make peace. Reconciliation is a very sensitive process and must proceed slowly and thoughtfully. Care must be taken to find neutral settings so that anger and blame do not escalate.

Anthropologists have noted a powerful mechanism for reconciliation in some cultures. A person who feels wronged or hurt seeks out the person who caused the negative feeling and gives him or her a gift. Period. This serves the purpose of stating that reconciliation and connection are stronger than personal differences. A variant of this for our purposes might be encouraging a hurt family member simply to seek out and engage the person who is responsible—or is perceived to be responsible—for the hurt.

The person who wants to end the feud must work on him- or herself (or with the person who is feuding) to take some responsibility for provoking the feud. Being able to say, "I understand that what I did hurt you" or "I understand that this business is very important to you and that you want to be recognized" demonstrates some openness to the other person. A very carefully written letter proposing a reconciliation meeting can even more fully open the door.

Reconciliation must proceed slowly, and without a rush to resolve issues. It is often best to start with areas of agreement, recalling what is good and positive about the family, the business, or their work together. Talking about what both people want to do or see in the business can also build a positive foundation for moving forward.

Family feuds are common, and many of them are so deep that they are hard to overcome. But it is a tragedy when a strong business and people who have so much to offer the family, each other, and the business find their vision narrowed and their fulfillment frustrated by the residue of long-standing family hurts, rivalries, and deprivation. When a family develops positive ways to openly express and deal with differences, the chances are much fewer that the situation will decay into a self-defeating feud.

Keys to Success: Overcoming Family Feuds

- Seek out and talk to people who have hurt you as soon as possible
- Have patience; do not try to kiss and make up in one step
- Take responsibility for the part of the hurt or conflict that you have contributed
- Involve others who know both parties to mediate and offer their observations, without necessarily taking sides
- Define what you want and what is fair, not what you don't want the other person to get; state this clearly and directly to the other
- Check out what you assume the other person has done, intends, or thinks before you act on your assumptions

3.7

The Disruptive In-law

In many families, the entry of new family members by marriage presents a challenge for the family business. First, the family must decide if the in-law can be considered for a role in the family business. This is challenging in that the new family member may have a different style or set of values and can become a disruptive force. Alternatively, many in-laws offer an infusion of talent and capability that the members of the family can't match. But including the in-law in the family business often leads to dissension in the family. This selection suggests ways to get the best from new blood while avoiding potential conflicts.

When a family meeting is being convened, things often progress smoothly until a family member announces plans to include his or her spouse. There is a hush, and the patriarch usually mutters something to the effect, "We don't consider them to be 'real' members of the family." The matter could rest there, but for the fact that other family heirs tend to be not so easily convinced, and this gives rise to such questions as, How do we define membership in the family? What is the proper role for the in-law?

Many families follow the route of royalty and tradition: Blood defines the family. A spouse is a visitor to the family, necessary to the process of creating a new generation of the family, but not really part of it. Other cultures specify that a bride leave her family of origin and enter the new family. Divorce is rarely an option, so family members might have lovers and occasional illegitimate children all outside the sphere of "family." These conventions are easy to follow in a society in which culture is unified by a shared tradition. Marriages are entered into at the direction of, or at least with the blessing of, the patriarch and personal choice is limited.

Today, even in the strictest societies, such traditions are harder to maintain. The authority of parents to choose their in-laws is breaking down, and it is the individual's prerogative to choose a marriage partner. The increasing incidence of divorce, and therefore families with children from more than one marriage, further complicates the determination of who is in a family and who is out. A family, one of whose members has a former spouse who raised several children and was a member of the family for many years, may have to contend with the individual's new younger spouse and a new set of heirs. Personal relationships and allegiances may conflict with formal ones.

In many cultures, the parents had a utilitarian agenda in selecting in-laws. Royal families would marry to cement alliances. In business dynasties, the marriage of cousins helped limit the number of heirs and unified ownership of large estates across family branches. Parents selected spouses for their children, negotiating with each other for dowries and other inducements offered and received. A new spouse would result from a good business deal between families. A family might select a son-in-law who could add value to a family business or receive venture capital from the dowry of a new daughter. By seeking spouses within a limited community, the cultural and class commonality between spouses was virtually assured: The future spouse was a known quantity, their families familiar to each other and comfortable.

Today's global world promotes free choice and cultural mixing. Young people meet people from many cultures and social classes at school. A wealthy heir may appear similar to a poor student, and they might fall in love in a community where they both fit very well. They feel they have a lot in common and within their world, they do.

Most young couples today may decide to marry without consulting their parents. At the wedding, the other family members may barely know the new entrant. Unfamiliarity breeds distrust, especially when the new person represents a different culture, religion, or social class. A new family member's poorer background can lead to tensions—within not just the family but the new couple as well. The heir and his or her spouse-to-be face issues regarding how they draw on the family's wealth to support their lifestyle. The heir may be concerned about the feelings that family wealth can produce in the new family member. The family may fear that their child's fiancé or fiancée has an agenda other than love; the family's suspicion not only doesn't breed trust in the new relationship but may in fact begin to destabilize the couple's otherwise strong and loving commitment. While the couple may insist their union is just love, there may be an element of rebellion in the attraction the young person from the enterprising family feels to one who embodies qualities and values that are the opposite of those of his or her parents. The endings are rarely as neat as those of films like *Meet the Parents* or *Guess Who's Coming to Dinner*, in which suspicion is transformed into trust, respect, and caring. In life off the silver screen, the suspicion often lingers for years, masked by politeness or tolerance.

The new spouse in fact has to enter two systems of relationship: In addition to the helping his or her mate create their own two-person family, the new spouse also enters the larger family of wealth, which may have an intimidating and even arrogant demeanor. The spouse's entry into the enterprising family should be accomplished carefully, thoughtfully, and with clear intentions. Although there is no substitute for the ritual of meeting the parents, the member of the enterprising family should also arrange a way to ease the new spouse into the business-and-financial world of the family.

Why should the business aspect of the new family concern the spouse? If care is not taken to bring the spouse into this part of the enterprising family, that family may express its distrust by keeping the new member permanently on the outside. In my experience, this leads to misread intentions and deepening suspicion; the entrant suspects the family doesn't and isn't willing to accept the union, and the family fears the entrant is marrying for money. Added to this, the spouse from the enterprising family has an inheritance and role in the family, which she wants to share with her spouse. If not discussed openly, this can lead to situations in which misunderstandings and hurts are amplified and grow into full-bore rifts. A young bride from an enterprising family may not completely understand the business affairs of her family, and her husband, a young and overconfident businessperson himself, may begin to think the family is not treating them fairly. If the two sides are somewhat distant, the suspicion increases, the young couple talks to a friend who is a lawyer, and he further fuels their concerns. The family may have been less than candid with their daughter about their distrust of her fiancé, but when they hear about this, they may get even more angry, which can lead to threats and finally a complete breakdown in communication. Each side thinks the other is the source of evil. A family feud is born.

Contrast this to a prominent business family who has a formal entry process. Young family members and their spouses to be are invited to a briefing held at the family's annual meeting that introduces the family's wealth, governance, and business structures. The young marrieds are told about the need for strict confidentiality, and they sign a confidentiality agreement. While the briefing is very detailed, the exact sizes of trusts and financial statements are not specified. At the end, the new family members know what to expect from their new family and what is expected of them. They can ask questions, and they get to know the family financial and business leaders in a personal and respectful forum. The new family member also learns why the family asks new entrants to sign a prenuptial agreement, although sometimes this is done privately.

The positive message is clear: The new member is welcomed into the family. But the new member is also apprised of the rules and traditions that have evolved over generations in the family into which he or she is marrying, and the new member is asked to respect them even if in their new family some of the values about money may be unfamiliar to the new spouse. Benefits and also obligations come with the legacy.

If a family has regular family meetings, the in-law should be welcomed into many of them. The presence of fresh views can be a healthy challenge to the family's entrenched ways of doing—and seeing—things. If the new person is from another culture or class, he or she will bring diversity to the family. Some families, however, include only blood family in their annual meetings, which will likely cause the in-law to feel estranged. A family might exclude all in-laws because they are concerned about one particular in-law, whom they consider excessively disruptive or disloyal. Other families welcome all in-laws into their families as full members. One prominent multigenerational family has an extreme policy that any in-law becomes part of the family, and even if he or she divorces—and the heir did not instigate the break—the former spouse can still remain part of the larger enterprising family organization.

The in-law can bring new skills, perspectives, and ideas to what may be the family heirs' narrow skill and personality set and may find working for the family interesting and fulfilling. Moreover, an in-law may be trusted in a way that nonfamily executives often are not. Over the years, a family can become so ingrown and insular that it may be in danger, and a new family member with new ways of conceptualizing and a fresh view can help them open themselves up and bring health and vigor back to the family.

Working alongside other family members, who may be brothers, sisters, or cousins of one's spouse, can stimulate family rivalries. The Kennedy family's prominent in-law Sargent Shriver was seen as a loyal family member who worked to advance the political fortunes of his brothers-in-law until he was asked to run for vice president by Democratic candidate George McGovern, passing over a full-blooded Kennedy in the process. In another family business, a brother-in-law was accorded great respect as an operations person, but he had to accept that a family member would be CEO. He always thought that he had to work harder and that his brothers-in-law had a much less vigorous work ethic. If one accepts that his or her role will always be secondary, employment can work well. But what of the family in which the father sees in his in-law a person with a work ethic and capability far beyond that of his sons or daughters, who see themselves as the rightful heirs? Family conflict can overshadow the business realities. That is why many families, deciding that the potential for conflict overshadows any benefit that the in-law might bring to the business, prohibit in-law employment.

A clear employment policy that sets out the criteria for family members working, advancing, and being compensated helps smooth the entry of an in-law into the family business. If these exist prior to the person's entry, the process can be much smoother. The inherent structure of rivalry between old and new family members can at least be balanced by clear policies. These help, but they cannot overcome entirely the feeling of entitlement that many natural family members have over newcomers. These feelings are very difficult to overcome and hence, very few in-laws become family enterprise leaders. The most prominent cases are those in which the daughter in a traditional family does not enter the business, has no brothers, and the son-in-law is welcomed as the successor. But in even the most harmonious families, the entry of an in-law is fraught with challenges, and the benefits of the in-law's fresh ideas are all too often lost in the struggle.

3.8

Advisers: How to Get Out of the Middle

When a family conflict arises, a family member or adviser often tries to step in and mediate. This can lead to the individual's being caught in the middle, with neither side feeling helped or understood. This selection offers tips for advisers and other well-intentioned mediators as they wade into family disputes.

There is nothing more ominous for a family adviser than to hear from a family member about his or her growing resentment or conflict with the family. Too often, the adviser feels helpless, seeing misinformation, misperception, or misplaced feelings begin to poison family relationships and undermine the family's financial health. The family member feels deeply wronged by some action and instead of facing the issue directly, builds up negative feelings that too often lead to his or her seeking legal redress for what are clearly personal as well as legal issues.

Family conflict is inevitable within an enterprising family consisting of multiple generations, family branches, and complex and valuable financial entities. The challenge for a family and their advisers is to find ways to deal with conflict that sustain the family's overall financial and business health while also respecting the personal realities and relationships within the family. Too often, once a family dispute enters the legal system, the process and the outcome may be destructive to both their financial and personal health.

Family conflicts undermine the family's ability to manage their wealth in several ways. The existence of the conflict makes it more difficult for the various individuals and entities to reach agreement on basic policies. Conflict brews below the surface and while the discussion centers on control or distribution of wealth, the real issues that lie below the surface—and are not discussed—center on family rivalries, fairness, and ancient events. To make matters worse, the conflict often preoccupies family members, who spend endless amounts of energy working on their own agendas while nobody in the family focuses on the external challenges of the marketplace and the slippery world economic picture. While the family engages in endless palace intrigue, the kingdom is under siege.

The hidden causes of family conflict lie deep in the family history. Some believe one family heir is unfairly favored financially. There is jealousy over who is closest to the parents, whose work is more valued, or who is more successful. There are secret agreements causing some family members to believe they are not being told the whole story or the truth. There are old hurts—such as one's spouse not having been welcomed into the family a decade or more ago or a scion feeling that as a child he was neglected by his parents—that lead a family member to feel entitled to something later on.

The legal and business system is ill suited to handle these issues. First, the issue that is being fought over—for instance, how family income is distributed—may not be the real issue. If the legal system is contesting a trust agreement or a family financial decision, it takes that as the real conflict; the legal system does not have a mechanism that would allow it to see below the surface. Therefore, the resolution tends to satisfy neither party. For example, sometimes, because of the deeper personal hurts, it is not clear what a dissident family member really wants. There are endless negotiations to buy out his or her share of a family enterprise or to determine a fair price for her interest, but the deeper hurts make it difficult for either party to come up with a reasonable figure. Instead of looking out for their own interests, family members are focused on what the other side will gain, and too often, a family member focuses the issue on making sure that the other party is the clear loser. This form of thinking makes it difficult to find a fair resolution for both parties—or either party.

The adviser, seeing the storm brewing in the family, often takes action that makes things worse. Since he or she often has a working relationship with one member of the family—a patriarch, board member, or family office manager—the adviser may feel forced to take sides and "agree" with her colleague rather than suggesting that there may be more to the story. If an adviser talks with only one person, she may not be aware of the different ways other family members see the issues. For example, some minority family members may feel less informed than the staff and family members who are in the office every day, or are working in the family business, and may make assumptions about what the family office does.

Some advisers are not comfortable with emotions in general and collude with an upset family member to sweep the issue under the table, as if it will go away. They don't want to stir the pot and face a conflict directly. Neither does the family leader. The outcome of this neglect or one-sided focus is that the dissident family members, who feel unheard and helpless, will try to empower themselves by obtaining the services of a confrontational legal adviser who will shake the family tree.

Once a conflict has entered the confrontational stage, it is harder to resolve. Each person, talking to people who are in his corner, gets more deeply convinced that his cause is just. The legal advisers strongly urge family members who disagree not to talk with each other because they may hurt their cause. So efforts to reach a personal agreement are less likely. In addition, in the heat of the moment, a family member may say and do things that add more hurt and distrust to the relationship. Everybody becomes captive to the legal process, which can never achieve real family justice, because it is only concerned with legal and financial issues, not personal ones.

Of course, from within a family conflict, both advisers and members of the family can clearly see that the best and most-effective measures are those that could have been in place in the beginning to prevent the conflict from getting out of control in the first place. A family can initiate several forms of prevention. Although I have mentioned these before, they bear repeating: Families can, first, have informal activities to get to know each other and build trust. Families that have annual picnics or all-family meetings have a chance to get to know each other, and even to breach sensitive topics in informal settings.

Second, there is a need to communicate more than what the insiders—the family members who work within the family enterprises—think is sufficient. You can't communicate too much, and the communication process has to be extensive enough, at a minimum, so that individual family members get to talk about their concerns and receive complete responses. A family adviser who takes time to educate and share trust or business information with an upset or confused family member can be practicing preventive medicine, even if the questions and time can feel frustrating. A family often has a regular forum, an annual meeting during which financial and business information is shared and the family has an informal exchange about it. Of course, the family members must understand the need to keep these discussions confidential and agree to do so.

And finally, it is preventive for the family to create agreements about major issues—such as the overall mission and goals of family enterprises, how a family member can sell his or her shares, how dividends and compensation are determined, conflict of interest policy, and employment and decision-making authority about family ventures.

But hindsight is not insight. Families get into conflicts, and the adviser is sometimes in the best position to help move toward resolution. The adviser often has the ear of all the key people and can persuade them to come together to work on a solution. There are several foundations that help an adviser take on the role of mediator. First, the adviser has to make clear that his or her role in the conflict is to speak for the whole family, to be the voice of the business, or a fair witness, rather than taking sides or working for one part of the family. This

126

can be tricky, but it is possible for a person to make it clear that for purposes of a single issue the adviser is taking on this mediator role. This role is not that of arbitrator—a person who makes the decision—but of mediator, whose task is to create a safe setting for the family members to come together and find their own resolution.

A good mediator moves in certain ways to help create trust and engagement in the family. First, he or she can help the whole family create a setting in which family members feel comfortable sharing their feelings about the issues. The mediator might say that the initial meeting will not focus at all on what to do, but rather on making sure that each person gets to say what he or she wants to say and that all the family members get the information they need into the room. The phrase "go slow to go fast" suggests that a family has to decide that they won't have a quick resolution of an issue that has taken many years to grow into what it is now. Second, the adviser should begin with the positive—a discussion of the personal values of each family member and what is working well in the family. The focus should not be on "who is to blame" but rather on what can be done to move forward. Avoiding a climate of blame and recrimination is a key element of positive conflict resolution. And finally, the goal is to get the bystanders—the family members who are in the middle and have good relations with both sides of the conflict—involved so that they may act as helpers and show each side that there is more to the story than their own views.

When a family develops a conflict, as is inevitable in a large, complex, and wealthy family, the adviser is in a position to make a great deal of difference. Instead of feeling caught in the middle, and helplessly watching the family go downhill, the adviser can take action and become a family mediator, helping the family resolve conflict in ways that preserve both the family relationships and their wealth.

3.9

How to Hold an Effective Family Meeting

Throughout this book, in selection after selection, I will suggest that the family should have a meeting where they discuss an issue. A family meeting is a gathering of all family members in a quiet and comfortable place—for instance, a vacation home—with the specific aim of talking openly and honestly with each other about their feelings, issues, and desires. This simple activity is the foundation of many of the best practices for sustaining family enterprises. This selection offers some guidelines for holding meetings that leave everyone feeling included and that lead to productive outcomes that people feel positive about implementing.

Family meetings are a time-honored practice of families who want to talk about the personal side of passing on their wealth, family business, values, and tradition of achievement and good works. Many of the family's concerns involve the family business but include people (e.g., nonactive owners, spouses) who are not formally part of this business. Meetings might include discussions about values and mission, about family participation in wealth management, about compensation and distribution of funds, about fairness, and about how the family's wealth will be used to make a difference for family members and the community. These meetings can include a few people—parents and their adult children and spouses—or many family branches and sets of cousins.

The meetings need not lead to votes or decisions. But these events provide opportunities to unearth and explore differences and discover ways to be fair to everyone. And if decisions are made, in such areas, say, as inheritance and generational transition, family members will better understand the intentions behind those decisions.

The greatest value of such conversations is sharing and passing on **legacy**—the values that one generation honors and lives by and wants to transmit to future generations. These values concern the importance of family connection and the family's ways of doing business, giving back to the community, and raising children. Legacy is an implicit contract and responsibility that accompanies inheritance.

Major Purposes of a Family Meeting

- To foster healthy communication among all family members
- To pass on family values, such as work, education, community, integrity, respect, and loyalty
- To communicate core money values and their relationship to wealth management
- To communicate with the younger generation, opening up a dialog about their ideas and intentions and assessing their developmental readiness to handle money
- To deal with a change or transition in family circumstances, such as the sale or acquisition of a business or the death of a family member
- To achieve an emotionally healthy transfer of wealth
- To overcome a conflict

There are many formats for a family meeting, but they have some elements in common. They should be held in *comfortable* places, where there is no disruption. Phones and other intrusions should be kept out. There should be sufficient time to keep the meeting somewhat open-ended. It should be as *inclusive* as possible, with all family members invited.

A meeting sets up a *process* of communication. In many cases, families open up issues for which there may be no clear and easy resolution. Or there are more issues than can possibly be covered in one evening. Sometimes a meeting is extended to a one- or two-day event. Some families have regular meetings, once or several times a year. Continuity is important. Many meetings have a facilitator, a person who agrees to keep the proceedings on track and make sure that everyone participates. In some families, this role is rotated; other families hire an outside consultant for this role, at least in the beginning.

At the first meeting, the family should agree on a set of guidelines—a **Family Code of Conduct** (for more on a Family Code of Conduct as part of the mission statement and constitution, see "Why Enterprising Families Need a Constitution" and "Defining a Family Mission and Crafting the Constitution," in Part II)—for how to listen to each other, how to maintain order, and what sort of behavior is expected during the meeting. (This Family Code of Conduct may also be applied as a guide for family behavior in other contexts.) The meeting needs careful and clear preparation and follow-up. An agenda of issues and concerns should be established to guide it, and these topics should be available to the family members in advance. If the meeting leads to decisions or other outcomes, these should be recorded and distributed to family members. If someone agrees to do something, that also should be recorded.

Ground Rules for Successful Family Meetings

If the family is to agree on and articulate its **Family Code of Conduct** at its first meeting, the meeting must be one that encourages thoughtfulness, productivity, and collaboration. The following ground rules have helped many families create a successful and inspiring meeting in which they can begin to learn to work together by drafting the guidelines that are the Family Code of Conduct:

Create an environment in which people feel respected.

The family can't just call people together. Family members need to feel that they can talk about emotionally charged and difficult issues without recrimination. The convener needs to make clear what will happen and how it will take place. A good way to create a firm foundation is to pledge that confidences will be respected and that everyone will try to maintain a positive perspective. Another form of respect is avoiding nonessential discussions that create discomfort. In one family meeting, for example, it was agreed that an issue would be dropped if even just one hand was raised in objection.

Set your mind-set for "open" when you begin.

If you enter a conversation with the primary intention of making your own points and convincing others you are right, you won't get far. One of the treasures of a family conversation is discovering something about someone you have known and loved for many years that you didn't know or, more likely, hadn't heard before. In one family gathering, the discussion of career and family dreams helped the patriarch see that his children had very different visions of their futures than he did.

Conversations are about discovery, not making decisions.

Yes, a decision must be made, eventually. But a conversation is not a debate, and there will be plenty of time to come to a decision later. The purpose of a family meeting is to explore what people think and to devise ways to turn those thoughts into action. In one situation in which parents were setting up a complex estate plan, they were open to listening to the fears and concerns of their children after it was established that the purpose of the exchange was to share ideas, not talk the parents out of any choice they wanted to make.

Talk about your history.

Initiate a conversation about legacy. For a business founder, this would be a place to talk about how the firm was created, what it means, and what makes him or her proud and satisfied. The founder might talk about struggles, choices, and what he or she knows and how this knowledge was acquired. Legacy conversations are important. They are a living will and should be recorded, even videotaped. The family's job is to appreciate and listen. Certainly you may ask questions or request more details, but under no circumstances should you disagree or add your own ideas. This is about understanding where you have come from and what you are heir to. Once family members begin to share stories about their history, many families will have talks lasting late into the evening.

Begin with what you agree on.

When family members see how many important things they agree on, it may be easier to place the differences in context. For example, a family divided about the future fate of a family business began the conversation by articulating the many values they agreed on and discussing how much they had in common. This exchange enabled them to be more flexible when making their difficult decisions.

Take enough time, and stay in the room.

Avoid unrealistic hopes, such as expectations that people will change, that conflict will end, or that one conversation will do the trick. Agree to meet for at least a set amount of time. Get people to pledge that they won't walk out, or if they do, they will come back when they cool down.

Don't interrupt.

Some families love to interrupt each other. This is a sign that people are not listening; they think they already know what the other person is saying. A ground rule that people can talk until they are finished, and that the others will hold their comments until they are done should be established. Some families use a device like a "talking stick": The stick signifies who has the right to speak—you can only speak if holding the stick—and is passed from speaker to speaker. This technique almost always slows down conversation so that many people have a chance to be heard without being interrupted.

Slow it down.

Sometimes, a single phrase can upset many participants. When tempers begin to boil, the coolest person in the room should step up and say, "Let's slow down." Ask each person to take a break, sit quietly, and then explain slowly, without interruption from other family members, why he or she is upset. Silence can give people a chance to reflect and reconsider. Agree to disagree, and listen to what the others have to say, *even when you find it very painful.*

Put the toughest issues aside.

If this is your first family meeting, don't discuss how the inheritance should be allocated. Talk about simpler issues. Work up to the tough ones in subsequent get-togethers. The feelings of a generation can't be resolved in one meeting. After working on less-contentious issues, a family develops effective ways to move into more-difficult ones, and has more commitment to doing so.

Speak for yourself, not others.

Use the word *I*, not *we*. Take responsibility for what you feel, and share those feelings. Don't presume to speak for others or attempt to express what they feel or want. They are there to tell you themselves. One family matriarch who routinely talked about how "we" feel was able to see that these were her own thoughts and feelings and should not be imposed on others. She was finally able to hear and understand that some of her children had very different ideas and feelings from hers.

Encourage everyone to talk.

It is helpful to start a meeting by going around the room asking all family members to say what is on their minds. If someone is silent, or if one or two people are dominating the discussion, it is helpful for the facilitator to ask those who are not talking to speak up.

Avoid criticism or blame.

There may be strong feelings about past events. People may be angry and hurt, and may want to blame others. This is inevitable, but not productive. Instead of focusing on the past, try to stick to what people want to do *now*. One family repeats the following whenever a family member begins to use past behavior to blame others: "Let's not look at who is responsible; let's solve the problem."

Get concrete.

Family conflict builds up over many small events and misunderstandings. Over time, these misunderstandings can develop into huge and hurtful areas of disagreement. When you unearth such a problem, take time for each person to talk about what happened that hurt him or her. Resist the tendency to interrupt. Be sure to say what you really think.

Write down what is important.

Some things that are said—perhaps stories, values, or even understandings—are important enough to record. A useful aid is a large sheet of paper on the wall, on which people can record what they want to remember. Because people's memories are not completely reliable, if you don't write down minutes, decisions, and understandings, you will lose valuable information and a useful reference tool.

Follow up with individual conversations.

You can't always say everything you want to in the group. Sometimes, you need to have one-on-one talks. Agree at the meeting to hold some individual conversations among people who have the most difficulty talking with each other. One family uses the following plan: When two people say they will have lunch together or arrange for another joint activity, one family member writes down that agreement, and a third party makes a phone call to make sure the meeting took place. While some felt at first that this was too intrusive, in time they began to see its value. As one family member said, "Sometimes it's hard to pick up the phone even though you agreed to do it at a meeting."

Practices for Overcoming Family-Meeting Difficulties

The family must remember that they spent many years avoiding issues, and they will need to allow some time to unlearn this harmful practice. Some common challenges arise repeatedly when a family tries to set up meetings:

Some people don't want to participate.

Family members should be encouraged to come to the meeting. However, a meeting can be held even if one member is not willing to participate. In fact, when a family forges ahead, the reluctant member sees the cost of not participating and often decides that the family is really willing to listen to long-held grievances or concerns.

Deep-seated attitudes that inhibit money communication need to be challenged. Fears of retaliation for expressing one's point of view must be neutralized. Family members who are more comfortable with disclosure can demonstrate the benefits of communication, if the conditions are safe and the outcome of their communication will not be disastrous. Those who hold both emotional and financial power need to be heard by the family and recognized for their authority, and then they need to be contained in the overall process.

Some people can't get beyond their own opinions.

There are always family members who seem to feel they hold a monopoly on morality. If conditions are safe, a facilitator can challenge some of the assumptions that underscore such a person's rigid point of view. This can lead to a more-constructive dialogue, opening the door to conflict resolution or to the recognition that further communication would be fruitless. In the worst cases are people who are so self-involved that they are psychologically unable to empathize with or understand the validity of the ideas and opinions of other family members.

Some people are highly impaired.

Some family members are too disruptive to effectively participate in a family meeting. They may have personal problems that are too great or views that are so upsetting, angry, or rigid that they cannot follow the ground rules for participating in a family discussion. They erupt or storm out, or they make impossible demands. When this happens, the family leaders should have individual conversations with these members. This often requires professional help. The emotional issues are deep, difficult, and painful.

Some people are concerned about upsetting others.

Because money is a difficult, conflict-laden topic, some family members may passively drift toward the feeling that they do not want to upset people. The facilitator should clarify these concerns directly, pointing out that they are normal, based on taboos about communication regarding money. And then he or she should *encourage involvement*.

Keeping people to their agreements; follow up.

In a meeting everybody has good intentions and lots of energy. Then they go home and nothing happens. The family needs to appoint someone to keep things moving ahead. And the family should schedule a follow-up meeting to make certain that progress is being made. However, they need to be gentle with each other when things don't happen as quickly and easily as expected.

These ground rules and practices can help any family begin to hold successful family meetings.

 **Part Four**

The Rocky Transition From First to Second Generation

Over generations, every family faces a mixture of planned and unplanned family-business transitions. Some transitions, like leadership succession, can be anticipated and a strategy developed for their implementation. Others, like the sudden death of a family member or an unforeseen opportunity to sell the business, are unexpected and require immediate entrepreneurial responses. In family enterprises, all transitions—planned or unplanned—entail consideration of both rational business dimensions and emotional family dimensions; successful transitions depend on engaging both the family and the business leadership in the decision-making process.

Although it is not always possible to predict specific transitions—such as those mentioned above—a family gains strength by preparing itself to manage transitions in general before they arise. Some transitions can be anticipated, such as the inevitable family changes that occur when young people grow up and elders leave the field. If the family organizes its pathway to prepare the next generation for the elder generation to move on, it creates internal strengths to manage adversity. By creating mechanisms to manage unavoidable transitions and by preparing emotionally and strategically in advance for these transitions, a family will more likely have the strength and versatility to approach unexpected transitions as opportunities. A family's transition, for example, from ownership of a single business to that of a larger enterprise, requires both a shared family vision and a planning process involving multiple generations. The experiences of numerous families who have successfully navigated the transitions required by the inevitable and constant changes a thriving family enterprise encounters provide helpful lessons.

Unfortunately, when addressing natural generational and business challenges, families tend to focus on *individual transactions* rather than *transition processes,* and most professional disciplines reinforce this thinking in their training and practice. Sales or acquisitions of businesses are almost always viewed as transactions entailing discrete steps bounded by tight time frames. Similarly, transfers of stock from one generation of shareholders to another typically occur as part of an estate plan and are seen by many families and advisers as requiring only technical, legal, and tax advice, often with no consideration of the family dimension of the inheritance. Even leadership succession is viewed by most business leaders and advisers as a transaction in which one person replaces another in an organizational role.

A family can draw on a number of business factors to objectively assess the pros and cons of the available options for the sale of the family business. Still, one of the principal factors that influence the decision to sell or retain the business is the family's vision of its future as an enterprising family. If the family's vision of itself is limited to that of owners of an operating business, the family will find it difficult to agree to a sale. Or if the family business has not diversified or created enough wealth to provide opportunities for future generations, the family may view a sale as threatening. On the other hand, if the family sees itself as an enterprising family with multiple assets, the sale of its business can be an opportunity to begin the transition to ownership of more-diverse assets.

Whether the chance to sell the family legacy business is unforeseen or has been anticipated for some period of time, the decision to sell it can be the most wrenching decision a family will ever have to make. While many business sales are planned, other opportunities occur at unexpected or even inopportune times. To overcome the natural emotional resistance to such a sale, family leaders can use appropriate family governance structures to address nonbusiness factors and to develop a shared vision of the family's future.

After the sale of its legacy business, a family becomes another kind of business entity. The family may elect to invest its newly liquid assets together following the sale of the business. By doing this, the family makes a new start with the opportunity to diversify its holdings to reduce risk and provide for the growth of assets that will accrue to the benefit of future generations. This is more than a financial decision; the sale of the business heralds a major work transition for the family members who are employed there and represents the loss of an opportunity for the next generation. By redefining the family's identity following the sale of the family business, however, the family can set the stage for continuing its legacy as an enterprising family.

The selections that follow suggest that families shift the focus and reframe business transactions by viewing them as transitions involving multiple interconnected elements—some of which have to do with family dynamics—rather than discrete actions. By understanding these transactions as part of a larger process, families and their advisers will be in a better position to prepare for and manage the transitions they will inevitably face. Family members and advisers can benefit from understanding how family dynamics influence decision making in business transitions and from applying that understanding to the transition processes. By understanding that all business transactions require family transitions, families can approach change as not only unavoidable but also as offering opportunities for future success.

By clarifying their mission, including the family's values and goals, enterprising families can define the key elements of the family legacy that are shared by everyone and in so doing diminish the risks to family unity. External factors, those beyond the family's control such as industry trends, economic conditions, and the competitive environment, present opportunities for and threats to the continuation of the family enterprise. Planned processes aid a family dealing with both generational transitions and those occasioned by external factors.

The following selections explore issues related to family-business transitions and ways in which these transitions can offer opportunities for the future success of the family enterprise. By viewing these processes as family-business *transitions* rather than *isolated transactions* and being alert to the ways in which they offer opportunities for future success, family members and professional advisers will be best prepared to manage these transactions and take advantage of opportunities when they arise. In the following selections, I cite best practice solutions and offer processes for addressing the major transitions that an enterprising family can expect to face as it moves between generations. These include leadership succession; business diversification; shifts in asset ownership and identification; sale, recapitalization, or continuation of a business; merger or acquisitions; and minority ownership of assets. Examples of families who have successfully addressed these transitions illustrate the importance of integrating knowledge of family dynamics into business decision making and present methods for implementing this understanding so families may best accomplish these transitions in their own family enterprises.

4.1

Navigating the Inevitable Transitions in a Family Enterprise

Although a family may not be able to predict the exact nature or time of a transition, such an experience should not come as a total shock. Most transitions are dictated by human biology—the growth and development of family members. The family can be aware that such transitions will occur and be more or less prepared for them. This selection shows how a family can plan for family transitions.

Perhaps the transition most familiar to family enterprises is leadership succession. In any organization, the transfer of power to a new leader is a sensitive process. For family enterprises, leadership succession is even more complex since it most often involves both business and family leadership roles. When a family business transitions to new leadership, the successor must take responsibility not only for strategic management of the business but also for stewardship of the family's assets. In many cases, the next generation of leadership candidates includes family members, which means that the transitional process will include emotional elements.

When Harold Torrington indicated to his family and management team his intent to step down as CEO upon reaching his seventieth birthday, his daughter, Ellen, and nephew, David, were considered candidates to succeed him. In 27 years as the second-generation leader, Harold had built the family's building materials company into a diverse network of four operating companies with assets valued at more than $450 million. Harold's brother had served as the company's vice president of sales and had retired five years earlier but continued to serve on the board along with one of his two sisters. Harold's siblings were pleased with his leadership of the family enterprise and the wealth that he had created for family members. Harold's intention to retire signaled a transition in leadership of both the business and the family.

Harold Torrington's decision to step down was seen a mixed blessing for the family: It signaled the end of an era of business success for the family, and it produced anxious feelings among family members over what they considered to be a contest between his daughter and nephew over who would be his successor. Although the company's management team and family members all wanted the leadership-succession process to be fair and objective, family pride inevitably led family members of both generations to favor the selection of a member of their branch to serve as the next CEO. The family sought out their primary advisers for assistance in proceeding with the leadership-succession process.

At some time, almost all family enterprises will face leadership transitions similar to the Torrington's. Many will view leadership succession as a transaction with winners and losers, a view that can be destructive to the family and detrimental to business. But others will approach it as a process that begins long before leadership authority is transferred and continues well into the next generation. Seen as a process, leadership succession entails many steps, including the following:

- Entry into the business of new family members
- Education of family members
- Mentoring and development of future leaders
- Planning for retirement
- Teamwork as intergenerational leaders
- Transfer of authority
- Support and accountability for new leaders

Thus, leadership succession is best practiced as a multigenerational process, taking place over many years, instead of a transaction involving only successor selection and transfer of power.

Control and Minority Family Interests

When enterprising families undergo a generational transition, power is usually conveyed to one family member or a select few members of the next generation. When the transition is focused on leadership of the family's operating business, control may be conveyed to a CEO who also serves as chair of the board. In such cases, control of the operating business is clearly stated. Often overlooked, however, is responsibility for stewardship of the family's assets, which typically accompanies the operating responsibilities. The stewardship role may be unclear to other members of the inheriting generation of family shareholders; control over the family assets can be controversial in such transitions.

Despite his relatively young age of 37, Kevin Kohl was welcomed as the natural successor to his mother, Allison, when she announced her early retirement as second-generation CEO of the family's real estate business due to the return of her breast cancer. Kevin had joined his mother immediately after graduating from the Wharton School with an MBA, and by the time she retired, he had worked at the right hand of the company's general manager for five years. No one questioned Kevin's passion for the business or knowledge of real estate. However, less than a year into his tenure as CEO, numerous family shareholders voiced dissatisfaction with his leadership of the family enterprise.

Unlike his mother, who went to great lengths to meet with and inform her aunts, uncles, and cousins of the status of the family business, Kevin preferred to consult with independent board members and consultants he had hired to advise him on and execute real estate transactions. Family shareholders found themselves reading about the latest development project in local newspapers long before they had received any notice as shareholders. When several family members expressed concern about the family's holdings in the face of the downturn in the real estate markets, Kevin dismissed their concerns as "reactionary" and not helpful to management. After two quarterly board meetings during which concerns raised by family members of the board were not addressed, a group of ten family shareholders, representing two branches and 40 percent of the outstanding shares, offered their shares for sale back to the company.

Family transitions that result in significant changes in business conditions or expose family shareholders to increased risks can be very disruptive. Because the sale of shares of stock in family enterprises are rarely permitted outside the business or family, minority shareholders can be made to feel captive to the wishes of family management. Often the value of their shares represents a significant but nonliquid portion of the net worth of these family members, and in such cases, ownership without trust in family leadership can become an area of contention. Family members who seek to liquidate some or all of their shares are restricted by buy–sell agreements and by the lack of a market for their stock. Such shareholders can be made to feel disloyal or mercenary if they seek to sell their shares. To prevent family or business disruptions, family-leadership transitions need to address both business and family-ownership concerns.

In all business enterprises, there are dynamic tensions between the interests of management and those of owners. In family enterprises, these tensions can result in open conflict if family interests are not properly addressed. Generational leadership transitions should clarify the management responsibilities being assumed by the new leaders and ensure that family and business decision-making structures are employed to help family members communicate openly while addressing the interests of all shareholders. In addition to issues of the role clarification, performance measurement, compensation, and accountability that are part of any leadership transition, family transitions need to sort business from family issues.

Major Transactions and Family Transitions

Perhaps the most monumental decision a family can make is to sell the family business. Mergers with or acquisitions of other businesses have similar impact on families who own assets in common. In each case, the significance of the transaction can set off emotions and other dynamics that challenge family identity. In transactions like these, families can benefit from transition processes that provide for open discussion in advance of making decisions, clear governance structures through which the transactions can be vetted and approved, and lots of family work following the transactions in order to establish new identity and shared visions of the future.

As the most-effective generational leadership succession can involve years of preparation even though the actual transition occurs at a specific point in time, so too can a family-business sale, merger, or acquisition, which similarly takes place at a specific point in time, benefit from the family's reviewing their shared interests and legacy in advance. The family will benefit from this preparation as well. Decisions to pursue major transactions, like the sale of the family business, should be made only after taking into consideration the risks presented to family unity. In fact, intergenerational discussions undertaken in advance of the sale or acquisition of family assets can provide family members with opportunities to strengthen working relationships and prepare them for a new future together. Clarifying their mission can reduce the risk to family unity presented by such a transaction, as the enterprising family will have already laid the foundation for determining what they expect or need from the transaction in order to preserve the family legacy as they move forward.

Often those responsible for pursuing transactions can provide the family with substantial insight by presenting objective data about industry trends, economic conditions, the competitive environment, and other forces for change external to the family enterprise. Similarly, families can benefit from an objective assessment of their company's strengths and weaknesses and projections of its future successes and challenges. By sharing an understanding of changes in the marketplace and considering strategies for moving forward, families can use their governance structures to make objective decisions about pursuing transactions proposed to them.

After three generations of success in textile manufacturing, the Abromowitz family found it impossible to compete with low-cost manufacturers from China and Southeast Asia. On the advice of its industry consultants, the family and the company's board agreed to accept a purchase offer from a global competitor. Surprisingly, the decision was not an anguishing one for the family. Instead, the third-generation cousins engaged the fourth generation of 20- and 30-year-olds in a process, led by a family enterprise consultant, to explore their options for working together following the sale. Over a one-year period, the family developed a new mission statement and vision for the family's future. With an eye to the fifth generation yet to come, the family decided to invest their newly liquid assets together, established the Abromowitz Family Foundation, and formed a family council to represent the family in documenting its proud legacy, providing financial education to family members, and planning annual family retreats. The family emerged with a new identity and totally new family enterprise.

Enterprising families that enter into major transactions often need to redefine their family vision by continuing the family-transition process following the transaction. Often, the sale of all or portions of the family's ownership of operating entities provides liquidity that was not available to prior generations. In such cases, families might consider to what extent they want to invest together or how their new wealth will define their family identity. Liquidity events provide families with opportunities to explore additional dimensions of the family identity, including intergenerational family gatherings, family governance structures, shared philanthropic endeavors, or programs to educate and engage younger family members. It may be helpful for families to understand that younger family members—their next generation—will be responsible for extending the family legacy into the future and to provide them with major roles in the family-transition processes following major transactions.

4.2

Succession Begins on the First Day of Work

Succession—the shift in power, ownership, and authority in an organization— is made more complex in a family business because the successors are the offspring of the current leaders. A family leader must learn that succession is not the act of naming and installing the next leader. Rather, it is a process of entry, education, and mentoring, and involves several stages shifting from generation to generation. This selection presents a model of the stages of succession and explores the challenges to be faced at each.

Too often, a business owner comes to me with a problem of succession when it is too late. A potential heir has been working in the business, and the owner thinks the heir does not have the capability to take over. A key employee has quit, because she doesn't feel there is a place for her in a family business. Two sons who work in the business aren't getting along, and the owner isn't sure that either one can take over the business without bloodshed. A son is concerned that his father won't give up any control or give him any responsibility in the business. It goes on. The family moves into crisis intervention mode to try to straighten things out.

Facing such families, I wonder, Why did they wait so long? Why didn't they talk about these things before? Why did they let things go so far with each of the major parties having such different sets of expectations? Things have simmered below the surface, with negative feelings being suppressed or ignored, for so long it often seems as if everyone wants to keep the issues of succession under the table until they bubble up in a crisis. A great deal of anger and resentment, or too deep a crisis, can mean the prognosis for the continued success of the business is guarded at best.

Long-term preparation—not only of the individuals, but also of the organization—for succession involves guaranteeing that all generations involved share a mind-set that ensures the business will continue to thrive. Succession, as we have seen, is not a isolated event or a coronation, but rather a process that, especially as the business environment gets more complex, global, and competitive, must be carefully staged and anticipated. The heirs to the family business are not receiving a prize; they are taking responsibility for a legacy. The mind-set of the older and younger generations must be that the long-term security of the business rests in putting the business into the hands of capable, committed, and prepared heirs who are ready to take the business to the next stage of development.

I have identified **four stages of succession.** By taking care in the early stages, you create an environment in which the final stage is relatively easy to manage. If you don't begin to think about the next generation on the first day your son or daughter comes to work, you make your own job harder.

Stages of Family-Business Succession

Stage	Business Focus	Development Task
Apprenticeship	Learn about business and other options	• Get work experience • Pursue education • Discover passions and explore options
Career Commitment	Develop credibility, expertise, and track record in the company	• Receive feedback about skill • Learn all aspects of business • Work with mentor
Two-Generation Partnership	• Develop teamwork with family members in two generations as well as nonfamily leaders • Set vision for family and business future	• Achieve business results • Overcome blind spots, deficiencies • Develop network of relationships outside the family business • Work with next-generation team
Passing the Baton	• Strategic plan for future • Settling of new leadership team	• Refine leadership skills

Stage One: Apprenticeship

When a potential successor first comes to work, it is rarely a conscious choice. In secondary school or before, members of the next generation are asked to help out. They are proud to be helpful after school and during the summer. If you listen, there are also opportunities for conversations about what it might be like if they wanted to work in the business and even about your dream of passing it on to them. If there are several members in the next generation, the question of how many of them can find places in the business will surface, and they may wonder if they can curry your favor only if they enter the business. The key is to talk about issues, making it clear that the future is open and that you have a long time to work on these concerns. Making your expectations clear early, and frequently, will help the rest of the family define their own choices and direction.

The key conversation you need to have with the next generation is about the need for them to develop their skills and find their passion. It is not enough to have opportunity; they have to demonstrate capability in running the business, which comes from education and varied job experience. Family members who enter your business without having worked anywhere else are severely limited. They may never know what other options they have or may feel they have no options at all. They may be trapped in a gilded cage and fear the outside world. Or they may have no idea how other people run a business, and how competitive and difficult work can be. They also may lack self-esteem. By receiving a paycheck on their own and meeting the challenges that come with that, they develop skills and a sense of their own worth.

The development task at this stage is for the young people to discover what they really want to do before they settle into the business. Their wealth brings a wealth of possibilities, and they need to be encouraged to explore them. Also, they need time to learn about themselves in order to escape the power the older generation may have over them.

Stage Two: Career Commitment

At some point, a prospective successor shifts from working a casual job in the family business to working with the possibility that this will be his or her career. The person makes a commitment to the family business and expresses a desire to have an impact. Several things must be accomplished at the time of career commitment. First, expectations have to be shared with the family members that run the business. Does the individual expect to be given the business after a period of time or to have the option of buying it? Will the business be shared with other siblings or cousins who may not work in it? What does a family member need to do to be eligible to take over management, and perhaps ownership? What can he or she expect to earn? How will she be paid? What does she have to produce?

All these questions are difficult to answer, but if there is no talk about them, the usual result is that each person has his or her own expectations. These will likely be wildly different and will lead to conflict eventually, when one or more individuals find their expectations are not being met. These conversations are hard. They involve talking about quality of work, about the dream of the business owner, and about the feelings of different siblings. They are especially difficult if there is more than one potential heir. More and more today, heirs entertain the possibility of a sibling or even cross-branch partnership running the business, while traditional entrepreneurs think that they must name one person as the leader. What can in-laws or women expect? Is there a double standard? What if they take some years to work outside the business, while a brother or sister works there from day one? How are the different sets of experience considered when making succession decisions? By talking up front, you can keep runaway expectations within bounds.

If there are several people interested in the family business, or the business is large and complex, or there are several family branches, I highly recommend that expectations for family employment be made explicit and that they be written down. This means that a family will have to come together regularly to work out the ground rules for the incorporation and development of the next generation. The alternative is for family members to feel they face a Byzantine court of family intrigue rather than a business with clear goals and direction.

On the developmental front, making a commitment to the business marks the start of a period of intense personal development. A young heir should work with a mentor and establish a plan for professional development, which includes education, feedback, and conscious attention to skill development. A committed family trainee should continually ask, "What do I need to lead this business, and the family, in the next generation?" Every year the trainee family members and their mentors should check in with other family members and set some milestones.

The trainee stage develops through several steps. The potential successors may be put in charge of new business ventures, initiatives, marketing plans, or stores that offer them a chance for real responsibility. There will be candid evaluations of their successes and their areas of development. They should also have a chance to learn every phase of the business, to see the big picture and go over financials, and to be an increasing part of decision making. The mentoring and support they receive from their parents and other key older employees can be one of the major satisfactions that next-generation prospects have during this often-prolonged stage of development.

The matters of evaluation, roles, and compensation are crucial. Family-business scions may be too hard or too soft on their offspring. They may hold them to an impossible standard to which they never feel they measure up, or they may be so forgiving that the heir never learns discipline and how to deliver results. Neither of these poles allows the heir to develop effectively. One pole promotes rebellion, anger, or departure; the second fosters an insecure or dependent heir who is not capable of making tough choices or seeing new directions. Therefore, during this phase it is most important that the evaluation and promotion of heirs not be just the purview of the patriarch, but be shared among the leadership team, possibly including the board. Generally, family members develop best, and family strife is lowest, when the parent is not the sole decision maker.

Within the business, a family heir expects to be on the fast track for promotion, but the track should not be so fast that the young executive does not have the time to develop solid relationships and achieve clear results. As a young person moves through the business, the other employees will be checking him out, seeing if they can trust his skills and wondering what sort of leader he will become. A young person needs solid and lengthy stepping-stones that offer him enough time to develop his own team of young leaders and become credible to the company at large.

Stage Three: Two-Generation Partnership

The longest period of succession is one that rarely gets attention. As people live longer and are less likely to want to retire, two generations will work side by side for many years as partners, not equal partners by any means, but the partnership has to be dynamic, and the participating members of the younger generation must continually progress in the company. If the potential successors are capable and energetic, how many years can each keep the same job or be an assistant manager? How long before each individual wants to exercise more responsibility?

This intergenerational partnership must evolve, with control and responsibility flowing from the older generation to the younger. But many families get stuck in their roles. The family leaders (usually) like what they do and don't see any need to let go. Also, they have trouble remembering that their sons and daughters are now grown and have children. Each generation has trouble changing: The older generation resists allowing the younger to innovate and modify the business. The younger may be reluctant to take the reins and demonstrate what they can or will do. For this reason, many capable heirs leave or choose not to enter the business.

Often, members of the next-generation management team find themselves working together. If it looks as if the next generation is likely to employ or experiment with shared sibling or cross-branch leadership, they *must* begin practicing working together during this stage with the goal of shared leadership having been made explicit. Many elders keep their own counsel and do not want to tip their hand by picking a successor or delineating intended roles. They set the stage for competition, which may be destructive. For successful transitions to occur, the members of the next generation need to know they are not competing; they are preparing to share stewardship of the family business, and to do this successfully, they need to cooperate.

The job of shared leadership is made easier if the successors have distinct areas of interest or talent and are given responsibility in those areas; for example, one individual may excel at external business development and another at internal operations. By asking their successors to have a hand in determining the composition of the next-generation leadership, elders foster a healthy collaboration in that generation. I have seen too many intergenerational teams in which each potential successor has an intense personal relationship with the patriarch, and the members of the "team" are such rivals that they avoid or do not trust their peers. (If it looks as if there will be a gap in the leadership team, as there is no one in the next generation willing or able to take on a necessary role, recruiting of new blood should begin at this point).

As well as seeing that the two generations involved are working effectively together, the other task of this era is to begin to create a renewed vision for the business. For almost every business, the success of one generation can last only so long before a new vision, a new direction, and innovation must emerge. The older generation must set their heirs free to begin to create and implement new programs with a view to the future while the two generations are still working together rather than waiting until the earlier one is gone. The next generation should be encouraged to pursue some new directions, perhaps diversifying, maybe thinking of new business configurations or ventures. The process of formulating a vision must include exploring and evaluating many of the old ways against the landscape of the present with the intention of retaining those ways that are still valuable or can offer instruction going forward.

At this stage it is helpful if the family comes together as a whole to listen to the voices of family members who own the business but who do not work in management. The family group needs to have a say and a means to express any concerns they may have about the succession process.

Stage Four: Passing the Baton

If you cook a roast for too long it becomes dry and tasteless. If you hold on too long, your business can lose value or potential successors. The right time to initiate the generational shift is usually before the older generation is ready to leave. There is a time when the energy of the business will begin to flag if a new team does not take over. After 10 to 20 years of leadership, a business owner should think about moving on.

At that time the owner needs to determine specifically who will inherit the business and how the leadership transition will be accomplished. The succession process can take several years, during which the previous owner might stay around in a clearly defined role as an elder—or the business owner may move on to industry leadership or to a position managing family investments. The transition process itself is delicate because it likely involves not only family members but also outside managers, companies, and potential owners: A key manager may want to own a piece of the business; a larger company may offer to buy the business; outside investors might come in as partners, offering added business capital. A next-generation buyout may include a team of family and nonfamily owners.

The new generation does not inherit "business as usual." There is no type of business today that is not vulnerable to larger business rollups, international competition, and the need to rethink how the business is operated. That is one reason the wisdom of many years of ownership may not be suitable for a changing environment in which new threats have emerged. The new team needs control over the business so they can renew it and lead it in a new direction.

Keeping the Succession Process on Track

You can easily pinpoint where your business is in these four stages of succession. Look at the tasks of the earlier stages and see if you have successfully accomplished them. If you haven't, the family may need to get together and have some serious, in-depth intergenerational talks. To achieve a graceful succession, you need to pay attention and move your business and your potential successors through each of these key stages. Looking ahead to the next stage and predicting when those involved will be ready to move to that stage will also aid in a smooth transition.

4.3

Minority Family Owners:
Creating a Family Marketplace

When a family hands the control and leadership of a family business to a leader from the next generation, his or her siblings or cousins are often left with major shares of ownership in the business. The leader must manage not only the business, but also the relationships with these minority family owners. They are often not happy, and mutual suspicion and distrust may emerge. The minority owners often want to know how they can sell their shares fairly.

No source of misunderstanding can cause more havoc for an enterprising family than disputes between "insiders," family members who own shares and work in the business, and "outsiders," family members who have ownership but do not work there. These conflicts may have nothing to do with family dynamics because similar conflicts erupt between shareholders and management of nonfamily businesses. But because family members are involved, of course, the emotional stakes are higher.

Here is a common scenario: A family founder has established a thriving business and wants to pass it on to his children. One of his sons works there and is slated to take over leadership in the coming years. But since this is a family asset, the parents have gifted equal 15 percent shares of the business to each of their three sons and their daughter. They are leaning toward offering most of the remaining 40 percent ownership to their son in the business, with cash and real estate to the others.

Sounds familiar and depressingly normal and reasonable. But issues arise between the siblings about this arrangement. First of all, the business successor brother wants all of his parents' shares to be given to him, allowing him majority control of the business. His brothers and sister are upset, because they feel that it should be passed along equally; they are also upset about his salary, believing it is much too large.

The diverging interests between ownership and management in a family business are clear. The nonmanaging siblings want their asset to be "worth" something. They want a regular return on what may be their major investment. The son in the business wants to reinvest profits in growth and development, for the future of the business. And, of course, he thinks he more than earns his salary.

This tension exists in all companies. Witness the controversies in public companies about executive pay or dividends versus reinvestment. Investors often feel shortchanged by management. But in a public company, investors can vote by exiting from the investment, and there is a public market for shares. In a closely held family business, the lack of a market leads the minority family owners to feel they have precious little influence on or leverage for their interests.

The traditional family business had a paternalistic family leader who decided how much to distribute to family shareholders. He (usually) would say that he was responsible both for looking after the needs of family members and sustaining the business. Although this may have been his intention, family members may have resented and disagreed with his paternalism and even believed there was a degree of self-dealing in salary and benefits.

The family has to separate business from family issues. Even though the son has contributed to the growth of the business over the years, like any key employee, he has been well compensated by the owners. He really has no right to be given all or most of the business for his service. His brothers and sister have their own right to inherit the business as family members.

A family asset is not an asset to a minority family owner if he or she cannot enjoy it. Many family heirs feel frustrated because they own shares in huge and valuable businesses, but they cannot afford to buy a home or set themselves up in their own businesses. The resolution of these issues is to create a family marketplace for the business.

The family market is premised on the principle that family members who inherit shares of a business must maintain their ownership voluntarily. If they are captives of the business, or do not think that their interests are represented, their frustration will build into anger. If family members inherit ownership, the family should find a way to offer to buy the shares of those members who do not want them. A family exit strategy will allow a family heir to decide to invest in another direction, possibly sacrificing the shared family enterprise for personal financial autonomy.

If the family creates exit strategies for its members, the next-generation member or members who move into leadership in the business experience more freedom because family members who are not satisfied with the rate of return on their investment can leave. This exit strategy may also require that the family business leaders take some new actions. The next-generation successors may have to arrange to purchase more ownership from other family members by recapitalizing the company. Firms like de Visscher & Co., in Greenwich, Connecticut, specialize in helping family members recapitalize their businesses without sacrificing family control.

The family market can also help when there is a brewing conflict in the family regarding the passing on of ownership shares, as in the example above. A contentious and damaging situation may be averted by allowing the managing son to purchase his extra shares from the parents, offering them cash that they can distribute equally among their other heirs.

4.4

Should I Sell the Family Business?

The sale of the family business is not just a financial transaction. The business is often the glue that keeps the family together. Its sale profoundly affects the family and the members of the next generation. This selection presents some of the consequences of considering the sale and offers suggestions for how the sale can be accomplished by a family in an open and proactive way.

For many families, a family business is like the preferred child. It gets lavish time and attention and is a showpiece while the other—human—siblings are relegated to the background. It is the pride and joy of the parents, who may seem to be living their lives through it. The trophy business brings them renown, status, and importance in the community. With such a deep emotional connection to the business, it is unthinkable for many families to consider selling it, and none of the other "siblings" would dare bring up this option. For this reason, many families find it difficult to consider selling the family business.

But there comes a time in every enterprising family's life cycle when a sale will have to be seriously considered. Not taking this seriously endangers the enterprise the family has spent years growing and nurturing. Consider a recent example of a family with a strong car dealership that had lasted nearly a century. The family was dedicated to keeping it in the family and had begun to develop a next generation to run it. Then they received an offer from a large company that was acquiring many dealerships, offering a price more than the family had thought the business was worth. But how could they sell? The message from the buyer was simple: "You can sell to us, or we will buy your close competitor and with our deep pockets, we will run you out of business." The family hung on proudly and declined the offer. Within ten years, the franchise was fighting for its life, with a set of car brands that were losing market share. Is this a family tragedy in which emotion should have been challenged by reasoned thinking based on the realities of the current business world?

There are internal and external pressures for a sale. Externally, the global marketplace is changing, with offshore competition and rollups of smaller businesses, and a family business that has been successful in a small market niche for many years is not guaranteed success in the future. When an offer emerges, the business has to look seriously not at its successful past, but at its future prospects and strategy. Also, the business may need an infusion of capital at the very time when older family members want to be assured of retirement income, and younger family owners want returns on their investment. How can they balance these competing needs?

Internally, as the older-generation leadership ages, they have to look at the capability and desire of the next generation to lead the business where it needs to go. If both will and skill are not there, they should consider passing the business outside the family. If there is a family leadership candidate or candidates, the family should be sure that the potential successor/s can deal with the future challenges. Another internal challenge is in the area of ownership; it occurs when some family owners want to have access to the capital that is locked up in the business and the other owners have to figure out how to buy them out.

In one family, there were capable leaders in one family branch who wanted to take over. Another branch wanted to exit the business. The marketplace was such that there were several buyers who had expressed interest in the business. Rather than hide or jump to a decision, the family considered its options carefully. They quietly listened to offers, with the understanding that the family successors could also make a bid and their bid would be somewhat privileged. But in the end, it was decided that the best option was to sell. Each of the two family branches had good business ideas, and each branch soon became involved in new ventures that were successful. In some ways, they built on the family legacy of entrepreneurialism; in other ways, they were freed from the past and able to move forward in new directions.

With all these pressures, can a family reasonably expect that the family business will continue to offer the returns on the family's investment that it has in the past? When is it time to say the business has been a real value to the family, but it cannot reasonably offer such return in the future? Added to this, having all the family's net worth in one major asset is a source of risk that a family might not want to shoulder. And finally, the growing number of family members who want returns on their ownership adds more pressure to the business. When a family tries to hold on to the family's legacy business, it will have to deal with all of these issues. If the family leaders are holding on to the business for emotional rather than business reasons, they are highly likely to run into trouble.

Consider the benefits if a family decides to sell the business when there is an offer on the table. First, the family cashes in its success and is able to diversify its assets or divide them among family branches or individuals. Second, the family does not have to deal with the awkward issue of making sure that family leaders can develop the business to the next stage of growth. Finally, the family business does not drain capital from the family.

By selling the business, the family, through a new generation, can make a new start as a financial family, with investments in real estate, new ventures, and other areas that the new generation can operate responsibly to provide return to the family. The freedom from the legacy business allows the family to come together as a new generation and reinvent itself in a new form. Many of the conflicts in a business family over income and management of the business are ended, and the family has a new playing field on which the next generation can make their mark. And of equal importance, the legacy and retirement income of the founding family is assured. The elders are not dependent on the success of their heirs for their own livelihood, and they can live comfortably with little risk for their own futures.

A family who is not open to considering a valid offer for its business and does not consider the future prospects for the business against the alternatives runs the risk of a healthy and productive business suddenly hitting a crisis and losing a great deal of its value. Or a family may place its future in the hands of a new generation of leadership who are not able to compete. A third possibility is the family has handed off a business that does not have the capital to develop and innovate. All these scenarios are equally frightening.

The sale of the family business is not the end of the family as an economic or shared enterprise unit. Rather, a sale is a moment of rethinking and balancing of the past with the future. The family has a legacy of capital, skills, and relationship that offers it advantages if it acquires or moves into a new business area. The relationships and capital of the family can be leveraged in new ways. At the same time, with a liquidity event, the family has the option of allowing "free choice" of family members, so that members of the next generation do not have to be captive partners. Some can go their own way, while others can take what they have inherited from the family and build for the future.

4.6

Becoming an Enterprising Family

Although the establishment of a family business is a foundation of the family's wealth and identity, in many families, the decision to sell or diversify the family assets from one business to several is just as important a marker. This may mean a big payday for the family, but it also creates a huge shift that must be addressed in the nature of the family. This selection defines the issues that a family must anticipate as they look toward this transition.

This selection was written with Fredda Herz Brown of Relative Solutions.

When family leaders make major decisions affecting the future of the family business in the absence of clearly spelled-out decision-making policies regarding a sale, merger, or acquisition, it can have devastating effects on family members who worked in the family business and saw themselves as possible next-generation leaders, as we see in the Bolton family.

The Bolton family owned a large plastics manufacturing firm that had received a number of patents for products it had developed during the 50 years it had been in business. Like other industries, the plastics industry was undergoing a consolidation, with manufacturers buying related manufacturing companies and taking over distribution channels. The senior Bolton brothers, Kevin and Brian, now in their late 60s, were proud of what they had accomplished by significantly expanding what had been a very small company inherited from their father. They fully expected to keep it in the family for the generation to come and had already been joined by two members of the third generation; each of them had a son who was working in the family business.

In keeping with the family employment policy, each of the children had entered the firm after spending three years in positions in another company. Both young men, one 30 and the other 38, enjoyed their work and were active in the industry. While the family had often discussed the challenges facing their firm, they had never established a solid succession plan or made a specific leadership decision. As is often the case in such situations, the third-generation sons expected to become the next-generation leaders.

One day a competitor offered a huge premium over the current value of the Bolton's company for it to merge and become part of a larger distribution network. Kevin and Brian did as they often did, put them off by saying they would think about it. This time, however, they did think about it, and together decided it was time to achieve some liquidity by agreeing to the merger. The day after consenting to sell 49 percent of their business to the other firm, the brothers announced the change to their sons and then to the family at a previously scheduled meeting.

Kevin's son was at a senior level in the company; Brian's son was more junior. Both were extremely upset. It was not clear whether they were distraught over the decision to merge or over the fact that they felt marginalized by the decision-making process. It is clear that they felt their opportunity for leadership, and that of the future generations, had been cut short. The other members of the third generation were married with children of their own and were working elsewhere. Brian's daughter and her husband were investment professionals at a large New York trust company. They understood the need to diversify the family holdings and therefore the need for liquidity. They envisioned helping the family choose an investment strategy and advisers.

One of the conditions of the merger was that the family would maintain operational control of their company and that all currently employed family members would continue to work in the business. The older generation would remain in place for three years; the younger generation could make their decision about length of employment when the option went into effect in ten years. Although they would not be out of a job, the two sons felt that it would no longer be "their" company, and they didn't know whether they wanted to stay under those conditions. They were upset that they had never thought about or planned for such an outcome.

A Change of Focus

While it would be easy to see the $40 million Bolton deal purely as a financial transaction, it was really part of a process that occurs in families that share several assets together.

That process transforms a family from one that owns a business and is building wealth to one that is able to experience wealth and build many other assets. The focus moves from a single business to many enterprises and opportunities. This transition brings up several questions and dilemmas for any family. Clearly, the Boltons' decision making was based on a variety of factors and, although the possibility of a merger had been anticipated and discussed for years, the decision was made more rapidly than anyone had expected because certain contingencies came together so quickly. When decisions are made rapidly without a previously communicated plan, family members, even those making the decision, may not feel prepared for its consequences.

One of the first decisions the Bolton family had to make was whether to handle their new liquidity together; that is, as one family rather than two branches. What will be their reason for being; what do they envision as the future of their family? For a family who has owned a business for generations, this may be the first time they have considered whether they want to remain together as partners. Although they are aware of the financial advantages of pooling their money—in terms of the access to investment funds and deals—if they have different values regarding money and investing, they may not be able to work together effectively. They need to reexamine their family values regarding business and wealth to see whether joint endeavors are desirable. And if so, whether all members of the family wish to participate; one or more members of the family may wish to secede from the family business ventures.

Fair Sharing

Deciding to share assets beyond the original family business also means that the Boltons must decide if they want to share the risks that go with the positives—not just financial risks, but risks of human capital. Sharing assets means that all members and branches of a family are joined together, and what befalls one also affects the others. So, for instance, the Boltons will have to consider the potential situational and normative changes their families will experience over the next few years and how these can be anticipated and planned for. Family groups at different life stages, or with different approaches to money, may want to invest their money differently. For example, some families look for new businesses to invest in that make use of their family talent, while others desire a more passive role in investments and seek a lower-risk portfolio.

If the Boltons decide to continue to share their growing pool of assets, they need to determine what decisions must be made and how they will make decisions together. The original plastics business will now be one of the holdings of the family, and some major decisions will need to be made regarding it in the next few years. The family must also decide what constituents make which decisions, therefore necessitating a structure that defines the decision-making process. Before the merger, the two older Bolton brothers made the decisions as leaders of the family business; who will now be part of the decision-making process? How will that choice be made? Some families want to represent family branches equally. Others want each individual in a generation represented. And still others opt for a small group of trustees or independent experts. These are value questions for the family, not correct or incorrect approaches.

While finding the best people to make decisions, a family may also view governance as a vehicle to develop the talent, capability, and engagement of members of the next generation. Making decisions helps the family develop the next generation as joint owners, stewards of the family's financial, human, and social capital. The degree to which young family members have the opportunity to work together will determine how well they can work through any difficulties in their governance as the family has defined it. But since the assets involved may be huge, and the consequences of poor or naïve decisions so costly, the family has to balance the desire to get people involved with checks and balances on what is decided. The hierarchy of the family business must give way to a new set of leaders who represent all the family owners.

An Enterprising Decision

For these reasons, the decision to sell a family legacy asset is a choice that almost always leads to a thorough reassessment and redefinition of the family's governance and rationale for working together. The effects of a liquidity event bring up questions for each individual as well as for the family as a group and may affect how they want to provide for the next generation and what they want to give back to society. While the decision to sell may have been made by the older generation, the choices in the areas discussed above concern everyone. Although not everyone will have equal say in every choice, the convening of the whole family (as defined by the family themselves) at a large family event, followed by the creation of task forces or working groups, is an effective way that many families address issues brought to the fore by the sale or ownership transition of their family business.

After a lot of planning, the Bolton family set up a three-day, whole-family retreat to explore the major issues confronting them, starting with what they want as individuals and as a family and proceeding to how they can use the financial gift to achieve those goals. A combination of small-group discussions and sharing with the whole group made for a high-involvement event in which everyone had a voice. It was pretty clear that this was a time in which the options were fluid, and the older generation did not have a strong preference for any particular path. They really wanted guidance from everyone.

Over the course of a year and after a half dozen drafts, the family crafted a statement of mission, which included their vision and values and set forth the key principles of how they would operate as a multigenerational family. Then, they set up structures to enable them to make decisions and to act on the values they'd established. They created policies that define clearly who participates and what entities make which choices for the family. For example, financial decisions would be made by an investment council, but decisions about family events and education would be made by a family council representing all generations. The family also began to define what the next generation can expect from the family—in terms of inheritance, education, support, and involvement—and what the family expects of each family member in return.

From owners of an original family business, a family such as the Boltons can evolve after a sale into a diversified financial entity, with family groups that support each member of the family in achieving his or her personal goals and the family as a whole in working together on shared projects like businesses, investments, and philanthropy. The work that enabled the Boltons to define these structures, processes, policies, and values represented a major commitment of time, energy, and funding for the family, but it provides a clear path forward, and it would not have happened unless, or until, Kevin and Brian made the initial decision to diversify the family from one legacy business to several family assets. Making such a decision is the beginning, not the end, for an enterprising family.

4.7

Surviving the Sale of the Family Business

As we have seen, the sale of the family business is more than a business deci-sion, it concerns the destiny of the whole family. This selection explores in more detail what the family has to do before and after the sale in order to successfully manage both the family and business dimensions. It looks at constructive ways to listen to the "voice of the family" both before and after the sale, and at how the family has to re-define and reorient itself in the process of transitioning from a family who owns and manages its own business to a diversified family with financial and other assets.

When a family has created a successful family business, the business is usually the major asset for sustaining the family's future, and the holder of its dreams and aspirations. The dream is to see it pass to the next generations in whose hands it will continue to thrive and grow. The reality, especially today, is quite different. Many factors interfere with the orderly continuity of this dream.

- The business may not continue to grow, as new competitors or mar-ket changes emerge. The company may need to invest heavily in new technology. And family members may want to harvest the value of the business. The business, successful as it is, cannot meet these multiple needs for capital.
- The next generation of the family may not be ready, willing, and able to take the reins and move the business forward. While they can hire outside managers, the family's leadership may become a stifling rather than a creative force.

For these reasons, today, more and more families make a decision that had previously been unthinkable—to sell the family business. Every year many successful, and in some cases very large, family business are sold. We have recently witnessed the sale of Wrigley to another family business, Mars, and the

163

sale of Budweiser to the large conglomerate, InBev. The sale is often marked by a trade article pronouncing the sale as the apex or crowning moment for the family in question. But as any family owner (and his or her advisers) knows, the reality is often quite different, with this milestone event just one step along a much longer path.

Some family members may believe that choosing to sell is a simple financial decision. I challenge that view and show numerous ways in which the sale of the family business is a major milestone for the family. Success for the family depends not just on making the right decision and getting the right price, but on how the family themselves approach the sale, on its impact on them as a family, and on how they redefine and reorganize themselves as a family after the sale. This selection will help families navigate this process, bringing it to a positive conclusion.

Deciding to Sell

The possibility of selling the family business can surface in several ways: An offer comes from a strategic competitor or other source, or the family themselves bring up the question because of issues in succession, a family member's desire to be bought out, or the need for capital for business development. Rarely is a family pleased to discover that a family member wants out and the others have to pay her. As I've mentioned previously, but would like to emphasize again here, the family business is more than a business, it is a sign and a symbol of the family's success, a center for their hopes and dreams, and a setting in which the next generation can grow, work, and sustain the family legacy. So the family members resist even the thought of letting go. However reluctant they are, at such times, the family must consider a sale. They can do it forthrightly and thoroughly, or they can limit their information, fail to seriously and deeply consider their options and the implications of the sale on the family and the business, and avoid facing the possible ramifications of the challenge on all levels and in all dimensions—including the business, family, and current market, among others.

Whether or not they should sell is the initial focus of attention, so I will touch on it before exploring pre- and postsale planning and execution. Most families want to keep the business in the family. Yet circumstances appear that contest their desire. First, the business may need outside capital, which the family cannot raise. In order to continue to compete, a business that has been successful for many years may need capital for expansion, acquisitions, modernization, or development of new products or services. Although the family might pick up a partner, the likelihood of their finding a minority partner for a closely held business is small. Related situations include a business that has offered a good return to many family members no longer being able to sustain its profitability or a strategic partner seeing a value in the business and offering a price that would give a much better return than the family members think the business would bring in the long term given today's uncertain future.

Does the family require a level of internal or external funding that cannot be maintained with the current capital structure? This can cause acute dissension within the family, especially when the company requires funding for rapid expansion of the business, while some shareholders (often not involved in management) continue to expect dividend payouts with which they can sustain their current lifestyle (it has been suggested that the dependence on regular dividends led the Bancroft family to vote to sell their interest to News Corp. despite their desire to remain a family-held business).

Family elements figure in the decision. While one generation may want to retain the business, the family may not have the motivation or skills in the next generation to run the business, and may not think that they will be able to find an appropriate nonfamily CEO. The family may be losing interest in owning or running the business in lieu of pursuing other endeavors. This can become an especially serious concern if ownership is 100 percent in family hands or management has a restricted or limited ownership say in the business. For example, a family may not have next-generation leaders who have the "will" or the "skill" to carry the business forward. Sometimes, a family leader persists in imagining that a son or daughter will emerge fully prepared to lead the business and interested in doing so, when in fact, checking with the candidates the leader discovers it is not high on any of his heirs' agendas nor are any particularly capable of taking the reins of the business.

The goal of keeping the business privately owned, particularly as a family enters the fourth and fifth generations, becomes more challenging as family members' economic interests become more fragmented. In addition any valuation discount applied to the business appears to keep the value of the business depressed relative to current market value.

While a business can remain a powerful rallying point for fulfilling the family legacy, mission, and community expression, it can also limit individual family members in pursuit of their own dreams. The collective interests of a diverse group of family owners must be balanced against the individual needs and aspirations of each of its owner households. Or, as the family grows, individual family members or branches may want to exit, and ask to be bought out. These factors increase the need and desire to sell.

One of the mistakes a family can make is confining the conversation about the sale to only a few individuals, usually the board of the family business. They look at the business case, but do not include or engage the rest of the family. When a family (and this is to a degree dependent on the number of family branches and adult households) has a clear and unified sense of where it is as a group, the planning and execution phases will be that much smoother.

When I ask board members why they do not consult family members on the sale, they cite two factors that lead them to limit information: the need for confidentiality and the fact that they have the legal responsibility and authority to make the decision. Both factors are important, but they need not prevent the board from involving family members in the conversation if the greater family understands and agrees to abide by simple rules: In a family dialogue, family members who are included must respect the need to keep things confidential. And they need to be aware that while they have an important voice and role in informing the board about their desires, their decision power is limited. The controlling shareholders will make the final decision.

The pre- and postsale periods are often similar in that they both require that the family have a well-defined sense of their involvement in the process, clearly crafted and understood rules of participation for individual family members, and an awareness of the specific roles and responsibilities available to them postsale. However no matter how prepared a family is, the postsale period will involve many of the same types of discussions the family held prior to the sale. It is impossible to anticipate and address in advance the tensions and confusion—especially regarding the roles, responsibilities, and rights of each individual—that may surface during the postsale period, partly because the sale is complicated by such ephemeral factors as the emotional ties family members have to the legacy business. In the wake of the sale, the family must move slowly through as many transparent and direct, but deeply respectful, conversations as they need to redefine themselves. Furthermore, all the stakeholders—people who are affected by the outcome—need to be involved in both the pre- and postsale processes in appropriate ways.

Before the Sale: Deliberating and Preparing

The steps a family takes preceding a sale of the business are often the most important indicators of a healthy family strategy, effective execution, and success postsale. Yet, too often the family has only a limited exchange and planning process preceding the sale, which leads to difficulty, confusion, or mixed signals after it.

Prior to a sale, the family should engage in two parallel conversations about the future: a discussion of the future possibilities and vision for the business, and a discussion of the desires and future vision for the family, including where the business fits into it. These two conversations are held primarily by different groups, but with a lot of cross-communication and cross-membership:

- The **business conversation** is led by the board, with input from the leadership team, the other employees, and the family (and nonfamily if there are any) shareholders
- The **family conversation** is led by either an ad hoc group of family members or the family council (for more on the family council, see "Sustaining Connection Through a Family Council," in Part II), whose job is to consider the business in the context of the family's hopes, dreams, desires, and intergenerational policies and activities

Most family businesses convene only the board conversation, and it is a limited one, focused on whether the business should be sold and for what price. The board often contains the main family owners and perhaps some independent, nonfamily members, but ideally it includes members of the next generation, who are expected to inherit and manage the business in the future. In the broadest possible terms, the board has to consider the question, Should the business be sold?

The board should take into account the future vision and direction of the business and whether the family owners have the capital and desire to steward it for the next generation. They directors need to look at the profitability and the degree of dependence family members have on a return. Often, the directors feel compelled to pay out dividends or distributions to family members when the business needs the capital for development. From a business standpoint, the board has to look at what the business wants to achieve and the amount of investment it will take to accomplish that. It also has to ask how likely that outcome is, how much risk there is that this goal will not be met.

If a family wants to consider selling the business, specific preparations must be made. A family business is frequently organized in an informal manner, growing as it has out of the idiosyncratic needs of the family founder-leader. To be sold, the business must have adopted clear and organized business processes. But a family-owned and -operated business often has a structure that is not ready for a sale. It may have a very rudimentary board, composed only of family members, or its operations and finances may be less than clear and transparent. In an example that is not unusual, when one industrial family business began to consider a sale because the family no longer had the leadership and commitment to operate the business, the family found that to receive good value for the business, it needed to recruit independent directors to its board and to prepare the balance sheet and operations of the business for future development. This entailed a major commitment by the family and took several years, but the family was rewarded by a sale to a strategic buyer who was able to provide the capital to expand the business into new markets.

The board cannot do all this without input from the family, especially concerning the family's goals and vision for the future. Does the family want to provide a setting for family employment for the next generation, and does the presence of the business provide a focus for family involvement in the community? The proposed family conversation includes not only the family members who work in and own shares of the business, but also other family members—spouses, parents, potential owners and employees, and members of the next generation. They may not all have a formal vote in the decision, but their opinions matter. Family members are connected by blood and a common heritage, and their needs and desires should be taken into account; they are the beneficiaries, and often the drivers, of the business.

The family has to convene itself to discuss these types of questions. This conversation can either be held at an all-family gathering called a family assembly, or by a representative group of family members who are designated the family council. Even if the family is unusually large, they may still hold a family assembly during, say, a whole-family retreat. Some families have established family councils that are already operating, while others may need to elect one to act as the center of the family conversations about a possible sale. This group of elected family members should represent all parts of the family. (For more on the family assembly and especially on the family council, see "Sustaining Connection Through a Family Council," in Part II.)

The whole family, or the elected family council, must examine the key questions about what the family wants for the future.

- Is a next generation of potential future leaders in development or ready to take over the business?
- Is the family willing to sacrifice current returns for future ones by investment?
- Is the family willing to continue to take the risk of having its assets largely pooled in a single legacy business, and is it willing to shoulder the risk of having so many expectations from a single asset, especially when these risks may increase due to numerous factors including the current market?

Often, different family members feel differently about these issues, and the family has a lot of exchange to do before they can come to consensus, if they can at all.

One fifth-generation family, with several hundred members, considered the sale of its legacy business after nearly 100 years. There were strategic and financial reasons for a sale, but the impact and will of the family were their prime concerns. The process of deliberating had several steps. They convened a whole-family meeting for all interested family shareholders (all family members were shareholders) at the expense of the company to present the idea. Then a series of small groups convened to discuss the idea and reported back to the board. After the board heard the feedback and the consensus that the family was ready to move forward, the sale proceeded.

Many families today engage internal and external advisers to explore questions such as why a family should or should not stay together, what this means, how a family's goals can best be actualized, and how to separate the family from the business. They may need several advisers to help them: Financial advisers and business brokers can help them prepare the business and find a market for prospective buyers or evaluate and negotiate with an interested buyer. Other advisers or consultants can help the family define their collective and individual intentions and values, will and desires, and balance the legacy commitment to the business with their desire to move in new directions and diversify their family portfolio.

If the family comes together without the assistance of an adviser, it is best that none of the family's business leaders guide the meetings. The family has come together because their needs are different from those of the trustees, managers, or even the family leaders who run the business. And for that reason, it is good practice to not have a business leader run the meetings or guide the process, though all of the family's business leaders clearly will be active participants, as family *members* not *leaders*. If a business leader guides the family conversation, other family members will wonder if he or she is presenting the choice and situation fairly and will suspect that the leader is pushing his or her personal agenda.

The starting point of the conversation should be defining the family future and determining whether this vision can be achieved without the legacy business. The family cannot expect to answer these in a single meeting, and they should not come together expecting to make an immediate decision about whether to sell. Rather, they need to be aware that they are beginning a process that must run parallel to and intersect at points with the board's business-and-finance-oriented conversation.

After—or at—this first meeting, the family will want to establish various working groups covering family governance, family office, family philanthropy, and the like, particularly for larger families with multibranch and multigenerational issues.

It is important to have clearly defined roles for participation and voting, especially about who has an advisory voice and who is a decision maker. In the family conversation, those who are to be heard but will not vote may include spouses and some family members or generations.

After the Sale: Redesigning the Family

The decision is made; the business has been sold. After the "liquidity event," the family faces a watershed transition. No longer a family closely tied to and personally identified by the family business, now they must manage and invest liquid wealth. They become a financial, or enterprising, family, with multiple assets and investments, and this demands new skills and a new design for the family. The old leaders and the old ways of working together have to be modified for the new reality.

This event initiates both a public and private family transition. The family is no longer associated with the business, which may even stop using the family name. The sale price is often publicly stated, creating the impression that each member of the family is now in possession of great wealth. Invitations to fund-raising events pour it. Family members who were employed in the business, or who planned to be, are now jobless, left to find other options.

All of these can result in a profound trauma to the "identity" of the family. In a way that is difficult to anticipate, the family feels a deep loss, not dissimilar to the loss of a friend or relative. The family may succumb to a sort of seller's remorse, that is, they realize what they have lost and regret the sale. I know from the psychological studies of trauma that such a profound transition is an emotional event, after which each individual, and the family as a whole, goes through several stages: shock, denial, anger, fear, depression, and questioning in response to what is experienced as an emotional loss.

The sale creates a new reality for the family. While the family may have designed a family trust or LLC to handle the cash from the sale, the family members have to face the question, Do we want to stay together as a family with shared assets or should we just distribute the cash to each family member? Many family members may assume that they will stay together while others will assume, with equal certainty, that the cash will be distributed. With the "glue" of the family business gone, what will be the family's focus, organizing purpose, and principle?

As during the presale process, the family should hold two related conversations: one about how they want to be organized in relation to their family assets, and one about how they want to remain connected as a family. Since there is no longer a family business, the question is, Who is to be part of this new conversation? It is hard for the family to engage this question actively. For many families, the presence of the business leader has meant that family members are not really participants, and certainly not decision makers when it comes to financial matters. So even though they may be told that they are being invited to be part of a discussion about the future, the old habits of being passive and getting "taken care of" are hard to break. Family members need to learn how to be active.

One of the perplexities that most confuses the family is the question of who decides and who is part of the discussions. With a long-standing family business, the family often has adopted a patriarchal structure, in which the family is taken care of by the business owner, who is usually the founder and sole owner. Other family members are not usually part of the board or business decisions, and after a sale, they may assume that they will remain in the background. They may not be comfortable with this, and in fact, they may be due a more-engaged role in deciding what is next for the family. One of the primary issues is, for a family, that the stakeholders—family members, next-generation heirs, spouses, and nonfamily board members, among others—have a place in the new family structure that is not yet entirely clear. So after a sale or business-ownership transition, the family may stick with its former structure, with the same family leadership, while moving slowly and carefully with much discussion toward a redefinition of itself as a unit.

The family may find it hard to understand what happens to the money after the sale. The deal is usually complex, often including a family trust or conditions that not all family members understand equally. If there is a trust, the role of the trustees and the ways that family members can participate in decisions are far from understood by all. So there must be a great deal of sharing of information and discussion about what this structure means for the family, as they also consider the ways that they will be together personally and the various family activities they will pursue.

One family with a successful business that employed many family members in two generations received an incredible offer from a competitor. The patriarch took the offer quickly, without consulting the family members who worked there. While the windfall was huge, the shock to the family was tremendous. Family members who had never worked anywhere else had to consider what to do with their future. The business had been the focus of the family's life for many years, and now was gone. The questions emerged: What was the family to do together? Now that they were not on the payroll, what could they expect? How was the family going to safely invest their funds, and who would be involved in their management?

The personal shock was considerable as family members felt adrift and disconnected. After a while, the family began to create a new design. They created a family office, and several members of the second generation participated in organizing it. They began to define services for the support and development of members of the second and third generations, develop careers, practice philanthropy, and do things together as a family. As a first step, they came together for a series of meetings to define the family mission, including their values and a vision of what they wanted to become as a family (for specific suggestions about how to craft a mission, see "Defining Mission and Drafting the Constitution," in Part II). When the question arose, To what degree do we want to remain connected and do things together as a family?, they answered that they wanted a lot of connection, but also support for each person in creating his or her own family unit.

They developed a family council to organize these activities, with an elected group of family members coordinating it. They began to consider which members of the second generation would be part of the board of the family trust. They also had to determine the specific role the family council would play in bridging the gap between family, business and investing endeavors, and other decision-making bodies.

As wealth transfers from a concentrated and nonliquid form to a more-diversified and liquid form, the types of advisers, structures, and skill sets the family need change as well, so that the family can most efficaciously create, manage, and monitor this new form of wealth as it evolves. They have to decide on the type of entity that will manage their investments. There are many options available. They can become part of a large financial institution such as a trust company or a multifamily office. Or they can consider forming their own family office, a structure that invests their money, takes care of the administration of it, and performs financial and often other services for family members. To establish a family office, the family must make decisions about who will lead this venture and how the family will oversee it. Because this can be a costly and complex entity, usually only larger families take this option.

Most families will engage a financial institution, multifamily office, or other investment firm to manage their wealth. But the family still has to create oversight, which includes forming an investment policy statement and a board to oversee the investments.

These decisions require professional advice, but the family must make them, and make sure that they are competently carried out. In their oversight, the family must benchmark the performance they seek and define their expectations of the financial managers. In addition to setting up and looking over the investment policy and process, the family must create a process by which family members will be kept informed and can participate. Some family members may have strong opinions, and the family's decisions may be contentious.

The family must decide what new structure and form it will adopt as an enterprise, and that concerns all the stakeholders even though, as I've mentioned, only some of them may actually have decision-making power. For the family to meet the needs of all its members, the whole family must first understand what is being proposed and then have a say in the conversations prior to the decision. An effective family will convene several family meetings to discuss these questions. The paramount one is, What structure will the family adopt for the next stage of its life? But following close behind are, Who will be on the board that represents the family owners? What are the procedures by which the family will be kept informed and will be asked to participate in discussions? It takes time for family members to understand that although they have a right to be informed and to share their ideas and concerns, the board makes the final decisions. Whatever organization or structure the family will adopt as an enterprise and engage to manage its wealth—a multifamily office, a financial institution, an investment firm—the family itself, perhaps through the family council, is an adviser, not a decision maker.

4.8

After Crisis Comes Growth:
Family Resiliency and Rebuilding Trust

So far we have looked at a range of possible transitions that face an enterprising family. Just recently, almost every such family experienced a huge financial transformation. As the global environment shifted, each family had to redefine its sense of wealth and determine the ways in which the wealth is still a resource for the family. This selection explores how the family manages major transitions. It looks at the personal and emotional stages through which a family and an individual progress after a substantial change and the ways a family can recover in a fashion that leaves them stronger and heartier than they were before.

The huge financial upheaval of the year 2008 deeply affected every enterprising family's experience of wealth. Families that spent with the expectation that their wealth would grow found their wealth had significantly decreased. For family members who are accustomed to receiving passive income, the upheaval has a deeply personal aspect, as they must adjust to new conditions that may be permanent. A family may have significant wealth but nonetheless need to move from one wonderful vacation house to a smaller one, resign membership in a club, or limit philanthropic commitments, leading to a feeling of loss and even public shame. While the family remains "wealthy" before and after the upheaval relative to the rest of society, its members feel a loss, compounded by complicated feelings of anxiety, distrust, and even anger and resentment. The safety and stability of their wealth, and their trust in the financial stewards who oversee it, have declined. As a result, many families have begun to review their expectations and assumptions about spending and lifestyle.

One casualty of the crisis has been the loss of trust in many sectors of society. Families have lost trust in employers, whom they'd counted on to provide for their retirement or even for continued employment, in government to make sure that the market and financial system functions, and most personally, in financial advisers and financial institutions who made promises on which they did not deliver. And most devastatingly, as a society, we have lost trust in the earth and the environment for having magically provided us with food, water, and a natural bounty that we thought would last forever—only to discover that, like the wealth of a dissolute heir, it may disappear in a generation or two unless we act quickly. What lessons are families taking from this loss of trust, and how are families best able to proceed? Trust is easy to lose and hard to rebuild. When it is lost, people tend to react precipitously and do things that upon reflection, are premature.

In responding to the recent financial losses, members of a family may decide to get together across generations to recalibrate their lives and expectations. Emerging from the shock and pain, they discover that many elements of their lives that they had considered essential or accepted without question in fact are not necessary at all, perhaps not even enriching. They may not even add to one's pleasure. Their new values center on what really creates quality in their lives, and they turn toward simpler pleasures, sustainable activities, and personal relationships rather than consumer behavior. The crisis may lead them to a fundamental reevaluation of the purpose of their wealth and the ways in which they want to make decisions about it and make it a part of their lives. I call this a **family sustainability conversation**, which involves reflecting on the family's values and lifestyle and resetting some of their practices and choices. While this "reset" was galvanized by the recent crisis, the process is not unlike the one that every family has to undertake periodically, as there are losses and transitions in the family, and in their business and financial ventures.

A wealthy family faces other disorienting losses and changes,. This includes the untimely death or disabling of family members, which are especially difficult to cope with if the family has put off realizing that such events may occur and preparing for them. People also leave the family through divorce, and stepchildren enter and leave. There are unintended effects of the sale of the family business or loss of value of family assets. Other generational transitions involve the loss of an older generation and the stepping up of a new one. While these transitions can be anticipated, *when* they will happen cannot be. Too many families put off making plans for them. When they come, they pack an added emotional punch because the family is not really ready or able to deal with them effectively.

Rebuilding Family Resiliency and Trust

In the 80s, while working with employees and executives in companies experiencing their first major downsizings, my colleague Cynthia Scott and I developed a model we call the transition curve—the stages by which an individual, group or whole organization experiences and moves through an unexpected, and often unwelcome, change. The first stage is **denial**. "Sure, we understand the theory, but we don't have time to think about it right now." Up until a few years ago, almost everyone was in denial about the impact of climate change and the need for sustainability.

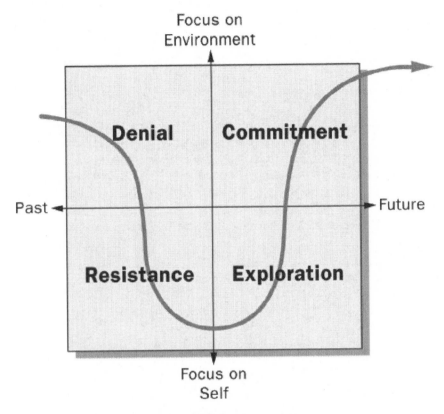

The Transition Curve

The economic shock awakened us from denial, sending us into the second stage, which we label **resistance**—the emotional rainbow of fear, anger, depression, and upset that follows a shock or trauma. In this stage, we look for someone to blame and dwell on what we are losing. We learned two things about this state: It is not good to take action when in this stage, and many people get stuck in it and never move beyond it.

At varying speeds, most people hit the bottom of the curve, acceptance of the change, and enter the stage of **exploration**, in which we accept the reality but instead of dwelling in the past and on what we have lost, we begin to seek out strategies for managing our new situation and for determining what we want to do about it. Instead of punishing those who created the crisis, we focus on developing societal and personal responses to reconstruct our lives within

176

the new realities. We redefine the situation, look around, talk to other people, experiment, and reflect on what we can do in an innovative and transformational period that leads to the final stage, which is **commitment** to a new path. In exploration, a family may also create a new **story** of who they are and where they are going. As families, and as a society, we seem to be moving from resistance to exploration in our response to the economic and social crisis.

Following the transition curve, individuals and families respond to the loss of trust in two major directions. They may act when they are emotionally sitting on the left side of the curve—in denial and resistance—by becoming more defensive, distrustful, and angry, as they focus on their feelings of loss and betrayal. By blaming others in their anger, they may act spitefully or impulsively, to their detriment. Other families allow themselves time and get together and are able to move across the bottom of the curve to enter the stage of exploration and move toward commitment to new conditions. They use the loss as a catalyst to look forward, seeing their life goals with a different set of realities. They are "sadder but wiser." They move beyond their first emotional reactions to reflect and take responsibility for learning and taking action. They have moved from upset and blame of others to a perspective that allows them to focus on "what do we want to do now." This transition is equally important for families and individuals.

The financial crisis seems to have laid bare some aspects of our relationship to money. We may have seen happiness as buying more elaborate houses, cars, vacations, or personal goods. All of a sudden we can't expect to get them, or even to keep the ones we have. In many families, the conversation begins with what we have to cut back on and how we can live with less. Vacation homes and cars are sold, and families move into smaller quarters. So, we ask ourselves, are we less happy? Is our life over? While the reality is not as stark as that, for a family with major assets, it is important to have a time in which the whole family discusses their responses as the background for making decisions about what to do.

The family's response is complicated in any case, but even more so if different family members have different attitudes. If, for example, the elders become more distrustful while some members of the younger generation want to talk about what they have learned and how to move forward, the different perspectives can lead to conflict about whether they need to talk about the future at all. Too often the defensive attitude, especially in the elders, trumps the desire of other family members for open discussion.

How can a family and its individual members best move through the full transition process after the shock of the crisis? First, a family can't maintain that things are "just fine" and "we are handling it." That is a form of denial we call the Tarzan swing, in which a person feels that he or she has jumped like Tarzan grabbing a handy vine to fly over the chasm represented by the downward curve. Other families have a quality we call resiliency: They naturally allow themselves to experience the different stages of transition and, by listening to themselves, are able to look at what has really changed and address what they need to do differently to still lead a full life. They are challenged by a crisis to question how they do things and often come out the other side stronger and more capable as they use the crisis to develop new skills and awareness.

Resilient families exhibit certain characteristic qualities. They do not rush to make changes nor do they proudly assert that they are doing just fine. They resist the urge to strike out or take impulsive action, and instead take a "time out" to reflect and consider where they are and what they want. They acknowledge that things have changed; they work together to listen to each other as they move through the stage of resistance through the bottom of the curve; and then seek advice from a variety of sources as they enter the stage of exploration. After they deal with the emotional effects of a change or loss, they enter exploration with a desire to learn and the ability to question whether their old ways really are best for them. Instead of patching themselves up, they stretch for better solutions—which is why studies of the financial crisis have found that many families have reconsidered their basic structure and their financial advisers.

A family who lost significant wealth convened a family meeting, with three generations of family members including spouses. Many of them had never talked about the family's wealth, though they all were beneficiaries of it. Rumors had been swirling that there would be no more distributions, and everyone was upset. The family leaders and their money managers were viewed with suspicion as the family looked for someone to blame. At the meeting much information was shared, and many questions were answered. Family members remarked that they were glad that the family had finally shared this level of information and wished it had happened earlier. As a group, the family agreed to take a "time out" from making decisions or changes. The first goal was to understand and learn.

As they saw how much the family had lost, they began to consider how the loss would affect them, and what was really important. They talked about what they valued as a family, and what they wanted from their lives. Money was not the central value, though members of the older generation had feared it would be. As they got to know where things were, the family agreed to begin a process of talking to other financial advisers and reflecting on how they would manage their wealth in a more open way than they had in the past. They agreed that the major decisions would be made together by a new family board, who would then delegate further choices and options to a smaller group of family and non-family leaders.

While they ended up making changes in their financial management, what was most important to the family was the feeling of shared engagement and the fact that the family members who were experts were taking the time to help other family members learn. They also felt good that some of the major decisions were shared and that after they delegated responsibility, they could count on regular briefings and discussions. So for this family, the crisis was a catalyst for major changes in the direction of discussion of what was important to the family and the sharing of information and some decisions. The family grew as a result of their loss.

After such a crisis, trust must be rebuilt in a family's personal network, especially with advisers. As family members enter the phase of resistance, the propensity to blame can be joined by a planning process based in distrust. They don't reach out to advisers and other resources, who have let them down. Instead of engaging their advisers, the family leaders avoid them and impulsively seek other venues. They never get a chance to potentially heal the rift or understand other points of view.

Often, the family has placed its desires and intentions into trust documents that separate the use of their wealth from the decisions about what to do with it. A professional trustee is put in the role of referee to make sure family members abide by the parents' wishes. The system and division of roles lacks flexibility and a way for trustees, grantors, and beneficiaries to engage each other. It is especially difficult to deal with the unanticipated financial crisis. In fact, the presence of a trust and trustee may have unintended negative effects on the beneficiaries. While the beneficiaries enjoy the fruits of the family wealth, they feel that even after the death of their parents, they are in an eternal state of childlike dependency, coming to an adult authority figure for their needs. The financial loss is that much more devastating because they are not prepared to take care of themselves. This may result in a terrifying experience of personal helplessness.

Now, this was clearly *not* the intention of the parents who set up the trust. They wanted to ensure that their wealth was used by their children responsibly and in line with their values. Their expectation was that by creating certain conditions, they would guarantee the wealth would more positively and effectively help their children and heirs. By limiting full access to the wealth, they expected their now-grown children would create their own wealth to support their families. In many cases this is the effect. But I find that in almost every family, this is not true for all inheritors. The effect of "incentive" trusts is different on different heirs and on some may lead to misunderstanding, bad feelings, and difficulty growing up.

The elders want not simply that the next generation be "happy." They want them to exhibit the old-fashioned virtue of character by using the wealth not just for selfish consumption but for supporting future generations, for doing significant and important things, and for serving the community. But the parents cannot achieve their goal solely by legislating rules about inheritance. Development of character in the next generation demands an active engagement, in which the elders act as mentors for a period but in the end must let go of control and allow their heirs to define their own destinies. Letting go and trusting the next generation is often difficult for the elders, who have a long history of exerting control and vigilance over their affairs. Many elders need to learn this as a new skill.

Advisers have a rough ride when they are the focal point of a crisis. To help families progress along the transition curve, they have to change their tactics as family members go through each stage. When a family is in denial, the adviser has to gently but firmly help them see the realities they must face. In resistance, when the family is upset, the best that can be done is to offer a listening ear, without trying to "fix" a feeling or solve the family's problems. But when the family accepts the new reality and begins to enter exploration (and remember, this can happen at different times with different people), advisers can be a resource and can help support and focus the family's learning. At this point, not earlier, they can help convene family educational meetings and help families redefine their values and their approach to their wealth. And finally, the family, not the adviser, makes decisions that commit them in some new directions. The adviser has to gracefully accept what the family chooses.

Redefining the Dream and the Family Capital

Family wealth, as we saw in Part I (in "True Wealth: The Stewardship of Family Capital"), is not an inert pile of money sitting in a vault. The family capital represents a resource that the family has developed over time. It is an active force, a capability that opens up many possibilities and choices for the next generation. As advisers like Jay Hughes point out, there are many aspects of the family's capital. Even as the family has lost wealth, they still maintain the family capital in the form of family members' competencies and knowledge; their associates, colleagues, social circle, and relatives; the respect they have in the community; and the support they have within a growing family network. By looking at these nonfinancial sources of value, a family can see that their loss is confined to a smaller area than they may have originally thought.

In many families, wealth comes from the creation of a family business. The value of this business is likely not strictly financial; in fact, the family cannot realize the total financial value until it sells the business. The value of the business comes from the visible leadership of the family, which provides jobs and support to the community. Family members earn money both by actively working in the company and passively sharing in its profits. A family member can benefit by working in the business or by community involvement, occasioned by the family's standing in the community. A family member inherits community status and opportunities in addition to financial wealth. All of these are elements of the legacy of the family's capital, which can be transmitted to the next generation.

Therefore, when a family considers what the next generation will inherit, they need to look at more than money. Who will inherit the family's seat on the board of the symphony? Who will represent the family on the board of a public company in which they invest? Who will be on the board of the family foundation? Who will serve on the family's board of directors? These inherited aspects of the family capital are often not clarified in trust documents or estate plans, yet they are real and important enough for siblings to fight over or to cause them to resent each other. In fact, before making inheritance plans, the family should define and articulate clearly what they want their wealth to achieve for the coming generations. This is the family's vision, and although the formal choice of how the inheritance is passed on rests with the elder generation, the entire family has a responsibility to talk through the elements of the cross-generational vision and agree on its form if the outcome is to match the intention.

The feelings within a family about inheritance and use of family money are so powerful that many families want to deal with such explosive feelings by avoiding them, denying issues, and not trusting each other enough to talk together openly. In many families, young people are told in a variety of ways, "We don't talk about money." Yet these parents send messages to their children every day through what they say to each other and how they themselves deal with their wealth. These mixed messages are fodder for comedy acts and can cause cynicism and negativity in their children. A young adult may wonder why she is given an allowance when the family buys her whatever she wants, and why they talk about sustainability but own three houses and many vehicles.

As the family faces a financial crisis, or another potential loss in a major transition, as they move through denial and resistance, toward exploration, one important task is for the family to undertake an **inventory of family assets**, in which they look at their family capital in the broadest sense. In a series of family conversations, they begin by asking the large question, What do we want for our family wealth? This is a larger question than how they should invest, whether they should have a family business, who should inherit what, or who should be the family leader. After losing a percentage of their net worth, the family might also consider the questions, How much is enough? What do we want our wealth to do for us and for future generations? What is our legacy as a family? How do we want to help individuals in the next generations as a family? The conversations stimulated by these questions are the foundation for choices about the future of the family wealth. Coming up with an answer is not easy, not quick, and not simple.

Two important elements of the gatherings in which discussions will take place are who should attend and who makes the decisions. Some families want to talk with only natural family members, and the presence of married-ins can be a source of contention. Siblings, step-siblings, and other relationships and connections can also complicate attendance. The age at which children are to be invited is also an issue. The rule of thumb is that there can be different conversations for different people, and it may not be practical or workable to include everyone at each meeting. Also, some family members have special needs or status that makes it hard to include them. Regarding the second concern, including individuals in a family conversation during which family members talk about their values and their desires does not mean that they will have a vote in the decision. The family elders, or decision makers, listen to the input and then decide. The principle is that family members should have a voice, not necessarily a vote.

Several surprises emerge when a family plans together regarding these large questions about the future of family wealth. The first is often that having a house or a car, a new kitchen or a fancier interior does not really add to one's overall happiness. Remembering Maslow's famous hierarchy of needs, a family begins to see that once they have something they want or need, having more of it doesn't make for more satisfaction. A bigger something is not intrinsically more fun; it actually may not satisfy an inner urge at all but rather a social urge to have higher status in relation to others. When everyone in society suffers together, the loss of luxuries does not have the same sting.

The family may make another discovery. As they talk about cutting back, and perhaps decide to take a camping vacation together rather than a luxury cruise, they are actually getting closer and often having more fun. They are engaging with each other constructively, helping each other solve a shared problem. As they do this, they are also talking in a new way about their relationship to money and wealth. They ask, What do we want to have as a family and what do we want to give to our children? Of course, money is important in paying for education and raising a family. But a family who are conscious of their gifts can offer far more than just money to their next generations.

In learning to view money in a different way, we can learn something from one of America's wealthiest families. Over six generations, this family has amassed billions of dollars. However, in the transition to the seventh generation, the family made a discovery that seems obvious. While as a family they are fabulously wealthy, the number of people in the family will soon exceed 1,000. While they all can inherit some wealth from the family fortune, the family can no longer make every family member rich. So like many families, they are experiencing a wealth downsizing over generations. The family, who get together for a whole-family retreat each year, have found that they offer family members far more than financial wealth. As a family they have an incredible group of educated and talented people, spanning many professions and achievements, which teaches us that when young people seek our resources—whatever they may be—and learn from them, they often discover unexpected opportunities for their own development and career. As a family, they offer seminars and other learning activities, and provide their members with a rich tradition of fun and positive relationships. So although they will be offering less financial wealth to the next generation, the human and social capital they offer is, as the commercial says, "priceless."

In this selection, I have suggested that to rebuild trust and family alignment after a loss or transition, a family has to take the time to reflect on what has changed and do this with their eyes open. They need to be available to their own feelings and concerns and those of the other family members, and to the possibilities, information, and knowledge of outside resources. In times of stress, a family must fight the desire to turn inward and hide, and instead reach out, listen, and learn under difficult circumstances. They need to take the time to reflect before they take action. They need to create discussions with many family members, and they need to become open systems in which information is shared and concerns are communicated. All these principles—collaboration, listening, and reflection, openness internally and externally—are qualities of resiliency, the ability to bounce back after a crisis by learning and growing, rather than risking never recovering by turning away in what will almost certainly be a futile attempt to make everything right again through the dangerous path of contraction.

 **Part Five**

The Personal Challenges
of Succession

Succession, as we have seen, is a process not an event. It is also a personal experience for everyone involved—not only the person or persons being groomed for succession and the family leader, but the entire family and the business as well. It starts with a period during which the elders—and possibly nonfamily business leaders—prepare the members of the next generation for leadership roles, helping them learn and grow in the business. After this comes a period during which power, ownership, and authority shift from one generation to another. This section explores personal aspects of the succession process in depth, developing some of the themes from the previous section about family transitions. Leadership transition in the family enterprise demands the same straightforward process other organizations employ. However, family enterprises present more-complex conditions for leadership succession, primarily because successors include not only employees but also relatives. Unlike nonfamily successors, family members have personal relationships outside the business that influence the way they are treated in the leadership-succession process. In addition, most family successors are either current or future owners of the family enterprise, and their ownership may influence the manner in which their relatives view them as potential leaders in the business.

Succession is a challenge for the next generation. They see great works that have come from their elders and wonder what they can do to follow them. Although succession proceeds most often from a male patriarch, increasingly, the issue of different genders comes up as succession can cross genders and there are more and more female business leaders. The issue of finding the most-capable leader—especially when the candidates are brothers and sisters, cousins and in-laws, and outside managers—is so complex that too many family leaders just avoid it. They put off thinking about it, or expressing their thoughts, which only further complicates the process and engenders dissension among family members. In the following selections, I suggest ways to transparently manage the succession process over time so it does not result in family members feeling that some have been anointed as winners while others are losers. The selections focus on how the family can create conditions to grow a new generation of family and enterprise leaders.

5.1

Dutiful Sons: How to Succeed as Heir to a Great Entrepreneur

It is hard to be empathetic to the dilemma of the (usually male) heir who fol-lows in the footsteps of a larger-than-life father. The path of the younger son is very difficult. This selection looks at what constitutes success for founder's son: success in business, in the family, and in his personal life—that is, in his sense of identity and well-being—using the stories of some prominent scions of the great wealth creators as examples.

What an act to follow. Your father is Tom Watson, Henry Ford, John D. Rockefeller, or George Bush. You may even share his name, but the life ahead of you seems fraught with peril. How can you possibly succeed? Everyone is waiting for you to fall. Your father, while a great man, has not exactly been easy to live with. He has been absent for long periods in your life. And when he is around, it is hard to get airtime or attention. He tends to be overly critical of you. You love and revere him, sure, but you are also a bit angry with him. You often wish you had a normal, human-size father.

Sam Bronfman was such a larger-than-life father who developed Seagrams into a powerhouse that included many global brands of spirits and at its zenith was the largest distiller of alcoholic beverages in the world. His son Edgar was a worthy heir, taking over the family empire and modernizing, enlarging, and diversifying it manifold while maintaining a vast charitable empire and act-ing as a family leader. But his tenure began in an entity that was confronted with a fairly commonplace, but significant, challenge: It needed to grow and develop quickly as a company to respond to increasing opportunities and an increasingly competitive market. Edgar couldn't afford a misstep. He needed to think quickly, act fast, and be versatile—but continually vigilant—to avoid the landmines strewn about the landscape. It required that he bounce between tact and daring, independent action and subservience, as he struggled to come after the powerful, mercurial, and willful Sam.

Edgar's first life task, like that of many successful heirs, was to gain a modicum of separation from his family, with whom he had grown up in splendor in Montreal, replete with lavish attention and a fair degree of isolation from worldly realities—not a good training ground for achievement. Everything is taken care of and risk is nonexistent. This may be good training for a crown prince; it breeds a monstrous sense of entitlement. How does a scion develop the desire to excel, the skill to achieve success, and the prudence to balance the many crosscurrents present in a business family?

Edgar made several moves that seemed to help him develop his natural talents. Attending college in the United States, he developed an identity as a rebel and came close to getting expelled. Going to work in the family business, he established himself in New York, where he was far away from Sam at least for some periods of time, as his father shuttled between Montreal and New York. He developed his own style of management, more informal and team-oriented than his autocratic father's, and he brought in his own team. Even though Sam was around much of the time and made sure to overrule many of his son's decisions, Edgar was able to disagree and take his own counsel. However if pressed, he knew he had to defer to his father. It may have been that the blend of the two resulted in more-effective leadership than either of them alone would have provided.

Any succession rivalry between him and his brother, Charles, was cut short in the first days of their careers, when the two mutually agreed that Edgar would be the visible heir, and Charles would be the silent partner. Thus, by not only acknowledging their differences but using them to the best advantage, they avoided the toxic rivalry that has resulted in both personal and professional disaster for many famous wealthy brothers. This also likely helped ease the difficult life path so often given the younger brother in such a powerful and wealthy family.

Although Edgar played the role of mogul with relish, enjoying his wealth and the social position that comes with it, his success was in part due to elements of his nature that may seem to contradictory to his upbringing—balance, dedication, self-awareness, among others.

He was a diplomat, harmonizing his desire to achieve with the needs of his father, his brother, the rest of the family, and key employees. Unlike the entrepreneur who listens to nobody, Edgar was a good listener and collaborator. These seem to be the character traits of the successful family business heir.

Contrast Edgar with another heir, Gene Pressman, whose father Fred developed Barney's into a leading clothing store in New York. Gene was a poster child for entitlement, living lavishly and spending without limit until he finally bankrupted the company. He seems to have inherited his position from his father without either of them having given a thought to the skills the position would require or the help he would need to run such a company. Impressed by his confidence and showmanship, his father let him to take over, but did not oversee or challenge him. Raised in privilege, he appeared to have relied on his own fantasies for counsel, paying no attention to limitation or risk. He listened to no one, in the family or outside. Rather than acting as if he understood that he was responsible for stewarding the business and leading the family with compassion, an eye toward their interests, and concern for their desires, Gene seemed to care only about overshadowing his father. It was competition out of control, and it cost the entire family its future.

The challenges facing a second-generation business heir usually lie in several areas: coming to terms with Dad, gaining real competence in a world that tends to defer to you, developing legitimacy in your own right, and developing a sense of stewardship over the family's assets. The second-generation heir is a leader, but not of the entrepreneurial sort that most founders are. Heirs come from another world altogether; they did not have to make it on their own, and they have to navigate a family-and-business world that is already populated with a diverse and colorful cast. They fail if they don't develop the skills, sensitivity, and identity necessary to balance the existing demands of the enterprise and the family while adding their own unique contributions.

The most overwhelming challenge is to come to terms with Dad. While he may say that he wants you to succeed, you have to wonder about his behavior. Some dads create pliant, uninformed heirs who will do anything to please them. Tom Watson Jr., of IBM, wrote in his biography of the brutal and demanding treatment he received from his father and presents his work as a lifelong quest to prove himself worthy. The fact is that many entrepreneurial dads do not know how to create successors and are somewhat ambivalent about them. For every heir that worshipped his dad, there is one John D. Rockefeller Jr., who moved his family from infamy and focus on oil to an investment and philanthropic orientation that continues three generations later, and one Edsel Ford, who was ground down and degraded by his father and finally met an early death from illness.

The key seems to be taking a tactical and strategic stance toward Dad. He has the power, until he dies or relinquishes it. The heir must find domains somewhat removed from Dad's influence where he can grow, develop, and exercise authority. You cannot impress Dad with your day-to-day achievements; you need some distance and separation. An effective heir doesn't try to stage a palace coup either; he learns to adapt to Dad as most often the strongest element in the environment. That said, the heir also has to develop the ability to confront, argue, assert himself, and even sometimes manipulate situations to make sure that his voice is heard.

Developing competence and self-awareness in a world of privilege is another task. Like Edgar Bronfman, who had to put some distance between him and his family early on, an heir has to escape the nest. In the past, this was done by going to war. Today, an experience in another business, developing skill at competition of any sort, or overcoming a self-created personal crisis through exercise of will (e.g., overcoming drugs or poor relationship choices) can get things started. One must conquer several demons. The demon of privilege and entitlement must be overcome by developing a desire to achieve on one's own. For a young heir, getting a small paycheck on one's own or building a small business can be as meaningful as creating an empire. One must learn to filter reality from deference and fantasy. Learning to trust other people stems from being able to distinguish between those who will tell you only what they think you want to hear and those who are genuine. One is able to make this distinction, and therefore begin to trust others, only after having developed the self-awareness and interpersonal skills known as emotional intelligence (some of these skills are presented in "Moving Beyond Emotional Reactions to Effective Family Communication," in Part III).

Another task is to develop legitimacy in your own right. When a young heir enters the business, it is a public event. His reputation follows him ("He is a fool." "He is a rebel." "He is thoughtful."), to his detriment. It helps to come with a reputation for having done something ("He was a star at this investment bank," or "I hear he was a fine lawyer"). The key is not to start too high and to take a role that allows you to do real work. Don't be Dad's personal assistant. Go to a division in which you will be able to learn from those around you. Take responsibility and gradually begin to make decisions. Two fifth-generation Ford cousins—Bill and Edsel—worked for years in midlevel executive roles, until Bill was plucked from the ranks in his early 40s and made chairman. While being a Ford was key, he did not get the job on name alone. He had an independent reputation as a reformer who was prudent, sensible, thoughtful, and environmentally sensitive.

Finally, an heir must develop the attitude and behavior of a family steward. He should never feel that the inheritance is being given to him alone. An heir is being asked to take on a responsibility for the family, which means that perhaps unlike the father, the scion's role includes family leadership and respect for all family members. The successor must not let the business overwhelm all other considerations, but must remain close to the rest of the family, who as the "owners" give the leader legitimacy. The good heir is steward of the family, using the skills of emotional intelligence to solicit opinions and remain alert to different needs, helping family members to find good paths in life and to get support for their choices and endeavors, and making sure the family develops procedures to assist all family members in making their way. Heirs that neglect this aspect of leadership find themselves isolated, rejected, or resented and never fully develop themselves as leaders.

Being a successful third- or fourth-generation heir almost without exception requires a broader mix of leadership skills than was demanded of the founding entrepreneur. Regardless, there is no doubt that succeeding as a dutiful son (or daughter, but that is another story) demands a vastly different sort of leadership. It is not easy to preserve the family business or fortune as an heir. Whatever one is given demands careful nurturing and development, because a family fortune can be lost as quickly as it was gained. Sadly, Edgar's Bronfman's heir, Edgar Jr., who had many of the positive qualities of his father, but perhaps not all of them, lost much of the family's fortune through a series of bad business moves, which also severely alienated his uncle Charles's side of the family. Being a third-generation heir can be hell.

5.2

When Succession Crosses Genders

The previous selection looked only at male successors of successful men. This one looks at a much less common pattern—that of a woman succeeding her father or a man, his mother. This unique pattern of cross-generational succession is much different from that of father to son (and perhaps mother to daughter). We present the stories of some prominent, and some lesser-known, young men and women who have taken over a family business from a parent of the opposite gender. Each of these paths is quite different.

This selection was written with Fredda Herz Brown of Relative Solutions.

Hugh Hefner revolutionized the magazine industry in the 1950s, making *Playboy* a production with himself as the star. In many ways, the magazine was a chronicle of his own lifestyle and ideas. Yet this self-appointed role model for New Age males lacked a male heir. His daughter, Christie, grew up with her divorced mother under a different name. Father and daughter got to know each other only cautiously and with infrequent visits. During one such visit, impressed by Christie's thoughtfulness and intelligence, Hugh made her an incredible offer: Why not join the business?

"Hef started saying in interviews, 'Oh yeah, Christie's going to take over the company,'" she later recalled. "And I thought, 'That's an interesting idea.'" She accepted, and after not even ten years with the company, ascended to the presidency of Playboy Enterprises. Then, in 1988, she became CEO. She remained the leader of a quintessentially male-oriented company until early 2009. Hef later remarried and sired more children. While he still garners attention and embodies the magazine, Christie was clearly in charge for more than two decades. Hef occupies his special "emeritus" role (a role that, among other things, enables him to spend most days lolling about in pajamas at his mansion where he in fact actually works, reviewing proofs in his bed). Their roles were very different and highly complementary. "He has turf and I have turf," Christie said. "We respect each other's abilities and don't try to do the same thing."

Most families are run by a highly effective cross-gender team—the parents. Equally effective is a cross-gender team that spans two generations—father and daughter or mother and son. Such pairings can create a special bond that serves as the basis for a powerful leadership configuration.

"Gender sameness" often produces a rivalry that complicates father–son and mother–daughter relationships. But gender difference allows an opposite-sex parent to appreciate a child's talent without feeling threatened or superseded. And because sons and daughters feel protective toward their opposite-sex parent, they can serve comfortably as stewards and cheerleaders, especially when they enjoy the requisite authority to take action when needed.

You don't hear much about the blessings of cross-generational succession because it's a relatively new phenomenon. When business was a male preserve, a daughter who expressed interest in the family firm was roundly discouraged. Katharine Graham, who stunned the business world in 1963 by taking over her family's *Washington Post*, enjoyed an opportunity that a generation earlier was considered unthinkable for another equally bright and capable newspaper heiress, Iphigene Ochs, the only child of *New York Times* patriarch Adolph Ochs.

Two generations after Katharine Graham's accession, partnerships' crossing genders and generations elicit not curiosity as much as envy. Many cross-gender business successions seem characterized by patience and willingness to allow the older generation to linger without the heir's feeling diminished, frustrated, or stifled. In these partnerships, the son or daughter feels fully empowered and fulfilled without having to push a parent aside. High-profile examples of this phenomenon abound almost anywhere you turn.

Surely only a daughter could respect and appreciate Hugh Hefner's idiosyncratic role at Playboy Enterprises. Though father and daughter were rarely shown together when Christie was CEO, in that capacity she steadfastly defended Hef's various bizarre "perks"—an outsize salary and residence in the company-owned Playboy mansion, among others—and respected his creative decisions about maintaining their flagship magazine's traditional format.

At the same time, Christie engineered the company's successful entrée into new fields like cable TV and licensing. She is credited with boosting Playboy's profits and stock price to all-time highs—no mean feat in the fickle world of publishing. It's difficult to imagine anyone else, especially a son, achieving that balance. While it was a roller-coaster ride for the company, Christie was generally considered a good strategic and operational leader.

The Lauders

Estée Lauder grew up in Queens, New York, and began to sell lotions and beauty products out of her home in the 1940s. She was one of only a handful of women business founders in her generation. The company grew, so when her oldest son, Leonard, completed a stint in the Navy and graduated from the University of Pennsylvania's Wharton School with a business degree, it seemed natural for him to work there. He joined the company in 1958. His partnership with his mother thrived as Leonard oversaw incredible growth by professionalizing the company's management structure, creating its research-and-development labs and spearheading its international expansion into a global giant with more than $8 billion in sales in 2008.

Although Estée Lauder Companies went public in 1995, it remains firmly under family control, with the family owning almost all of the voting shares and occupying key positions. Leonard's wife remained a senior VP, a position she still occupies; Leonard became chairman of the company (a position he held from the public offering through summer 2009). Also on board are their son, William (who is now the company's executive chairman, having recently ceded the CEO position to a nonfamily leader), Leonard's brother Ronald, and Ronald's daughter Aerin.

Interestingly, each of these well-known successors has a long-term partnership with an opposite-sex parent that's remarkable for its harmony, its synergy, and the special regard each has for the parent. These heirs are not simply waiting to ascend the corporate throne. They seem to be engaging in a special continuing relationship that's a reward in itself.

Fathers to Daughters

One quality seems to characterize the style of a daughter moving into her father's business—patience. In each case we look at here, the daughter understands that there are issues, emotions, and complex roles to navigate, so her instinct is to slowly develop trust with her father and other employees.

Another unique quality daughters generally possess—and bring into their father's business—is the absence of entitlement. They recognize that to succeed they need to prove themselves—to their father and to the company—and in a number of situations we have seen, proving themselves includes building credibility outside the family enterprise first.

Moreover, unlike many sons who can't wait to push a stubborn dad out the door and streamline the company, daughters seem tolerant and even fond of their fathers' foibles. The desire to serve their father and the enterprising family—a quality often attributed to women in nonbusiness families—seems a greater motivating factor than the desire to aggrandize control and power.

Alan Bressler's father launched Agar Supply Co. by selling pork to restaurants in Boston's Chinatown and subsequently expanded into meat distribution and processing. By the time Alan inherited leadership in the 1970s, Agar Supply was a large independent food-service-and-supply company servicing restaurants and groceries throughout Greater Boston. In the early 90s Bressler faced a classic succession dilemma: Food service was an unglamorous and very male business, but he had no sons—just three daughters born within three years of each other. Increasing competition and changing markets demanded that he focus on renewing the business immediately, but these same conditions and his lack of sons left him with difficult strategic choices.

Bressler's eldest daughter, Karen, had an MBA in international business and was quite successful in a company that imported and sold toys. But she was also raising her own young child. To her surprise, Bressler asked her to try out the family business. "I didn't need it," she recalls. "I could get a lot of jobs. But because he was my father, and he asked, I decided it was worth a try."

She quickly discovered that Agar Supply was, as she said, "a very 'guy' place," full of long-term employees uncomfortable with change. That didn't deter her because she had no particular interest in running the place. "My strategy was to keep to my area, do my job, and get results," she recalls. "I let trust and familiarity build slowly, and I waited for them to warm up to me."

Karen worked with her father on some major strategic changes. The business needed more space. It was time to think about moving out of Boston and offering a wider range of products and services.

The process was anything but smooth. At first, Karen recalls, "there wasn't anything for me to do. Then, as jobs came open, I had to 'swim' with each assignment." As she took on each job, "there were things for me and Dad to talk about, and he got a sense of me and my work." While father and daughter looked for a role that would match her growing competence and authority, the company's president resigned, so "I took the initiative," Karen said, and assumed the president's responsibilities.

Within a few years, Agar Supply moved to a suburb of Boston, expanded its products, and revamped almost the entire management team. Working together throughout the 90s, father and daughter had virtually transformed the company. By the time Alan was ready to retire in 2000, it seemed natural for Karen to take his place.

It Works in India, Too

Like Karen Bressler, Charu Modi Bhartia was asked to join her family's business after earning an MBA and working for a U.S. company. Like most Indian businesses, her family's companies were traditional male preserves, so she had many reservations. She was asked by her father to return to India and in an unusual gesture, to join the family's multifaceted business empire. Her role required that she work with her father to launch two entrepreneurial ventures in health care and education. While developing her relationship with her father, she created firm boundaries and had realistic expectations.

Slowly, she gained her father's trust. "I don't confront him or speak out in business meetings when others are there," she said. "I confront him in private, where I can ask him to explain his position and talk an issue through." The relationship is cemented through a daily father-daughter lunch at home. "I feel like a real partner now," she said. "My business is about a year from being profitable, and I am starting another venture for our family."

The Schneiders: From Emotion to Trust

Most fathers and daughters share a natural closeness. But translating that emotional bond into a trusting business partnership takes some doing. On the one hand, the father instinctively presumes that his daughter will always be his little girl whom he must protect (and who in turn protects him, albeit emotionally). On the other hand, the father needs a business colleague with authority, capability, and the aptitude to win and lose her own battles.

Frank Schneider, a Denver family business and turnaround consultant who has developed and sold several professional-services businesses, looked ahead at age 65 to a comfortable, active practice with a small, one-person, consulting firm that could support a flexible lifestyle. To his surprise, his daughter Kim Schneider Malek, an MBA who had been working with a large company, asked if she could join him.

He was reluctant at first. He had worked for a year with his son, Brad, who opened an affiliate office in Chicago in 1995. After two years, Brad left to assume leadership in one of his wife's family's businesses. Kim, as a middle daughter, played a role in the family that was conciliatory and diplomatic, "making her supportive of me in ways that her brother was not," Frank said. "Brad was more like me, and had we been working together in the same office, we probably would have had some clashes." After working with Kim on several engagements, Frank saw the benefits of their collaboration. "We are polar opposites," he said, "but we respect each other and value our differences. This has become one of our competitive advantages."

Kim experienced a particular work–family conflict that often seems to be present when a daughter collaborates with her father. "My father wants me to devote myself to the business and our clients like he does, which is very time-intensive," she said. "But he also wants me to bear and raise his grandchildren, which is fighting for the same time. He has genuine conflicting commitments for me: advancing my career in his business and perpetuating future generations in his family." To be sure, Kim said, she feels this conflict as well.

The presence of brothers in the business can lead to an intense rivalry if the daughter is chosen as the successor. In a public company, the father was founder and icon of the product. The mother was a strong personality, active in her own ventures and community affairs. First, their eldest daughter entered the business, followed by their son several years later. The daughter was serious, dedicated, and patient, learning her role and taking on many jobs. In contrast, the son focused exclusively on his area of interest: marketing and promotion. He presumed that he and his sister would share leadership, but their father thought that she was the natural leader and let it be known that she was his designated heir. This led to a deep rift and a feeling of betrayal on her brother's part.

Mothers to Sons

Mother–son working partnerships are more complex, partly because they're less common. Much depends on how the mother originally reached the top. A mother, like Katharine Graham, who became CEO through the death of her husband, may be more tentative or conflicted about her abilities. A visionary founder-mother like Estée Lauder, on the other hand, was confident, clear, and assertive about who she was, what she was doing, and what she wanted. The mother thus seems either to exult in playing the father role or suffer the burden of trying to succeed him.

In each path, the son has a different image of the mother. Leonard Lauder had to perform at the top of his game but still accept that he would remain in his mother's high-profile shadow as long as she was alive and her work attracted the spotlight. Little did he know she would continue into her 90s. Donald Graham, by contrast, may have felt a calling to protect and support his mother in her role.

Kathy Gardarian founded Qualis International, in Orange County, California, in 1988, to sell and distribute packaging products to retailers like Home Depot. Her only son, Leo, came on board two years after his mother started the company, fresh out of college, at age 23. The business was growing fast, and she needed help building the distribution system for its products. The special relationship between the son and his mother, who divorced when he was nine, enabled Kathy to let go and trust Leo in ways that, as a controlling entrepreneur, she might not have trusted someone else.

"We have always been best friends," Kathy said of her son. "He knows me well, and we have a remarkable ability to diffuse the stress levels for each other. Having a male counterpart in this male-dominated business is a real asset. There are still some clients who are more comfortable doing business with a man."

At first Kathy functioned as Leo's mentor. "At the start, he was afraid he couldn't contribute anything," she recalls. "He needed help to get his confidence up. He was very concerned that he not disappoint me and hurt our relationship. He felt he had to prove himself to me. It was never verbalized, but I know it was a struggle for him."

Over the past 20-plus years, Leo has grown with the company as Qualis International expanded to numerous distribution centers nationwide and increased its revenues to more than $20 million annually. While Kathy remains the sole owner, Leo was promoted to president several years ago and is on track to eventually inherit his mother's ownership. Although Kathy is still active, and seems proud of her business's being—at least for now—"100% Woman-Owned," as her website says, she spends a lot of time serving on boards and pursuing her personal interests, giving more and more authority to Leo. Although Leo doesn't do everything her way, she said, "I am so lucky to have had this opportunity; his presence has freed me up."

Not every mother–son partnership is so lucky. Florence Kaslow, a family-business consultant and psychologist in Palm Beach, Florida, has worked with several families involving single, self-made CEO mothers. Unlike their married counterparts, each of these women acts as both head of household and company president. In many of the families with which Kaslow has worked, the mother was successful as a businesswoman, but as a parent she was resented by her sons because of her frequent absences and limited involvement with the home. In these and other similar situations, the mother wants her son to succeed, but he isn't always up to it. Unlike daughters, many sons of enterprising families do feel a sense of entitlement, exacerbated by the feeling that their mother's devotion to her business deprived them of an essential element of a traditional childhood. The mothers, feeling guilty about their lack of familial participation, believed they "owed" the business to their sons but were increasingly disappointed in their performance. In such a situation, when the mother brought the son into the business as a partner despite her concerns about his abilities or commitment to doing the hard work his position required, the resulting partnership often led to the sale or decline of the business.

Mother-mentors often expend much of their energy curbing their sons' overconfidence and eagerness to take the helm before they are ready. In other cases, the son develops such a close relationship with his mother that he's hard put to feel as close and responsible to anyone else—his wife, for example. While daughters feel responsible to their fathers and to their families simultaneously, sons feel responsible and dutiful to their mothers both personally—to the exclusion of their own families—and professionally.

Successful cross-gender, cross-generation partnerships share one common theme: the respect and trust that opposite-sex parents and offspring feel for each other. This leads to great tolerance and to the ability to be attuned to each other's needs. If this basic building block is in place, the benefits and special features of this tricky relationship should outweigh the liabilities.

5.3

Making the Right Choice for a Family Successor

The family-business patriarch often wrestles silently and internally with the great dilemma: which of his offspring will be the next family leader? This selection suggests that this internal process may itself be less than optimal, in that it does not allow the whole family, especially the members of the succeeding generation itself, to take part in the decision making and to take responsibility for making it work. I suggest an alternative: a mentoring, assessing, and decision-making process that is open, transparent, and collaborative.

One of the calls I get most frequently as a family-business consultant is from a family patriarch who wants help with the momentous choice of naming the successor-leader of the business. The leader-founder wants assurance that he is making the right decision, and he thinks that "assessment tools" can take away some of the risk and help him pick the right person (or ratify the choice he has made). Although such tools may indeed produce important information, they cannot predict the future.

Often underlying the request is a family dilemma. One family founder had to choose among three major characters: An older son had entered the business soon after college and assumed he would take the reins. He worked diligently, but was not very outgoing or expansive. His daughter had gone to a top business school and was a partner at a leading strategy consulting firm. She had been calling him and challenging him with ideas for how the business could expand into global markets. The third potential successor was his operations guru, a talented nonfamily executive who had crafted the company production and supply chains. He seemed indispensable to the future, but would he want to work with the founder's son as co-leaders?

The founder faced this challenge in silence—talking to his wife only, while the three candidates each felt avoided, deserted, and confused. Finally, each one sought him out privately and gently voiced concern about the future. He didn't want to hurt his son, though if he took his daughter's or the executive's concerns seriously, that would be the outcome. His solution was to hire an executive coach for his son. When he announced this to the son, the son felt undermined and confused and didn't understand what his father hoped to gain from this or why he felt it necessary to hire a "trainer" for him as if he were an incompetent child. The coaching went nowhere.

Succession is a challenge unlike any a founder like this has faced. Each previous hurdle was one the founder (usually a male, though today that is less frequently the case) could handle directly. But trying to handle succession in this way—by himself alone—sets the stage for disaster. The founder cannot control the outcome, and the consequences of his making a decision and then changing his mind are unthinkable. So the controlling founder must select people that he trusts to find their own way in unfamiliar territory. He has to learn to let go and not expect to control the outcome.

Also he must face some uncomfortable facts about the future. First, the nature of the business in the next generation will be very different from what it was in his generation. Globalization, greater size, competition, new technology, and changing demographics all will make for a future that is quite unlike the past, with the result being that next-generation leaders will have to manage a very different business from those that exist now. If the founder picks someone who pledges continuity with the past, he or she will not succeed in shepherding the business through the next generation. In many cases, the founder has to understand that one of the earmarks of success is that the business has outgrown even his formidable skills. Like Moses, the founder may never see the land to which he has brought the next generation.

So the new leaders must take the organization to places it has never been. Who is best prepared to do that? This puts the potential candidates in a new light. Loyalty to tradition and continuity are not the best qualities to select for. In most industries, a business will eventually need to address questions about whether it can compete on its own or needs to be part of a larger entity or coalition. The family business may be absorbed into a larger entity, and the family may not control the offspring of what was once its company. Or the business may expand, but that may require bringing in new partners who will want to have a say. Who is best suited to manage those changes and will have the courage to make the hard choices?

To lead the family business, the successor will also have to lead within the family. The founder did not face this sort of challenge; he was the unquestioned leader, and the family had to respect that. But the next-generation business leader will be answerable not just to him- or herself but to the whole family. So in addition to vision, courage, and skill at navigating in a global environment, the successor must have the diplomatic skills necessary to gain the agreement of the family shareholders. Is there a person in the family who possesses these two sets of qualities? The founder may have to select more than a single individual—say, one to lead the business and another to steward the family. Succession, the founder must learn, not only requires paying attention to more than just the business, but also may mean not choosing only a single leader. Naming a business leader and ignoring the family shareholders could lead to the self-destructive conflicts that have brought down major enterprises. Clearly, the founder contemplating succession faces an even more complex dilemma than he ever imagined.

To this mix he also must add consideration of his own future. With today's life expectancy extending very close to the century mark, the founder must ask, What role will I take in the family if I give up control and select new leaders? His greatest fear is that he will have no role at all and will instantly become irrelevant. How can he find a constructive role that is different from that in which he has become comfortable? What would that look like? In the 1980s Yale business professor Jeffrey Sonnenfeld set about finding out how CEOs who had left their companies handled this. In his 1988 book *The Hero's Farewell: What Happens When CEOs Retire*, Sonnenfeld presented his findings, which suggest that the way these leaders see themselves strongly impacts the way they act upon leaving. He found that among the predominant exit styles are some—such as a former leader's meddling in company politics from the outside—that can damage both the company and the family. The leader vainly tries to preserve his ties to the business in an attempt to preserve his sense of self, which he can't separate from the company. Other leaders, whose identities are not fused with positional leadership, deal with their retirement more creatively, by moving on to other activities, for instance, or finding a way to advise the company without stepping on the toes of the new leader and the next generation. Some family leaders stay on for a while as board chair or help the family pursue entrepreneurial activities like real estate or new ventures while leaving the core business to their heirs.

Back to the original question, How does a family leader-founder select a successor? Some leaders avoid the question, put it off, or keep their own counsel, to the frustration of everyone around them. Too often, the founder feels this isn't something that can be discussed. Choosing to act on the basis of this feeling is almost never wise, and often ends up harming the family and the business. To avoid conflicts in both arenas, the family leader must start by addressing openly the above issues in various ways within the family and the business. It may be true that the final decision regarding succession will be made by one person alone, but that doesn't mean that many people can't deliberate, plan, and explore different avenues transparently in a forum including all who will be affected. The decision can be consultative and collaborative without being democratic.

Members of the family, family and nonfamily executives of the business, and even outside advisers could and should be engaged in the process of inquiry into the future. A large family with a complex business or group of businesses might convene several task forces to explore different elements of the family and the enterprise with an eye toward preparing for the future. They might create a family task force to look at where the family is going and a business task force—maybe including some outside advisers with more in-depth or broader business experience than most of the family members have—to look at the future of the business and the environment in which it is situated. The business leaders might also have a succession task force that reviews talent development and assesses how the family and the business are preparing future leaders within the company. These are not one-time meetings. Each is an ongoing process that may be punctuated by reports, conclusions, and action steps at key choice points.

The family founder is no longer alone with the succession choice. The decision will now be much more informed, as he will have much more information with which to work. While the future the successor will face cannot be predicted, it can be looked at directly, and certain general trends can be highlighted. The various task forces can each describe the environment that the family and the business will be facing ten or more years out. Starting with the future, they can work backwards, asking what each area needs from leaders right now. Two things will have been accomplished by the family founder who sets up such a process: First, the whole family-business system will have received the message that the future is part of their current responsibilities. Second, the discussion of who will be "picked" to lead will be located within the broad context in which the leaders will have to serve. A family or nonfamily member who seeks leadership will have to demonstrate his or her ability by participating fully in one or more of these task forces. These groups will offer multiple opportunities for people to demonstrate leadership skills and make themselves visible.

Returning to the dilemma of the founder who is trying to choose among three candidates, we can now see that instead of trying to decide—in his head—whom to select as a successor, the family founder can invite all three candidates to work together to chart the future. It may be clear that his daughter, by taking leadership in the task force for the business future, is the best leader. Seeing his sister in action, the founder's son may learn that, indeed, he does not have the skills to shepherd the business. The founder may discover that he does not feel comfortable naming the nonfamily executive as sole leader, despite his qualifications. But a combination of the candidates may become co-leaders, with the daughter as chair and either the son or key executive as CEO. In any case, the conversations about who will be the successor are now very different in both the company and the family. Many voices have been heard, and many people have stepped up to envision the future. Having listened and learned how people think (on their feet as well as in prepared, tightly controlled settings), having seen how they frame discussions, and having watched them interact and in action, the founder will have greater trust that a new generation can take the family and its business where they need to go.

5.4

Nonfamily Executives:
Augmenting the Family Talent Pool

An enterprising family may spend an inordinate amount of time looking at the small number of family heirs in an attempt to decide who should run the business. When it does this, it often overlooks the possibility that both the family and the business might be better served by a nonfamily leader. In fact, a family often resists or avoids creating a climate that would support leaders from outside the family, which can be fatal. Too often, family enterprises inadvertently make themselves unattractive to talent from outside the family; this is self-defeating. In this selection, I present some of the ways a family can create a team of family and nonfamily leaders to steer the business forward.

Every family business that grows beyond the "mom and pop shop" stage faces the need for experienced, highly talented professionals from outside the family. Some of the most successful family enterprises have found their nonfamily executives to be among their most valuable assets. But the contributions of key managers at family firms are rarely touted in the media. Many families fail to recognize how important attracting and retaining nonfamily professionals is to sustaining their success.

Families need nonfamily executives for a variety of reasons, but the factor that most often spurs families to look outside for a business leader is the lack of sufficient family talent to lead the family enterprise—a situation that inevitably occurs as the business grows. Family companies also seek nonfamily executives to contribute specific skills, add diversity to their organizations, or offer new ideas or creative, strategic thinking. Some families seek nonfamily professionals to prepare succeeding generations for leadership.

A family business can grow much faster than the family talent pool of executives needed to lead it. At some point, a family must begin to recruit outside talent. But working for a family business can present special challenges for nonfamily executives, and making the decision to go outside the family's tight circle can present special challenges for the family. Not all families are clear about the benefits they can derive from engaging nonfamily executives, and not all executives are interested in working in family businesses.

A great nonfamily executive can bring a lot to the business, offering business skills and an objective view that contributes much to the company's management. The presence of such a person can bring credibility and capability to the family business. But too often, families focus on the benefits the nonfamily executive brings to their business to the exclusion of how they can benefit the nonfamily executive. Or they wait too long before bringing in the people they need, do not recruit the level of talent they need, or inadvertently discourage the people they hire by making it difficult for them to do their jobs well.

While nonfamily executives fill a variety of roles, they tend to be most prominently featured in key supporting leadership roles, such as chief financial officer, chief operating officer, or general manager, chief technology officer, and vice president of human resources. However, evidence points to a recent trend to engage nonfamily members as chief executive officers in family enterprises.

The dynamics between nonfamily executives and family members vary according to the size and nature of the enterprise. In some organizations, family control of ownership is less centralized so the executives must answer to multiple family members. In other companies, the ownership structure is simpler, making the ownership dynamics more consistent and clear. Large family enterprises tend to have more-formal governance structures that provide clarity for nonfamily executives.

In some companies, family dynamics are more overt; in others, nonfamily executives are insulated from most family issues. Some family enterprises that are unclear about leadership succession and business continuation pull key nonfamily managers into the succession process or other issues inappropriately, and the nonfamily managers are faced with addressing both family dynamics and business issues when making decisions that should not be in their purview to begin with.

It is not easy being a nonfamily executive. They are willing to take on major responsibilities often without having the opportunity to participate in ownership—although some of them eventually are awarded a share of ownership. Often they face a slow pace of change in the senior management ranks and may even have to step aside as family members rise to key leadership positions. In some family enterprises, family membership and loyalty trump experience and performance. In these cases, nonfamily executives can be left behind, even treated unfairly, while working long hours and performing admirably.

The Family Mediator: Avoiding Triangles

Perhaps the most confounding element of a nonfamily executive's job is the intrusion of family dynamics into the business. Nonfamily managers often find themselves engaged in what family systems professionals refer to as triangulation—a dynamic we explored earlier, which can have a disastrous effect on all involved. Triangles are created when a person who is not a member of the family is thrust into an inappropriate third-party role in a family relationship and is forced to mediate between two others. Usually in enterprising families these are siblings, generations, genders, or working and nonworking family members. Although triangles can be created in which all parties involved are family members—as we saw in "Conflict, Emotions, and Family Dynamics," in Part III, where such a dynamic involved two sibling managers, their CEO father, and their mother, who was not involved in the business—here we focus on those involving nonfamily executives and members of the enterprising family.

In this type of triangle, a family member creates a strong bond with a nonfamily executive, or takes advantage of a bond that already exists, instead of facing an issue in his or her own family. The executive may have a special relationship with one family member; for instance, he may be close to one of the parents as a business colleague, and the parent may confide her feelings about another family member to him, putting him in a bind. The executive must be aware that this can antagonize an already dysfunctional family relationship. Instead of becoming a sounding board, the executive must make it clear that he is not comfortable hearing about personal or family issues or he thinks such issues should be dealt with directly by those involved. The nonfamily executive needs to remove himself from the situation or risk having his participation in family relationships impede his progress in the business.

A nonfamily executive who must resolve differences between a retiring CEO and a next-generation family member must understand the implication of his or her interactions with each family member and the way in which her role affects the parent–child dynamics. It behooves nonfamily executives to gain an understanding of such dynamics so that the executive does not unintentionally contribute to misunderstandings, conflicting interests, or family rivalries.

In one large family business, for example, the father retained the title of chairman and brought in a nonfamily member to serve as CEO. Four second-generation family members reported to the experienced nonfamily professional. The father continued to give directions to his children working in the business, and many business decisions were made at the family's weekly dinner. The father gave little guidance to the nonfamily CEO and isolated him from the company's board. The nonfamily executive lacked the authority necessary to manage the company effectively or provide leadership direction for the family members reporting to him. Aware that the father had failed to recognize his contributions to the company's success and give him the authority commensurate with his responsibilities, the nonfamily CEO accepted an offer from a public company and left the family-owned business.

Many nonfamily executives are forced to contend with issues such as family conflict, favoritism, avoidance of responsibility, lack of access to information, and inadequate succession planning. They often find themselves in the middle of family situations without having the ability to understand the dynamics or respond in a way that can help resolve the situation. As in the example above, in which information critical to business operations is disseminated at closed family gatherings such as informal dinners rather than in senior management team meetings, nonfamily executives can be deprived of information they need to effectively carry out their responsibilities. Healthy family dynamics can make nonfamily executives' lives comfortable, but negative family patterns can induce excess stress, making their involvement in the company unbearable.

Recruiting and Retaining Nonfamily Talent

To recruit the talent that they need, family members must be clear with each other about what they are willing to offer the nonfamily executive, and they must show the same face as they begin to recruit. The family must prepare itself for the entry of new talent by clarifying its own policies and practices for family employees. While an executive may be comfortable knowing that a family member will probably head the business, the presence of several family members within the company can present a real barrier to attracting talent. Nonfamily executives need to know that they will be evaluated and offered opportunities for advancement based on their performance, not on the basis of family politics. The nonfamily executive who supervises a family member requires clarity about what is expected of her in the roles of mentor and assessor of future family leadership. If these roles are not clearly delineated and defined for the nonfamily executive, the executive who tries to fill them will find it hard to be candid. If the family itself is not clear about the nonfamily executive's roles and responsibilities, the executive will be even less so. The executive needs to feel that her future is dependent on performance, not on making political alliances with family leaders.

An independent executive may believe the family has a culture of loyalty and obedience, rather than a focus on measurable results or performance in the marketplace. An environment resembling the town in the fable "The Emperor's New Clothes" may result when everyone knows that something is greatly amiss, but no one feels comfortable saying anything about it. What type of executive is attracted to this sort of business? One of the signs of a dysfunctional family-business culture is the inability to tolerate managers who are more talented or capable than the family owners. And the only executive who knowingly accepts a position in such a business is one who thinks loyalty is above capability and whose primary qualification is his or her willingness to be obedient. A culture of loyalty and obedience severely inhibits a family business's growth, innovation, and development, and an enterprise with such a culture fails to attract capable, highly motivated executives.

Other family businesses suffer from a variety of maladies that inhibit successful performance by nonfamily executives. Some family businesses that are inward-looking—that is, in which family members compete with each other for status in the company—may neglect to focus on the market, customers, and true competition with similar businesses in the external market. Other family businesses are overtly political, requiring that nonfamily executives ally themselves with one faction of the family or another and intentionally recruiting executives whose willingness to subordinate themselves is greater than their talent. In such companies, family rivalries are imported into the family business to the detriment of not just the family, but the nonfamily executive, the business, and all who work in it. Family businesses with these disorders fail to attract the most-capable nonfamily executives and if they are successful in hiring top-flight talent, find it difficult to retain it. The nonfamily executives who remain may be the most loyal but not the most capable.

While dysfunctional family dynamics are not uncommon, fortunately, they are not the rule. Many family businesses have thrived for several generations because they successfully overcame these tendencies and offer real authority and responsibility to nonfamily executives.

Also the dealings of these families with nonfamily executives have several qualities that differentiate them from the inward-focused, politicized family businesses. The most successful family businesses recruit and develop nonfamily talent honestly and transparently. Take the example of a business owner who recruited a nonfamily leader close to his own age making it clear when he hired him that one of his responsibilities was to mentor his son. The nonfamily leader was 15 years older than the owner's son; his own tenure was not going to be more than a decade, and he was aware of this. Because of his openness, he was able to candidly talk about what it meant to have a limited tenure and how long his was going to be, after which the son would take over if he were ready. Such expectations were shared transparently and understood by the father, the son, and the nonfamily executive from the beginning.

High-functioning family businesses are candid with nonfamily executives about ownership issues. While it may be tempting to dangle vague promises for the future in front of nonfamily executives—promises, for instance, regarding distributions if the company were to go public or if ownership is diluted—a more realistic course would be to offer performance bonuses and the possibility of a large payout after a successful tenure. These are only a few of the many reasonable and attractive incentives family businesses might offer nonfamily executives.

Business-owning families enhance good working relationships with nonfamily executives by being honest about difficulties, even going as far as setting up a neutral party to mediate conflicts. For example, in one enterprising family, the family elder was candid about the difficulty he had sharing power, and he asked the nonfamily executive to help him with this. To give the executive an added incentive to put up with the struggle that would likely ensue, the elder offered a contract that had generous terms if the executive were dismissed. Other families designate independent board members or outside advisers to monitor the relationships of family leaders and their nonfamily executives. Such safeguards contribute to good working relationships between family leaders and nonfamily executives.

Transparency serves both the family and the nonfamily executive. Just as it is important to share financial and business information within the family, so too is it important to share such data with the nonfamily executives. If an executive is not trusted with financial information about how the business operates, he or she will find it hard to trust the family or be candid with them about these issues. Transparency can further benefit the family and its enterprise by providing the nonfamily executive with clarity about how best to make a measurable difference.

What Nonfamily Executives Need from Family Enterprises

Nonfamily executives need clarity not only about their professional roles but also regarding their relationships with family members. Clear and detailed family and business governance structures can help nonfamily professionals better understand and manage these relationships. Although nonfamily executives rarely have opportunities to receive equity positions in family enterprises, they require compensation and professional development plans that clearly link financial rewards to their long-term performance. These professionals are best served when succession plans for senior family members and executive management are made clear to everyone.

Lack of trust is the primary reason nonfamily executives leave family businesses. When the trust relationship between the nonfamily executive and the senior family executive is broken, the nonfamily member is likely to seek an exit. Contributing factors include being sandwiched between family management and family shareholders and situations in which the nonfamily executive's hands are tied by family control and family dynamics. Other factors that cause nonfamily executives to leave family enterprises are lack of authority commensurate with management responsibilities, unrealistic expectations on the part of the family regarding the executive's ability to clean up management or family dysfunction, and lack of appreciation by family members. The consultants also point out that some nonfamily executives leave because they simply lack the skills to meet both business and family objectives.

Nonfamily executives should remain "unsung heroes" no longer. Every family business that grows and moves beyond the first generation of ownership will require the services of experienced highly talented professionals from outside the family. Recognizing the importance of attracting and retaining nonfamily professionals, learning to manage family and business dynamics, and providing these essential personnel with the recognition and compensation they deserve are all essential to the future success of every family enterprise.

Effective family leaders are candid and up-front about roles, responsibilities, and rewards of family members. If the family has a policy about family employment, it should be clearly stated and shared with the executive. Nonfamily executives need to be confident that family members who are employees will be assessed on the basis of performance and can be challenged, disciplined, and even considered for removal from a position or the business. Clarity about roles, responsibilities, and performance measures affirms that the business is operated as a business and not an extension of the family.

Succession: Within or Outside the Family?

Leadership succession is an especially delicate process in all family businesses, and nonfamily executives can play beneficial roles. In some cases, the family shareholders may recognize that the nonfamily member is the best person to lead the company forward. In others, the nonfamily executive may be called on to mentor, develop, and in numerous ways prepare a family member to ascend to a key leadership role in the next generation. Still other cases call for nonfamily executives to share leadership with family members as part of the leadership-succession plan. A healthy family business can look at the strengths and weaknesses of family leadership and assess what it needs from nonfamily talent. In one company, a young family member was named CEO, and a nonfamily executive was named president, with authority over key functions. Finally, nonfamily executives may serve as objective assessors of the leadership needs of the business and advise the board and family about the leadership-succession process, and in most family businesses, nonfamily executives will play a significant role in this process.

Virtually every family business will face a time when its owners turn to nonfamily executives to play integral roles in continuing the family's success. By allowing for candor and real influence from the nonfamily executive, the family begins a process that may occur in family businesses that grow beyond the first generation. The business begins to pass partially into the hands of nonfamily leaders (after the second or third generation, the business may find nonfamily executives filling the preponderance of C-level positions), and the family owners take on new roles: as owners and stewards, sustainers of the family's values, and parents to family members entering or remaining in the business. Some family members decide to work in the business, in leadership roles or positions similar to those of other employees. The rest of the family must learn new roles as owners, board members, or active shareholders. In such businesses, a family member may become CEO not because of family privilege but because he or she is considered to be the person most capable of leading the business, sometimes in a partnership with key nonfamily executives.

Some businesses fail because they cannot make the transition from total dependency on family members, but the most successful family businesses recognize the value of highly capable nonfamily executives. These businesses continue through multiple generations by recruiting exceptional nonfamily talent and endowing them with the authority necessary to successfully manage the family enterprise, including working collaboratively with family leaders and developing the next generation of family leadership. Successful family businesses are characterized by their successful nonfamily executives.

5.5

Founders Succeeding in Middle Life:
Letting Go and Moving On

A scenario common to many family businesses is one in which a younger gen-
eration is ready to take the reins but the older generation is not ready to let go. This
selection presents a novel notion—that a family-business leader should let go earlier
rather than later and move on to another, more-generative life task. I present some
examples of elders who have done this, illustrating that it can be a positive life path
both for the older family leader and the son or daughter who is able to take over
earlier in life.

We cannot escape tales of traditional family patriarchs who are so fused
with the business that they can't let go. Two sons who built vast media con-
glomerates out of their fathers' original ventures—Sumner Redstone and Rupert
Murdoch—even though now in their 80s, show no signs of seeking out a life
beyond their enterprises. Redstone has capable nonfamily leaders in place,
but he had a well-publicized falling-out with his daughter, and Murdoch faces
the possible resignation of one of his sons and heir apparent (his daughter has
already left the organization). Neither has any plans to step down.

Two younger company founders may offer another path. Both Bill Gates
and Michael Dell stepped down from their CEO posts when they were in their
40s—not leaving their companies, but broadening their lives by balancing their
focus on company with a strong commitment to family and, in Gates's case,
philanthropy. Their great works may be in the future as well as the past, but in a
different arena.

Over the past century, the average life span in the developed world has
doubled. A longer life, combined with the likelihood that the patriarch's children and grandchildren will grow to maturity while the elder leader still has the
capacity and desire to work, presents the leader of a family enterprise with some
interesting life challenges. In the British Royal Family, the challenge of succession is no longer two-generational; a capable scion is now caught between two

215

generations. The queen shows no signs of retiring, and yet her grandchildren are already entering adulthood. Her firstborn son has moved through life with something of a career and identity deficit, which deepens as his sons grow older and his mother continues her reign.

When does a leader decide to leave a family business, and how is the decision made? In *The Hero's Farewell: What Happens When CEOs Retire*, which I introduced in the selection "Making the Right Choice for a Family Successor," Jeffrey Sonnenfeld identifies four styles that describe the ways in which various leaders of family enterprises exit their positions. The first two—the Monarch and the General—are forced out but try to get back into power. The second pair—the Ambassador and the Governor—leave their leadership positions in the company of their own volition and move on psychologically as well. The Ambassador stays on behind the scenes to help the company succeed; the Governor pursues other interests. The latter styles represent people who do not invest their whole identity in the business, but have a strong enough sense of self to see themselves as important even without a formal connection to the business.

A problem emerges when the founder-leader's personal identity is fused with that of the company. "I am the state," says this type of family leader, who may be convinced that the company cannot succeed without his leadership, which in a deeper psychological sense masks a fear that he is nothing more than the company. He doesn't see himself outside the business or think he has a life outside it, so the suggestion that someone else take over becomes an assault on his sense of self. (Yes, I am assuming that most such people are male.) This lays the groundwork for deep conflict when family members suggest that either it is time to consider succession or they are ready to take the reins. The fight between a father and son for control of a company is a deeply wounding war, which often becomes a Shakespearian tragedy.

What are the alternatives to a family leader who cannot let go and who may hang on too long or fight like a Monarch or General against his offspring? Other than in family businesses, the model of one's having a single career with a single company is dying fast. I think it is time to free oneself of the mind-set that views ascension to business leadership as the culmination of one's career and stepping down as tantamount to death, and I suggest replacing this with a mind-set that considers family-business leadership a period of service to the family in the *middle* of one's life with several roles and challenges still ahead. After retiring from an active role in the family enterprise, a patriarch or matriarch with this mind-set might say, "Well, I've given something to my family over the past decades, and now I want to serve in a different way." The next generation, who are itching to make their mark, would certainly welcome this, but it would likely take some selling to make it palatable to the elders.

For other people entering middle age, the challenges of multiple careers and the delight in shifting from one career to another are becoming more common. After a lifestyle crisis, such as losing one's job (or one's company), or a personal crisis, such as an illness, a person is forced to consider new possibilities. After the initial shock and despair, the new direction allows the individual to expand like a butterfly emerging from a cocoon and to find pleasure and meaning in areas that he or she previously had not even considered. Why is this difficult for a family-business patriarch?

It may be that leading a successful family business is both addicting and limiting to one's growth and development. The family-business leader—even more than other business leaders—may not have anyone who can contest his actions until the business suddenly crashes. He lives in a closed system; new information simply does not enter it. Key nonfamily executives are sycophants, and any heirs who confront the leader are automatically discredited. The business is wonderful, and the leader need not consider any other options for a good life. Outside forces that bring new information and challenge someone to grow do not get through the wall that bounds the system. The leader, who at first was visionary and inspiring, becomes stale, self-satisfied, and pompous. This is not good for the family business or the leader.

Now consider an alternative to this type of leader: the family leader who possesses the mind-set I mentioned above and who, therefore, sees business leadership as only one stage of growth and development. He or she started a business or succeeded the founder after serving an apprenticeship and developing the necessary skills. This leader defines a new vision and sets about putting it into action—a project for a person in his or her 40s. Starting with defining a new vision, a good family-business leader should maybe envision a 15-year run, during which the family would form a next-generation leadership group, comprising family members and nonfamily executives who would help with the succession process. After that time, most any corporate leader begins to get stale or to hold the next generation back.

With this as the guiding assumption in the business and the family, the CEO stage would lead to further innovations and changes, which benefit both the family and the business. At the end of the first decade of leadership, the leader's perspective and job definition would begin to shift. The leader would focus on becoming a mentor to the next generation of leadership. The next-generation leadership group would begin to take on more authority. I recently watched such a leadership-succession process unfold at a great company, closely held by the family but in an industry that is consolidating to the point that it might be best if the company were under new ownership. The father—a second-generation heir of another visionary leader—saw that his son, despite having some clear weaknesses, seemed ready to take on leadership. As a sibling in a large family, the father was used to holding back before making a decision and was much more cautious than his dad had been. The 62-year-old father decided it was time to step down. He named his 40-year-old son CEO and remained as chairman.

This is not uncommon, but the way he went about doing it made it successful. First, he moved out of the company, into a small family office in the next town. He made a point of not visiting the company very often. He met regularly with his son to listen to him and sometimes question his decisions or actions. He and the son together recruited three independent board members who were highly knowledgeable about the industry and were not old friends of the father's. The father left his habit of making intuitive decisions behind and instead probed his son and other executives about their plans, challenging them when he thought it necessary. He was like a professor running a seminar in corporate strategy. When the choices arose about the direction of the company, he deferred to his son and the next-generation family council, which the siblings had established (for more on the family council and suggestions for establishing one, see "Sustaining Connection Through a Family Council," in Part II).

But he was a young man who thought he had at least one more stage in his career. Freed of the need to focus daily on the business, he found his horizons expanding. Through his service on a university board, he was exposed to new ideas about education and global development. He became a prime resource for the university's development plan. He encouraged his family to fund and become active in a family foundation, which in its initial stages contributed to a variety of causes he'd suggested. As the next generation began to feel ownership of the foundation, they defined a more focused mission for it. In addition, looking at the family's portfolio, the father began to focus on diversification as a means to add wealth for the next generations by investing in a large land development project. On top of all this, he and his wife traveled, taking adventure and educational vacations, and he found the time both to read, a lot, and to get to know his grandchildren.

If you asked him, he would say this stage of his life is as rich and stimulating as the one that preceded it. He feels younger, and certainly healthier, than when he led the business. He is deeply proud of his children and their spouses for taking responsibility and initiative in their own lives and careers and equally happy about the way in which they are doing this. He has an opportunity to give back in ways that are both visible and personally rewarding. In short, by seeing his service to the business as only one of several life stages, he has grown in many ways, using the benefits of his wealth and his business wisdom to become an elder, serving his family, the community, and himself. He is looking forward to mentoring his grandchildren.

As life expectancy increases—and along with it the number of active years a person can look forward to—family leaders, like others in society, must begin to think of their lives not as a single ladder, but rather as a journey with several destinations. Business leadership may be one of the middle stages, so people need to develop a positive image of life beyond this and develop the motivation to achieve in the postbusiness life stages. Western society would greatly benefit by borrowing a concept that is central to many African and other tribal cultures: the notion of former leaders as elders whom others can go to for advise and counsel. As an extension of this, enterprising families might establish a group of former leaders whom these tribal societies call a council of elders. When a family-business leader in the United States routinely envisions his or her life after positional leadership as that of an elder—and the family shares in this vision—and imagines the work of a wise elder as a resource for the family and the world, both the elder and the world will benefit.

 **Part Six**

Developing Leadership and Teamwork in the Next Generation

The transition from an owner-managed single business to a team of siblings or cousins who own an enterprise comprising multiple family assets and
entities is much more complex than is leadership succession when both the
form of leadership and the form of the business are remaining the same—such
as, when leadership over a single business simply transfers from one person to
another. When leadership and the enterprise are undergoing radical changes—
and trying to adapt to a rapidly changing world—there is great potential for dissension in the family and tension in the business: dissonance that originates in
family dynamics but interrupts the life cycle of the business, conflicts between
owner demands for liquidity and the enterprise's need for capital, and fractious-
ness among siblings and cousins competing for leadership. There are no right
answers, but there are questions that need to be asked and patterns rooted in
past family relationships that need to be dissolved if the family is to sustain itself
successfully into the next generation.

The cousins, coming as they do from different family branches, have different views of leadership, especially regarding their own roles in the business
and the family. They need to broaden their notions of effective leadership if they
are to succeed as a team. Presuming each member of the next generation has
a highly developed and unique skill set, together they could form an effective,
efficient, and energetic unit that would advance the business and the family productively into the future—if they could get past real and imagined disappointments and slights stemming from family interactions. They also must figure out
a way to overcome the family tendency to hold one's thoughts close to the vest
until it is too late. Unlike most traditional father-owners or father-founders of
a legacy business, they need to share their views about the future and listen to
what others have to say—not just their siblings and cousins, but other family members and employees—to learn what each needs from the next leader
or leaders. In any type of business, the second generation needs to know more

about collaboration, teamwork, and sharing, because they do not have a single leader-owner who has the last word. Even if someone is designated the family leader, that person will have to struggle to retain legitimacy in the eyes of other family owners and to maintain their trust.

Determining the next generation's family leadership is more than a simple task of choosing the next leader or leaders of the family enterprise. The issues of leadership involve a complex set of interwoven tasks and choices, and fully addressing them demands that everyone in the next generation be involved. Each individual wants to develop his or her own skills, and the successful enterprising family will have many types of leadership roles that need to be filled. Maintaining robust family leadership across generations presents an especially complicated and difficult set of issues in a wealthy family with an enterprise containing multiple businesses and endeavors, all of which need talent and capability of the highest sort to become—and to remain—successful.

The family's inability to transcend family roles may limit its talent pool. When this is the case, strong, smart, and eager potential leaders may actually exist in the family, but the current leaders, confusing family roles with governance roles, aren't able to recognize the talent and abilities of these individuals. They are viewing the next generation through the lens of the family and do not see that youngsters have matured into capable and disciplined young adults. Family members must move past their own family biases before they can make both a realistic appraisal of what the enterprise and the family need and a realistic assessment of the talent available within the family itself. They must understand that within the family an individual who is able to both steward the enterprise and be an effective and fair family leader may already exist. But the family must be certain that the leader has both the commitment (the will) and the capability (the skill) to take on that role.

Leadership is certainly a popular topic in today's business world, but the discussions often focus on the qualities that are needed by a single leader and the leader's ability to motivate and inspire others to achieve more than they thought possible, to stretch beyond both their defined jobs and their self-imposed limitations. Family enterprises need multiple kinds of leadership to stay competitive and to grow. But rather than thinking of leadership as belonging to one person in the family enterprise, in which some current and future owners work in the business and some don't, it is useful to consider that multiple potential leaders may exist, each suited to a different role; for example, various family members may lead various businesses and endeavors in the enterprise. One may lead the stewardship of the family legacy and interests; another may head up the family's philanthropic efforts; another may manage the business; and yet another guide the family. If the family decides to organize itself in this way, the leaders must be able to work together as a team, whose interests and activities are aligned with the family vision.

Varied human and intellectual capital exists in every multigenerational family. The task is to uncover it, nourish it, and help it develop in line with individual interests and those of the family as a whole. Therefore, leadership, family dynamics, the current and future vision of the family and the business, and governance are intertwined. This section looks at pathways and actions a family can take to grow, nurture, and develop its crop of leaders so that they possess the finely honed skills required by the endeavor they will be shepherding, are aware of the sensitivity needed to harmonize the family's vision and values with the need of the venture, and each is highly motivated and energized to take his or her place as a leader, occupying a unique slot in the family enterprise and together filling all roles crucial to its continued success. The selections describe family leadership development and next-generation teamwork as part of a long-term process that is deeply connected to the family vision for sustainability and the needs of all the family stakeholders.

6.1

Knowledge Should Come
Before Power in Succession

How can a family pass on the knowledge and skill of the elder generation to their heirs? Passing control doesn't always include passing the knowledge and capability to run the business effectively. This selection outlines some of the ways families can pass on to the next generation what my colleagues and I call intellectual capital.

It seems like a long time ago, in the year 2000, when George Bush and Al Gore were pitted against each other in a U.S. presidential election. The media made much of the fact that they were both "fortunate sons" and grandsons of prominent political figures, the implication being that each had an unfair advantage in getting to where he was. But in every field, we find successful next-generation successors. This has been so since ancient times.

There are many families in which a parent moves a child or children ahead into public service with little preparation or effort, but this initial advantage makes all the difference. Many successful scions report that their parents did no more than open the door by helping them meet well-positioned people and encouraging them to spread their wings, and with this head start they are able to use their own skills to advance, though they sometimes return to their parents for coaching and advice. What really accounts for their success? Is it good genes, hard work, or unfair opportunity?

There have been accounts of growing up in the Gore family. Young Al was part of conversations with many of the leading political figures of the time, so political dealings were part of his everyday life. He had the opportunity to go to the best schools, and by all accounts, he worked hard to learn. He had a deep and impactful mentoring relationship not just with his father, but also with his grandfather. While the family had wealth and power, it appears that his most valuable inheritances were the learning opportunities his family afforded him and the time he spent with the elders. The family encouraged his personal development by offering young Al access to the knowledge and skills possessed by past generations.

To determine how valuable, and also maybe how rare, such active engagement can be, consider another style of family upbringing that might have occurred. Young Al could have been treated as a possession by his parents, trotted out for guests, but kept entertained and isolated in a gilded cage. Parental expectations of achievement and education could have been minimal. His parents, busy as they were, could have ignored or neglected him. They might have decided that children should not be exposed to the reality of their lives and passions. By doing this, the family would have deprived their son of an important part of his inheritance even as they gave him what they thought were "all the good things in life."

When a scion enters and works in the family business, any of these scenarios can apply: The heir can be mentored by parents and other wise nonfamily executives or left on his or her own. The heir can be challenged to learn from experience by being taken into places where important things get done or can be in a position where he or she works hard but not in meaningful or important positions. The heir can be assigned provocative and demanding roles and asked to produce results, or take home a healthy paycheck without working much. He or she may be pushed to learn and grow outside the family business or simply be introduced to a world of social prominence with other wealthy peers.

A parent who has created a successful business looks at his or her sons and daughters as a potential pool from which to locate one or more successors to lead the business and the family. But the parent should begin the grooming process early, many years before their children enter the business. Before they inherit the power and wealth of the family, heirs should have access to the accumulated wisdom of their elders. This knowledge is stored not just in their experience, but in the network of people they know, the shared trust they have developed, and their understanding of how things really get done.

Providing this wisdom to their heirs presents a challenge unlike any the elders have ever faced. First of all, they may not be aware of what they know. Much knowledge is what is known as tacit, visceral understanding, which its owners aren't really aware they have. It may be almost instinctive, so it is hard to put into words or describe to others. Because of this, a father-leader may opt for having his heir unquestioningly follow him around the business ignoring a critical element of mentoring, that of passing his knowledge on in words, partly by, say, explaining the business, his decisions, actions, and the like to the young scion. This has a dangerous downside: The young person can follow his or her father around for years and still not really grasp what he does or how he does it. Learning theorists have struggled to define the decision rules—known as heuristics—that make up creative behavior.

Tacit knowledge isn't acquired through imitation or observation. It seems to come from two mechanisms: placing an individual in challenging situations designed to unlock appropriate skills, and assigning him or her a mentor who will quiz her and exchange ideas with her. A young heir can be asked to try to work on a business alliance when he is not quite ready for this responsibility with the understanding that it will provide a chance for him to learn from his own mistakes, before he is put in a situation in which such mistakes could cause irreversible damage to the business and possibly exacerbate existing tensions in the family. When the heir makes mistakes or acts intuitively, he gets time with Dad or Mom. During these valuable face-to-faces, Dad or Mom can challenge his decisions—helping him see their weaknesses—in a straightforward and direct way that is not presented as criticism, but rather as encouragement, helping him refine his thinking and develop his skills. Dad or Mom may also ask leading questions or in other ways help her make a more appropriate choice and determine a more effective course of action. A noted business patriarch has a standing rule that he can always be interrupted to talk with one of his sons. This type of mentoring can raise questions and suggest resources, people to meet, and paths to take, helping the young person learn progressively and move forward when he or she is ready to advance to the next step.

Before succession occurs in a family business, there is a period—usually of more than a decade, and often as many as two or three—during which the two generations work side by side (as I discussed in the four stages introduced in the table in the selection "Succession Begins on the First Day of Work," in Part IV) in a growing partnership characterized not by a sudden transfer of power and control, but by a gradual shifting from one generation to the other before the succession procedure is finalized the family's knowledge and wisdom, the young person needs a variety of experiences within and outside the family business. As a sort of crown prince, the young person should spend time meeting with and perhaps working for related businesses. He or she might start at a similar business on another continent, where the family name is not known. After a period of time, when the young person is no longer a callow beginner but rather a capable young adult who possesses some professional skills, he or she might take a position in a key part of the family business and also spend time rotating through jobs or in a position that allows him or her to move through many parts of the business. The next stage of development might be working through a key challenge—opening a plant in Asia, perhaps, or purchasing a business, or dealing with a troubled division or area.

While the potential leaders are progressing on this developmental journey, the older generation should initiate a regular family forum for mentoring and discussion. For parents and children, this relationship that grows from this is the essence of the knowledge-transfer process. At this point, a young person and a parent advance beyond a parent–child relationship to become peers who respect and learn from each other. This takes a lot of work, and it not easy; some parent–child pairs never achieve it. But we also see examples of fathers and sons like the Robertses of Comcast, who—as we saw in Part I—worked together for many years, culminating in a quiet transfer of power that was accomplished easily and seamlessly.

Some families do this with one-on-one meetings, such as a weekly breakfast at which the two generations share what they are learning and doing in an informal seminar. Knowledge and skills are passed directly between generations. Trust develops. And the younger generation gains the elder's permission—implicit or explicit—to take a risk or move the business in a new direction.

Often, the younger person has been exposed in school and working outside the business to new ideas that can take the business into new realms. In a recent family-business forum at which four multigenerational businesses were inducted into their region's Family Business Hall of Fame, the third- and fourth-generation heirs talked about receiving the trust of their elders after they had earned their stripes. Each of these generations faced the challenge of having to reinvent some aspect of the business. As one son noted, this could not be done the first day of work, but only after they had shown that they were competent and that the innovation or change they were proposing was grounded in reality.

If a family is large, it may have more than a handful of family members in the second or third generation. In one family business that was started by five brothers of Chinese origin, who still run it with one brother being the CEO, nearly ten members of the second generation in their 20s are starting work in the company in various roles. The brother who is the business leader holds a weekly lunch-seminar for the group, during which they all talk about what they are doing. He may invite guests who are advisers or resources to discuss a key business decision. But the seminar isn't about operations; it's about learning. The founding brothers and the succeeding generation are aware that they have many years before new leadership is chosen, and the second-generation members feel comfortable getting to know each other and learning together. Over the years, the family expects to transfer the wisdom of the first generation to the next while continuing to help them develop their own entrepreneurial styles, honing their imaginations and deepening their skills as they begin to take the business in new directions. Members of the group are encouraged to bring new ideas to the family, where they can be explored and sometimes acted on.

The transfer of knowledge is not confined to the family members working in the business. There also must be a transfer of knowledge to family members who are shareholders. Many families fall apart because the family shareholders do not understand the complexity of their holdings, why decisions are made, or how they are expected to act as responsible owners. As we have seen, some families have annual meetings that include seminars or learning sessions about the family business. Several families with large businesses have annual visits during which key executives present news of the enterprise to the group of family shareholders, who are given an opportunity to talk about and learn from the company. Other families hold seminars about personal finance, spending, and investing, to help family members treat their inheritance responsibly. They also may have presentations about the family history and legacy, where elders talk about where they came from, thus passing on the shared knowledge of the past. All these activities develop the intellectual and human capital of the next generation of the family.

A family business or shared family assets offer the next generation tangible wealth, but that is only part of what members of the next generation stand to inherit. They also can benefit from inheriting some of the special knowledge and skill that the older generation has obtained through their success. This may include their being given chances to meet important and learned people and to gain access to special learning experiences that may end up being worth more than a financial inheritance.

6.2

Nurturing Talent Across Generations

Families who are successful over many generations often create very explicit and formal means to develop the skills and capabilities of the next generation. They adopt a set of rules and expectations for personal development. When a young family member chooses to work in one of the family ventures, the family has a clear process for overseeing his or her development. This selection presents some practices that a multigenerational enterprising family can use to help prepare young family members to be successful in the business.

This selection was written with Fran Lotery of Relative Solutions.

George is fifth generation and Sam, fourth, and although their family-owned companies are in different industries and at different stages of generational leadership, the two men have much in common. Both follow successful generations who grew the family business to exceed U.S. $100 million in revenue. Both enterprises are owned by two or three family branches, and at least five family members work in each business. George and Sam each feel ready to make his own mark in his family business. However, neither receives much, if any, feedback regarding how well he is doing, what he needs to learn, or what he ought to be doing to become an effective executive in today's economic climate, nor is either given information regarding the role he may play in the future leadership or management of the enterprise or encouragement, support, or suggestions for how he might add value.

Working with succession and leadership within a family enterprise, we find that frequently the current-generation leaders do not know how to set up a concrete plan for preparing the next generation of leaders. Combine this with the discomfort the next-generation working family members have about taking charge of their own careers—they do not feel free to make decisions for themselves because they have an overwhelming sense of obligation to do what the family expects—and a succession paralysis can set in.

Typically, a family career path includes the potential successor's rotating through the departments of the company to get to know the company, attending trade shows and professional organizations to learn the industry, and attending senior-management meetings. This "path" seems based on the belief that listening at the heels of the current leader is all the preparation the potential successor from the next generation needs. After this, so this way of thinking goes, he or she is ready to be anointed the next leader. It is unlikely that an individual who has been readied in this way will have had a mentor and even less likely that he or she will have been held accountable to a supervisor. Feedback seems almost nonexistent in this type of "development" and in fact appears to be the most difficult thing to give working family members.

George and Sam both face these impediments to their success. George joined the family business right after college. He grew up working summers in the business and appears to have worked his way up in the company. He now has the title director of marketing projects, but does not have any supervisory responsibilities. He is at a loss to define the kinds of experiences he will need as a future leader. And yet the time is nearing when he will have to take responsibility for guiding the business, as the current leadership is planning to step down within the next ten years. If George had gone to work in a company not owned by his family, he would have had to take an interest in his own career movement, because if he hadn't, no one else would have. He would also have learned to connect advancement with responsibility, performance, and salary.

In family enterprises, this developmental phase is often vague, and rather than figuring out for himself these very important aspects of work and making decisions on his own about how to advance his career, a family member like George is handheld through his "preparatory" stage—much like a child still under the guidance of parents, rather than a young adult seizing his independence and learning to become the captain of his own life and career. In the absence of a clearly defined developmental process for potential future leaders in a family enterprise, too much is left for others to decide, and the heir simply tags along without much thought to what he is doing or where is going or why.

One way to address this deficiency in family enterprises is to use a "360-degree" process of evaluation, which objectively and anonymously assesses an individual's weaknesses and strengths. First, key people who work with that person evaluate the individual anonymously by answering a number of questions about the person's performance, his or her ability to be a successful a team player or leader, and other aspects of the individual's workplace behavior. The results of these assessments are then compared with how the person views him- or herself. A variety of models are available, including those developed by the Center for Creative Leadership, Human Synergistics, and the Leadership Effectiveness Analysis (LEA). The Family Enterprise Leadership System (FELS), from Relative Solutions, which evaluates leadership capabilities in the next generation of family leaders, provides a snapshot of what stakeholders see as important and can be the foundation for creating an individualized development plan to help each person being evaluated take charge of his or her career.

George and Sam committed to a leadership development program that began with a Family Enterprise Leadership Assessment (FELS). The FELS and other tools, such as personality inventories, that identify thinking and behavioral styles are important in developing a baseline and a foundation for a leadership development plan. These objective assessments are beginning steps in shifting the mind-sets of future family leaders from observers of their careers to active owners of them. Along with this, the current owner's mind-set needs to shift from that of observer to mentor. By receiving objective and anonymous feedback from working family members, nonworking family owners, peers, senior leaders, and other next-generation candidates, George and Sam can increase their self-awareness and understand the impact their behavior has on others and on the organization.

The operative word is *impact*. Without feedback, George and Sam do not have the benefit of real learning and will ultimately not be able to add maximum value to the enterprise. George has been passive about his career, assuming that his uncles and father will let him know when he is ready to take on more leadership. Consequently, he is bored, aimless, and stagnant. He does his job, but it is clear from the feedback that although his raters see potential, his current performance is only average. Certainly, this is not the kind of evaluation a future leader would want to receive from shareholders, peers, working family members, and senior management.

Sam worked in an outside company for five years before being enticed to join the family business. Family-business leaders had the opportunity to observe Sam and the ways he handled each new challenge in his job. They knew he was adding value to the company he worked for because he was promoted and received salary increases and bonuses. When he decided to join the family business, the discussions centered on how the skills and experience he was bringing would add value to this company. Within a year, he was promoted to a vice president position. It was obvious to everyone that Sam helped close a very important deal and addressed significant tensions between the marketing and engineering departments. Still, he has been chided about how he treats other working family members in meetings, especially his cousin, whom he is used to teasing as this is a pattern that developed when they were young and has continued throughout their lives. Given that he has been told about this many times and has not changed his behavior, it is clear he does not understand the impact this familial one-upmanship has on stakeholders' confidence in his ability to be an effective leader. He remains unaware that others are uncomfortable witnessing the way he behaves toward his cousin, which they interpret as belittling and disrespectful. This diminishes his achievements in their eyes and undermines the confidence they would otherwise have in his leadership ability.

Without a process in place to give Sam regular feedback on how his actions are affecting others, the situation is likely to remain unchanged. Because there are no consequences to his behavior, and he continues to be promoted, he interprets the complaint as insignificant and petty rather than as an indicator of the degree to which others trust his judgment. When the results of the 360 were discussed with Sam, he grasped the feedback in a new way because it was not just an offhanded comment but part of a serious overall assessment from multiple stakeholders in the organization.

Both these young men—George, who is developmentally stuck in the mind-set of a child who knows he has his parents to guide him, and Sam, who is clueless as to how his behavior toward his cousin affects the way those in the workplace perceive him—need solid ongoing feedback and mentoring to develop as leaders. The feedback will be most useful if it is obtained from horizontal and vertical relationships with nonworking and working family, superiors and direct reports, peers, and key outside vendors and advisers.

Sam is a bit ahead of George in terms of knowing more about managing upward, taking a proactive position when it comes to his career path, and managing others, but both suffer from a lack of feedback about a) what they do that adds value, b) what detracts from their ability to lead, and c) what they need to do to align how they see their contributions with how others view them. Both would profit from a greater understanding of what it will take to build confidence and trust and to inspire others to follow them as leaders. Expectations and accountability are sometimes defined only for nonfamily employees because the leaders think that somehow knowledge and experience of the business will simply pass from one generation to another in the working family member's DNA. Getting real objective feedback from stakeholders helps the developing leader establish a baseline from which to grow.

Creating a development plan that is a combination of education, on-the-job projects or responsibilities that provide stretch experiences, and a group of key people who can serve as advisers and mentors to guide the developing leader and provide constructive feedback about performance will ensure that a next-generation leader is prepared when the family and organization are ready for the transition. Critical to helping the successor grow into the role of a family-business leader is encouraging him or her to take charge of her own leadership-development program. Developing this take-charge behavior, next-generation leaders such as George and Sam have the unique opportunity to break the barrier of discomfort associated with the feedback that so often exists in the family business. They can begin to engage the current senior leaders in an ongoing constructive program of building on strengths and mitigating problems or ineffective behaviors that get in the way of building credibility, confidence, and trust. Whether George or Sam join a university-based next-generation-leader program or become part of a program within their respective organizations, the key is that the program be geared to the individual and based on what George and Sam each need to learn to be effective and competent leaders within their family enterprises.

6.3

Leadership and Career Development
for the Next Generation

This selection outlines the extensive leadership development program adopted by one very successful family and details how each element contributes to the continued high quality of the family's many enterprises and the ability of each family member to succeed in life.

When a family is able to reach the fifth generation with a portfolio of thriving enterprises, strong and inspired leadership, and many family members preparing to take places in the business, something very special is happening. The Aboitiz family, headquartered in the Philippines, has been able to transmit a strong set of business and family values to each of its 800 family shareholders who live in many places around the world. The family's holding company and public companies in power, transport, food, banking, and real estate, with 22,000 employees, are all highly profitable.

Each generation, the family appoints a leader whose task is to bring each business to the next stage of development and help the family develop strong family leaders to participate in the businesses in many roles. The Aboitizes' practices can help other enterprising families understand what a family needs to do to keep its business strong over generations and to avoid the tendency to succumb to family pressures or conflicts that undermine the pursuit of business excellence. Their procedures and policies are clear and specifically designed to support and encourage family members to be part of the business while making it clear that decisions are made for the business, not the family. Explicit family values, practices, and governance mechanisms enable the family to manage the tricky path of keeping the family deeply involved in the enterprise while sustaining a strong, vibrant, and growing set of businesses.

A family faces some special challenges as it moves through generations. One of the most difficult is finding leaders who are able to maintain the unity of the family and take the business into new directions to continue developing the family's wealth. The Aboitiz family came to the Philippines from northern Spain. Don Ramon, assisted by his three brothers, helped develop his father's successful trading business. When the enterprise came close to bankruptcy, he returned from retirement in Spain to rebuild the businesses and pay off all the debts, leaving a legacy of trust and integrity that still inspire his heirs, generations later, and are at the center of the Aboitiz family values and notion of what it means to be a leader.

The next generation graduated from college in the 1950s and continued to develop the business by adding professional management. Don Ramon's son Eduardo took over as CEO and was a consolidator and corporate builder; he built the businesses into modern corporations by creating training programs, accounting systems, and clearly defined organizational structures while placing a strong emphasis on such values as ethics, meritocracy, fair play, and good business, thus translating Don Ramon's legacy and example into modern business practices. The company tries to base decisions—both operational and personnel—on data as much as possible. Family members are encouraged to enter the business and work in it—and many do—but everyone in the family understands that decisions are made for the business first, not the family.

Following his own policy, Eduardo retired at age 60 and passed leadership to his cousin Luis Jr., who was then in his 40s. At age 60, Luis passed the baton (though he remains on the board) to his cousin Jon Ramon, Eduardo's son, who will soon reach 60, at which time there will be another transition. With each succession, the family entered into more businesses and continued to grow each of them in terms of quality, cost-effectiveness, and responsible business practices. Today many of their businesses are global leaders in cost-efficiency, quality, and profitability.

Governance, oversight, and family participation take place through the active, highly professional work of the board of directors of the private company, which owns 50 percent of the public company and has annual meetings for shareholders just as a public company does. The board for the private holding company consists of seven family members; the public company board also includes two independent directors as well as family members.

I met Roberto, Jon Ramon's brother, who is chair of the family's public company and senior vice president of some units of the private company, at a family-business conference in Manila, where he explained how his family, over several generations, has nurtured and developed the talent, capability, and motivation of many family members. The family remains unified because of its members' strong sense of stewardship, "the belief that together we can achieve far more than we can individually." The company has a deep respect for talent, and within the family, there is a deep respect for the guiding principle of the primacy of making the best decision for the business, not for the individual or the family. Each value—transparency, openness, respect, customer focus, and social responsibility—is deeply held by each family member. Roberto remembers when some family members tested these values, and the family leadership had to challenge them. Some family strife has occurred, and family members have been asked to leave the business or take a leave of absence until they are serious about adhering to the family values and goals, including "business first."

The family understands that each of its members doesn't have to have every talent; with several hundred possible recruits, the family has a wide net with which to capture and develop talent. There is a clear path for a family member to enter the family business—a path that is attractive but also demanding. Once they are 14, young family members are invited to enter a summer program, where they can volunteer to move around the company for a few weeks seeing how various parts of the business operate. The family will create special programs so any family member, many of whom live abroad, can come and learn.

Roberto also speaks to each participant in the summer program, asking about his or her plans and reminding each individual of the demands working for the family entail. "After university, we don't hire them straight away, but we try to help them be placed with our contacts, to find jobs abroad," he said. His two sons work abroad for large banks. "They learn that there is a real world out there, and we find there is real value in building up their self-esteem and self-worth outside of the family umbrella."

Some family members return and announce they are ready to work for the family. "We submit them to personality and aptitude tests to see what is the best place for them given what we need. After they are placed, we evaluate them regularly as they begin working for a nonfamily manager. It is not easy, but it builds up determination to really want to perform. We have lost some along the way, and some have been asked to leave, causing family friction. But family members have to be the best, or others will not be motivated."

This is as it should be, and as it would be if they were not members of the family. But they are, and the family really values and encourages those who are able to shine under this microscope. "At the age of 35 or 40, if they want to enter the executive leadership ranks, a family member faces another challenge. In order to become senior executives within the company—now that they have proved themselves in operational management—they must develop their people skills and take a visible, accountable leadership role in the community. They are at the stage of leadership where we want to breed in corporate social responsibility, which is a major part of our business model and our values as a company," Roberto explained.

Each young family leader is involved in the community and society. The family funds several foundations and is part of a nationwide NGO, Business for Social Progress, which is composed of businesses that contribute 1 percent of their earnings to a fund that initiates social ventures in the Philippines. The family believes that a mature project that works for the good of the society outside the company is an important part of the family's social responsibility.

In addition to the unique career-development process available to each family member, the family also has several activities that help the hundreds of family members spread around the globe remain unified and connected with each other. Roberto chairs the family council, which is open to family shareholders who want to be involved. The council holds family reunions every three years. At the last reunion, more than 400 family members came from all over the world for two days of learning and fun.

The council has seven or eight members, who come and go, and is currently reaching out to the fifth generation. They try to pick future family leaders who are good communicators and who represent various family constituencies. "The council works as a communication tool, communicating what the business is doing to the nonbusiness parts of the family. In the past it was only men—the women were silent—but that has changed radically. Now we inform stockholders about how we work, what we are doing, and how we get paid. The idea is to avoid a festering problem and to deal with problems as they arise," said Roberto. The council has created a family constitution and acts as the focal point for family activities. In addition, it is responsible for maintaining the legacy of four generations of family enterprise.

From this example, we can distill several best practices that guide the rare family business as it moves from large to huge, over several generations. It develops an attitude that decisions are made for the business first. It creates and maintains mechanisms to sustain family unity and focus. It stands for clear personal and business values that inspire family members to be proud of their heritage and willing to put in the work to excel. And it establishes and adheres to clear and explicit governance policies and practices to nurture, develop, and bring into governance and leadership members of the next generations as capable new family leaders.

6.4

Creating Effective Management Teams

A family-management team is made more complex because the family members who must work together have a prior family relationship, which may be based on conflict, age, and gender rather than skills and roles. If the members of a family are going to be able to work together effectively, they will need to work hard to overcome bad habits stemming from their family history and the emotional patterns of the past. This selection presents some of the ways that a family can become a team that works together to make the business succeed.

In the Darwinian world of struggling economies, companies respond to pressure by looking to strong new leaders for salvation. Although the results of cleaning house are less than stellar, it seems almost quaint when a family business bucks the trends by supporting its leaders in ways that will encourage them to perform successfully over time and rather than having one fearless, undisputed leader, installs a team of family members at the top.

Many business sages proclaim that there's room for only one person at the top. Yet many family businesses have experimented with various forms of team leadership, sometimes with impressive results. A company that has thrived under novel leadership, J. M. Smucker, a publicly traded food-products business, reached the century mark under the leadership of fourth-generation co-CEOs and brothers Tim and Richard Smucker.

The Nordstrom family, owners of successful customer-focused shoe and clothing stores, has had two generations in which leadership was held by a team of family members: first, a team of three, second of four; it is now moving into its third generation of shared family leadership. The Nordstroms have also had great help from key nonfamily executives over the generations. As in many other family companies, the company's values and culture were set by the founders, and the next generations are raised and groomed for their roles by attentive and dedicated elders. A board with several prominent outside members, including a UCLA professor and a former U.S. secretary of labor, has been available to mentor the new generation, oversee the teams, and make sure the succession runs smoothly, amid the ups and now downs of the business world.

To be sure, there are disasters—one family heir fights with other family members for control; members of a family team have a falling out—but as family firms look to their younger generations and see many different talents, capabilities, and interests among their heirs, the attraction of forging a family team to lead the company is clear.

Not every family can create an effective team of siblings to share leadership of the enterprise. But when they can, the enterprise is enriched not only by the various skills and capabilities of the different individuals but also by the strengths of the individuals working cooperatively with a long-term, value-based perspective. But creating an effective, imaginative, and successful team is not done simply by delegation or election. The groundwork must be established many years before succession is to occur and the process of succession takes place over the intervening years.

Principles of Effective Family-Management Teams

After working with many successful and unsuccessful family teams, I have come up with nine principles that underlie effective family-management teams.

Trust is built by long-term fairness, dependability, accountability, and competence.
Trust is the currency that holds a family team together. Although this is true of every team, the presence of a family dimension, including deep family rivalries and emotions, complicates working relationships. To work as a business team, family members have to trust each other deeply and implicitly. This can't be legislated. Trust builds as family members learn they can depend on each other to come through, to be accountable, and to conduct their work with professional competence. Good intentions do not build trust; in fact, as trust begins to erode in a family team, each individual brings up his or her good intentions, which unfortunately are not supported by his or her behavior. It takes a long time to build trust, but one misstep can destroy it.

The older generation must mentor the new leaders extensively and actively.
Most effective sibling teams begin as intergenerational partnerships. The founder-leader must become a mentor-coach to his or her heirs. The elder generation helps bring each heir along, with power and control clearly shifting over time from one generation to the next. The natural rivalry that often exists in strong, competitive enterprising families must be tempered

241

by respect and cooperation.

I recently worked with a family team that had several fractious brothers, sisters, and in-laws. At the sudden untimely death of their patriarch, they floundered. While many of them worked in the various family businesses, each of them worked individually with their very controlling and secretive father. They had no history of working collaboratively or of considering themselves a team.

In contrast to this is the Mellon family (whom we encountered in "From Founder to Successor: Lessons from Nineteenth-Century Wealth Creators," the first selection in the book), whose founder, Judge Thomas Mellon, was an exemplary family leader. His leadership resulted in the family's second generation's becoming perhaps the wealthiest U.S. family in the early twentieth century. Judge Thomas, an Irish immigrant from the potato famine, was a creative and conservative businessman, but he considered preparing his sons to take the reins of the family enterprise his primary mission. As we saw in Part I, he took time with each one, seasoning them very early with responsible assignments, taking them into partnerships, and helping them learn from their mistakes. When son Richard wanted to join his brother Andrew, who worked with his father in their growing bank, he was immediately offered a full partnership. His personality was radically different from his brother's, but their partnership lasted the rest of their lives, and their varying talents and success in their divergent roles greatly enriched the family. The importance they gave to family partnership, trust, and collaboration, as well as mentoring, came from their father. He worked with them for many years, increasing their responsibility and authority. When they were ready to take the reins, and the time was right, he was willing to let go.

A family team member must carry his or her weight.

Too often a family will name a sibling to a management position without consideration of her ability to do the job simply because they feel it is her right as a family member. Seems fair, doesn't it? But, in fact, this places pressure on more-competent and -committed family members, who think that they have to carry their weaker family member. This can be unsettling for nonfamily executives and other shareholders. Too often, the family managers will do their best to deny or avoid the issue.

Family teams also break up when one member thinks another is not doing his or her share of the work. For example, the DuPont family had a strong troika of family members in the early years of the twentieth century. Then, as two of the partners began to spend more time away following pursuits such as politics and personal relationships, and the third member thought he was taking all the responsibility, the team broke down. One cousin forced a buy-out on the others, alienating him from them for many years.

Family teams must be anchored by a clear, definitive family shareholder agreement.
Families have a strong tendency to keep things informal. They believe their trust and love means they do not need formal agreements. This has a devastating effect when there are disagreements, which are inevitable. If there is a family-management team, the individuals on the team have overlapping roles as owners, managers, and family members. The family team must create a **family shareholder agreement**, which details the values and operating principles of the team. It should include information regarding the team's responsibility to the rest of the family, term of office, decision making, and accountability. For example, the third generation of the Rockefeller family, heirs of JDR Jr., consisted of five young men, each of whom evolved a role and responsibility for working with the family's diverse investments and philanthropic activities. When they were in their 20s, as they began their careers, together they crafted a thoughtful value-and-cooperation agreement, which specified that the welfare of the whole family was to be more important than any of their individual careers.

Communication must be continual and extensive.
Ensuring fairness and accountability in any team is tricky business. If siblings are a team, but each is also the sole manager of one or more diverse business areas, each has a great deal of autonomy to make decisions in his or her role as manager. However as partners in a team, each has a responsibility to inform the others about issues that may require decisions. This can short circuit potential misunderstandings and even lead to better decisions. Effective family teams tend to talk daily and give each other more information than they need. In families who have complex business interests, including multiple partnerships, the appearance of conflict of interest is often challenged. We have seen lawsuits for self-dealing that could have been avoided if the family team had talked before an individual took action or made a deal.

Teamwork does not mean equality.
Members of a family team of co-CEOs or a troika occupying the office of the president are not necessarily absolutely equal. The sharing of titles and leadership in effective teams is a mark of public family support and respect. In private, families often agree that one family member in the team will be the first among equals or that the family member who occupies the highest leadership position may in fact not have the strongest say in decisions. For example, in the Bronfman family, brothers Charles and

Edgar Sr., who were rivals when young adults but dealt with their contention early and effectively, agreed that Edgar would be the public leader, but that major decisions would be shared by the brothers, one in Canada and one in the United States. Every team has a natural hierarchy and division of labor.

The team must have its performance assessed by independent, outside board members who are tough and credible.

Teams and managers fail because of their blind spots. They may think things are going swimmingly and then find a deep fault in their business model or its execution. Family-business heirs tend to develop a sense of entitlement and are usually not given tough feedback on their performance. But running a business is not a family hobby. An effective sibling or family team must have an independent board or advisory group consisting of mature leaders who are able to tell the truth to emerging family leaders and be tough with them. The board members or advisory group also must be available and able to develop a trusting relationship with the family leaders. Sometimes, a new family leader has his or her performance assessed and is mentored by a key and trusted elder nonfamily executive. Either way, family members must have a way to get accurate information and a place to discuss it openly; they need an authoritative source who will tell them the truth, no matter how hard that is, and to whom they will listen, no matter how difficult it is for them to hear his or her suggestions or appraisals of their work.

The team must exhibit deep respect for the needs of other family owners and nonfamily leaders.

When there is a strong sibling team running a family business, two groups are often suspicious and feel left out—the nonmanaging family owners and the key nonfamily executives. The sibling team must be open to each of these stakeholder groups, sharing information, fairly allocating the profits, and listening to their concerns and ideas. If a sibling team is closed—and seen as working for itself—these other constituencies may challenge it. The family members can demand that they be bought out, that there be a change in leadership, or even that the company be dissolved. The key managers can vote with their feet, defecting to competitors if they think they are not being fairly rewarded or given real responsibility. Many effective sibling teams have strong outside managers on the business's **management-leadership team**. They often issue phantom stock or incentive compensation to reward and respect their contributions.

Nothing is forever; agreements must be flexible so the next generation may modify.
Retirement and letting go are difficult topics in a family team. A good team will likely want to stay longer than they need to or than is good for the company. A new generation is ready to take over long before the old generation is ready to step down. Many promising businesses have been eroded because the older generation would not move on. Effective teams have a clear sense of time, and provisions have been established for bringing in the new generation of leadership. Judge Mellon gave up his business interests to his sons when they were ready. He became restless. But instead of trying to get back in, or even act as a sideline adviser, he moved at age 75 from Pittsburgh to Kansas City and started a new business.

Family executive teams, or family-management teams, can be an effective way for families to manifest their values and to sustain a powerful company that both builds wealth and embodies societal values. But creating and maintaining a balanced and well-functioning team demands continual monitoring and attention.

Keys to Success:
Building Effective Family Teams

- Hold meetings to talk about all issues at least weekly
- Craft a family shareholder agreement, detailing the core values, operating principles, and rules governing the family team
- Define roles, responsibilities, and expectations of each team member clearly
- Have an outside group review the team's progress and assess the accountability and capability of each team member

6.5

How Brothers and Sisters Can Build a Second-Generation Family Team

This selection continues the discussion about how siblings, under the tutelage of the founding generation, can learn to shift their focus from the mentor to each other, building trust, accountability, and respect while learning to work together. It stresses the importance of open communication between the generations and among the members of each generation. Because renewing commitment to each other and to the business is essential to every generation's success, I suggest that enterprising families create a statement articulating the value of family unity and the other values that hold the family together. Each generation can renew its commitment to the family by reviewing the statement and adjusting it according to their ideas and ideals. In addition, this selection presents an example from one of the country's most powerful enterprising families.

I recently saw two families in which the members of the second generation were having a tough time working together.

The first family was reeling from the sudden death of their father. His five children—ages 20 to 42—each had roles in the family business and a very close relationship to Dad, who was at the center of everything. In the year that he had been gone, they had begun to bicker and resent each other, and the family's business suffered. It was becoming apparent that while each of his children had had a deep and positive relationship with Dad, they didn't have one with each other. They had all worked with Dad as individuals, and now that he was gone, they were finding that they didn't really know each other. And they certainly did not know how to work together.

Dad was very much still present in the second family, presiding over the business at 86, with no plans to step aside. While his three sons and a daughter expected to inherit ownership, they were aware of strains between the two who worked in the business and the two who didn't. They wanted to begin to think ahead about where the business was going, but every time they asked Dad about getting a consultant, he turned them down. They felt they couldn't move ahead.

These two families were experiencing a nearly universal reality of second-generation business families: The power and the focus of attention always point up. It doesn't matter if the father is benevolent or despotic, the members of the second generation do not see each other as partners, but rather as rivals for his attention. They look to the father not only as the person who will choose the business heir, but also as the source of love, personal validation, and of course, money. Their belief that their generation will have a winner—the one chosen to be the successor—and several losers—those who are not picked—tends to separate the members of this generation from each other.

Many families, as we have seen, who have a legacy of paternalism and dependency have created legal structures that hold adult offspring, who are quite mature and capable, in relationships in which they are treated as if they still are children. Some countries like the United States have trust laws that many such families take advantage of to keep ownership and control over assets in the hands of trustees, who make decisions for the beneficiaries. A trust created to keep a business unified or to avoid taxes is a vehicle by which the parents exert control over their heirs.

The emotional dynamics of families may largely account for the parents' insisting on treating their adult heirs as if they were still children. For instance, parents may vividly remember their children's irresponsible behavior, but later in life they don't have much opportunity to witness their offspring's mature adult behavior. So the parents conclude from the mistakes their offspring made as children that even as adults the heirs cannot act responsibly and need to be taken care of. The parents' own blind spots foster this impression. They find it hard to transfer real control to the next generation because they see them as eternal children. In turn, the kids become engaged in endless futile attempts to win their parents' approval.

The second generations in the two families above were discovering that leadership and control had to be very different in their generation if the business were to continue and succeed. But they were also finding that they weren't prepared to create a team that was capable of leading the family. In both families, all siblings would inherit ownership in roughly equal terms, making them business partners. They had to learn how to create a team to oversee the business and to continue their family.

The second family had to learn to question their father's resistance to their getting together. When they asked him what his concerns were, he replied, "The first thing you will decide together is that I am out," revealing his greatest fear. *Why do you need to get together? Wait until I am dead,* was the subtext to the father's response. The children assured him that they wanted to get together not to deal with the business today, but to consider how they would handle the business in the future. They were concerned that since they hadn't had much contact with each other, they wouldn't know how to be business partners.

As a generation, the heirs have to make major shifts of mind and behavior. The first is changing the mind-set, from that of children to that of adults and equals. They must move from operating as offspring of successful (and sometimes overwhelming) parents to working together as a group of equals each of whom has different roles, visions, and values in and for the family and the business, both in the present and going forward. Although as siblings they are a captive group of partners—that is, they did not choose each other—they have to learn to work together. And even though the temptation is to see the role of successor as a prize, if the business is to continue successfully into the second generation, the heirs must learn to see each other not as rivals, but as the members of a team. While the power and wishes of their parents are important, the heirs need to see themselves as having the power to make some shifts in their parents' legacy. They have to take responsibility for moving it forward themselves, without their parents. They have to grow up and become empowered. Their parents can't do this for them.

Every generation has to renew their commitment to each other and to the business. First, they need to decide if they want to remain together. Some siblings may be on different paths or simply may not be able to work with the others. The family has to provide a path and policy for a sibling to leave the family's unified business structure. Many family feuds brew because one member could not escape the others.

A new generation in a family can develop their unity and vision by creating a statement of who they are and what they want together. One famous example of this comes from the third generation of the Rockefeller family. A father and his only son and heir were followed by a powerful and fractious group of five brothers, all of whom wanted to be active in the family's affairs. As they grew up, they sensed the potential for conflict and disagreement as each brother pursued his own path. And so they got together and created a mission statement for them all as a unified family:

We, the undersigned, being brothers and having interests and objectives in common, have joined together in our desire to continue the tradition of public service and fearless leadership established by our grandfather and carried forward and extended by our parents. In uniting our efforts and coordinating our activities, we hope to be more effective in aiding in the preservation and development of the republic form of government and the private enterprise system which in our opinion have been fundamental factors in making the United States a powerful nation of free people...

In line with those convictions, we are prepared to subordinate personal or individual interests as and when necessary for the sake of accomplishing our broader objectives. We propose to use our individual abilities and those material resources that are at our disposal to further these objectives. By acting together with a common purpose, we will be in a stronger position not only to promote our common interests, but also to foster and effectuate our individual interests. We will be free to pursue independent and varied interests, at the same time taking full advantage of our diverse interests in the attainment of common objectives. Accordingly, we hereby form a partnership, the objective of which shall be to carry out the foregoing objectives.

While there were many strains in their partnership, this mission statement formed a framework for their cooperation for the next generation. Every second generation must find their own reason to remain together. Just being business owners isn't enough; they need a deeper purpose than one focused on the business. It must be crafted by the entire group together, not inherited from the parents or set by one family leader.

Another challenge for a second-generation team is to respect the leader of the family business—even if they were not involved in the choice of the leader—and to work with him or her. Although leading the business may be the most important task of the family, the family has other ventures—perhaps other assets, such as a family foundation—and shared activities that require leaders and stewards as well. Often the siblings resent the chosen business leader, and the business leader, given power by the parental generation, thinks that he or she does not have to pay attention to the other family members. Seeds of distrust are sown.

The second-generation leader must realize that family leadership involves collaboration and sharing of information and some power with other sibling owners. Dad's style of not sharing much information must give way to a desire to listen and a willingness to discuss and explore alternatives. The family leader should remember that his brothers and sisters are his business partners. The partners must craft a shared **Code of Conduct** about what they owe each other and what they want from the partnership.

A second-generation family business struggles with boundaries. The business may be growing, with more-professional management and more distance from the family. But since the family team has a controlling ownership in the business, they must see themselves as a team of stewards working together. The two families we saw at the beginning of this selection each learned how to work as a team to decide the direction and future of their family enterprises. They each respected the brother that was ultimately chosen to be the family CEO; but as a brother, the CEO got help from his siblings to learn to act very differently from the way their fathers acted. In neither family was the new CEO simply a solo entrepreneur or business leader, he was also a steward for a family, whose voice he listened to and respected.

6.6

Working for Yourself, Not Your Family

Too often when a young person pursues a career in the family business, the family automatically assumes that this is what the person wants. However, too many young people enter the family business for the wrong reasons. Later in life, they may regret the decision, thinking it was a mistake. This selection is a "letter" to a young person who is trying to decide whether to work for the family. It presents some of the considerations I suggest this potential heir take into account when exploring his or her career options.

To a Young Person Deciding Whether to Enter the Family Enterprise:

It is so easy to fall into the trap of working for your family's business. It is always there, available, and easy to start. And like a drug, it can lull you into danger and self-delusion. After a while, you can begin to feel empty, unexpressed, and less than alive, yet because of the perks and your own fear of life outside, you are afraid to leave. You begin to feel trapped. If you are considering working in the family business or find yourself working there, you need to be aware that what seems natural, easy, and available has consequences—and will affect your future.

If you begin working there too early in your career, you run the chance of never having the opportunity to grow up. You work for Mom and Dad, and get an allowance and other perks. You aren't really accountable for much, and others are always around to do your work. While this can be fun, and rewarding, I've seen many long-term casualties in businesses where family offspring started working and never left.

It is not bad or wrong to choose to work for your family. But it can be dangerous. It can be habit-forming, even addictive. Be aware of yourself while you work for your family. Consider what *you* want from your employment and examine your long-term expectations. What seems like a great option today can

250

be a prison, a source of frustration, or a good way to avoid the challenges and opportunities of the wider world.

If you do decide to enter your family business, do it with your eyes open. Take time to talk to your family, and clarify expectations, dreams, and possible futures. Watch your own personal and career development. This is a form of self-care.

Here are several ways you can respect and develop yourself while working for your family.

Learn before you earn.

School can be fun, but you should also take the opportunity to learn to do something. Consider the range of things that might be useful to your family to take its business in new directions or to just to be helpful. The world is changing fast, and whatever your family business is, it will need new ideas, new skills, and directions that you might learn when you are at school.

Do real things.

Get as far as you can from the executive suite, which is really a branch of your living room. Learn how the business works and take on some real responsibility. Run something.

Build a track record.

Face it. People won't be able to get past your name. You will have to work hard to get them to see *you*. Find something that you can put your stamp on, and do it well. And by the way, make it your own work; don't take credit for the work of others.

Get feedback.

The hardest thing to get from other people is the truth, especially about your work. If you cultivate people, especially the people who do the best work, and ask them to tell you how you are doing, off the record, you are at least likely to get unfiltered information that might be useful.

Find a mentor.

A mentor is not your boss, but someone who helps you grow and develop. He or she challenges you, tells the truth, and stimulates you. Your mentor can be a senior person in the business, though not usually a family member, or even someone outside. Sometimes a board member or family friend can serve this role. This is a person whom you can bounce things off and whom you can talk candidly with. A real resource.

Seek a variety of assignments.

You may be in the driver's seat someday, so the more people you know and the more you know about the business, the better off you will be. Move around in job assignments, and informally. If you have done well in one area, move on to another.

Attend to your development.

Many important things are happening, and when you have been working, you need to seek regular opportunities to learn more. You should especially seek workshops and learning opportunities in which you are an active participant. Don't sit passively in a workshop; do something with others. Experiential, active learning teaches you about leadership and your own limits and helps you stretch.

Take time away.

You have the luxury of not losing your job if you take some time to work away from the business. You should take some time before you work for the family or during a break from the family enterprise to work in another business, to see what you can do, and to see what life is in another world. You have to spend some time away from home in order to see your own place clearly.

 **Part Seven**

Creating Stewardship
of Family Wealth

Families who have amassed a great deal of wealth—more than they can use in their lifetimes—rarely take the time to consider how their wealth will affect their lives or those of their children. It seems self-evident that people will pursue wealth, and yet they rarely ask themselves why they do this. The presence of family wealth opens up possibilities for life. It creates opportunities and pathways for the family members who created the wealth and for their heirs. Amid all these possibilities, the ways a family plans for and uses their wealth is an extension of their life purposes, of what they value and what they want for their children and the people around them. Since there are so many choices about life path, direction, focus, and work, most enterprising families find that they cannot just let their lives evolve naturally but must be continually vigilant, thinking through their options and not just leaving them to chance. It is helpful for these families to take the time to step back and consider both what they want to achieve with their wealth and how they are going to go about accomplishing this. When practicing family stewardship a family, among other things, works toward using its wealth to have the greatest positive impact on a wider circle, not only family members in generations to come, but also the community and the world.

What future generations can expect from the family's wealth and how the family will use their wealth are not conventional topics for family discussions. Not every family member is going to participate in making decisions about these issues, but because the issues concern all members of the family, they all should all be part of the conversations about them, even if the reason for the get-together is simply for the family to learn the wishes of the wealth creator or elders. It is important that parents are willing to hear from their children and to acknowledge, but temper, their resistance if they feel their children's requests are not in line with their own values. By engaging all family members on these issues, a family can find a focus for their connection, which helps them stay together as a family as the next generation become adults and create their own families. In some families there can be huge differences between people's expectations or generations' expectations. Too frequently families avoid confronting these differences until they lead to litigation or have created deep rifts in the family. If they are discussed openly and at a point in the family's development in which there is still time to find a path that is comfortable for everyone, the family members are more likely to be able to sustain family closeness over generations.

As noted in Part I, family wealth is more than just financial. The family has wealth in a number of areas, including **human capital**—the skills they develop in the next generation—and **social capital**—the people they know, their goodwill in the community, and the resources that come from their success. Discussions of family wealth have to move from the financial to these other kinds of wealth (for a review of the dimensions of wealth I have identified, see "True Wealth: The Stewardship of Family Capital," in Part I) if the conversations are to be effective and useful. This final section explores how families deal with the special challenges that arise from the presence of family wealth and presents ways in which these can be addressed and overcome.

For a family who has a lot, the discussion of money is always emotionally charged. A family as a unit is founded by two people coming together from their own different families, who may have had very different experiences and values about money and wealth. The new family may have to overcome conflicts about spending, saving, and having money that stem in part from the varied experiences and values of the family in which they were raised. Money can become a way to control young people or to redress or paper over a parent's guilty feelings. This pattern often begins when a parent brings a child a present after having been away to make up for not being physically present enough in a child's life, or offers a gift as a way of trying to get a young person to do what the family wants him or her to do.

Money can also be a means by which an individual gains respect or recognition from the family. Earning a family salary and responsibly and capably fulfilling a clearly defined role in the family enterprise or making money on one's own are all ways that young people can prove themselves in—and to—the family. But simply making money is not the ideal way for individuals to gain approbation from their family or to develop their own competencies and sense of self-worth. To truly demonstrate one's own value, an individual must do something that makes a difference in and for the world.

Unfortunately, young people often develop the belief that growing up in a wealthy family by itself entitles them to part of the family wealth. They expect to continue to have a claim on this wealth even if they don't really know how much there is, where it comes from, or what difficulties, skills, struggles, and values were involved in making it. A major concern of enterprising families is raising children who don't develop this sense of entitlement, or if they do, will overcome it—perhaps with their parents' guidance—ultimately becoming productive and capable adults who are able to take care of themselves without a family subsidy.

Finally, the presence of wealth usually leads a family to ask, How much do we want to give back to the community? A very successful family is expected to give back, and if the family has a large presence in the community, they are known by how generous they are. Young people in the family may develop careers in public service, the arts, or areas like teaching in which the family only supplements their income. The second half of this section explores ways in which the enterprising family approaches the challenges of leaving a legacy of values and compassion and giving back to the community.

7.1

The Burdens of Wealth

Great wealth brings a young person both benefits and difficulties. This selection explores some of the issues that often complicate life for a person growing up in a wealthy family and presents ways that parents can help their children anticipate these and work through them.

Coming from a wealthy family can be quite a mixed blessing. Willy Vanderbilt, grandson of Commodore Vanderbilt, who built the New York Central Railroad, creating—along with his other railroads—perhaps the largest family fortune of the time, was healthy, wealthy, good looking, charming, and successful at running the family railroads. Yet, in a reflective moment, he conceded that wealth was not a solution for everything in life:

> *My life was never destined to be quite happy. It was laid out along lines which I could not foresee, almost from earliest childhood. It has left me with nothing to hope for, with nothing definite to seek or strive for. Inherited wealth is a real handicap to happiness. It is as certain death to ambition as cocaine is to morality.*

Is there something the family might have done to make him feel less hopeless about himself?

The shadow that weighs heaviest on the first-generation creators of a successful family business is concern over what inheritance will do for the next generation.

- How can I motivate my children to want to work? What should they do with their lives?
- How can I keep them from being spoiled or squandering the family's resources?

- Should my children inherit great wealth, or should it be given to a charitable trust or foundation?

"I came from a family with little means. My children always had more than they needed, but I am concerned about how their good fortune will affect their motivation and direction in life," said the founder of a large biotech company.

Family-business founders and their heirs come from vastly different worlds. Founders for the most part did not grow up rich and can remember the years of struggle and hard work that went into the creation of their enterprise. Their children, as industrious and disciplined as they may be, have never known real struggle. The fact is, they have always known that they are wealthy. Wealth is part of their identity, and it produces a curious ambivalence on their part. The family wonders how their children can learn the importance of persistence and of using their own skills to overcome difficulties when they have everything they want.

One liability of wealth for heirs is the feeling that they don't deserve their good fortune. In the 80s, John Sedgwick, who interviewed 75 heirs about the effects of their inheritance, wrote:

> For all rich kids, the act of inheritance is entirely passive. Yet this sometimes makes the guilt more severe, and more permanent. True criminals, at least, have something to confess. They can receive forgiveness; they can reform; they can put the sins behind them. But rich kids start to feel they are the sin themselves, and every crime that was ever committed hangs on their heads. They see the inequity that lies about them or read about it in their money mail, and they think they are responsible for it. Because they are on top, they must be squashing those on the bottom. This is the true embarrassment of riches.

Another aspect of growing up wealthy is the isolation it produces in the heir's personal life. Because an heir has a lot, he or she distrusts the motives of anyone who befriends her, let alone wants to date or marry her. So young heirs find themselves confined to a "gilded ghetto"; trusting other people is difficult as is understanding the lives of ordinary folk. This presents an immense challenge for a family, though not one likely to receive much sympathy. A wealthy family has to work hard to produce responsible, productive, and fulfilled heirs.

Practices for Producing Responsible Heirs

The following are some practices that next-generation family members find helpful.

Teach compassion.

Children are curious about money. They hear their parents talking about it, and they ask questions. Their parents may evaluate other people by what they have and how they use their wealth, attributing certain virtues to how families live. Talking about money and wealth is considered taboo in some families. This taboo in fact is responsible for the vague feelings of guilt that Sedgwick referred to above.

A family however needs to have open discussions about money and what it means to the family. These discussions form the basis for money values in later life. Children see rich and poor, and they want to understand why there is a difference. How does the family account for its wealth in these discussions? The most important qualities for a young wealthy person to develop are compassion for those who do not have wealth and appreciation that there is great inequality in the world. Talking about these differences and even having the children do charitable work during which they actually see and help those less fortunate forms the basis for personal compassion, especially if the parents present this work without condescension and with sincere concern for the plights of others. Performing work that gives a young person the opportunity to see, for example, how less-fortunate families live has a much more powerful effect on him or her than just writing a check, an act that keeps those less fortunate at arms' length. Also seeing firsthand the effects of good works, watching an at-risk child learn to read, for instance, can have a lasting impact on the young heir. As children grow, volunteer work in the community, in museums, with service groups, or for the environment should be a regular activity.

Finding a passion.

In order to feel alive, fulfilled, and productive, a person needs to discover something he or she can do that makes a difference. For the family-business heir, that passion may be continuing the work of the family in their business or generating new ones. But this presents two problems: First, the heir may think he or she can never equal the feat of the business founder, and therefore will feel no real satisfaction in his achievements. Second, there are only a limited number of places available in the family business, and these require specific capabilities that the heir may not possess.

So most family-business heirs will have to find their passion elsewhere. Some find it in spending their fortunes, but such passion tends to be empty. The greatest satisfaction is experienced by those family members who find a calling, not necessarily commercial, that makes a difference. Among the many possibilities, they may find careers connected with charitable works—preserving the environment, creating an art gallery, or developing urban schools. Or they may challenge themselves physically—exploring, climbing mountains, or sailing competitively.

"Do I have to work?" an heir will ask him- or herself and his family. I worked with two families of equal and substantial wealth. It was curious to me that in one of them, each young person grew up excited about developing a career and doing something in the world. Even though they knew that their income would be supplemented by the family's vast wealth, they each had a powerful urge to create their own achievements. The children of the other family grew up not knowing what to do. Their wealth was there, but the family had not helped them develop any motivation or structure in their lives that would help them find direction.

Successful families want their heirs to want to "work," even if that does not mean necessarily working for money. But heirs must have the support to explore many possibilities as they grow, and family must pass on—through their actions or the way in which they discuss or address their wealth in the presence of the children—the implicit message that while the younger generation may not be making money, they should find something productive to do that makes a difference in the world.

Responsible stewardship of wealth.

Not everyone can make a fortune, but too many heirs find spectacular ways to lose it. In big ways, and in little ones, the heirs of wealth are ripe for exploitation. The family can anticipate this by teaching them how to manage their wealth. The Pitcairn family, with scores of family members entering its fourth generation, created a seminar that introduces family members to their financial affairs and to ways in which one can make good financial decisions. Although only one or two family members work in the family's business, the family believes that every family member must learn how to manage money thoughtfully. Other families give their young sons and daughters a certain amount of money to manage, and then they receive the whole amount, including what they have made, when they reach a certain age.

There are also values that the family develops about their wealth. The wealth means nothing in itself; every family must tell their heirs what their family money is for. Is it for the personal pleasure of each heir, or is it something that is meant to be passed down to succeeding generations? These values underlie the understandings that come with the inheritance of great wealth. One of the most important decisions for a family—as we have seen—is whether to keep its wealth together in, say, a number of family investments. Family heirs must understand the reasons behind those decisions, because when they actually inherit, they will have to make the free choice of whether to stay within the family enterprises.

Inheritance without dependency.

Inheritance can take many forms. In some cases, through trusts and other vehicles, a person can inherit some of the benefits of an asset but not any control over it. Many heirs of great fortunes never really *have* their inheritance, as they have very limited control over it. A family may create a trust out of the fear that their children will use up their wealth. But in the end, the best insurance that the next generation will use their money wisely is not for the parents to take steps to prevent their children from having control over their inheritance, but rather is for them to take steps along the way to make sure that each heir develops compassion, passion, real work, values, and responsibility about money. In the end, the family must learn to trust that the members of the next generation will take charge of making their own ways in the world, will use their wealth to benefit the family and the community, and will make their own informed choices. By preparing their heirs for responsible and fulfilled adulthood, they increase the chances that their wealth will continue to make a positive difference in the lives of their family for many generations.

Keys to Success: Helping Young People Live with Family Wealth

- Talk openly with your children about your wealth and what it can do
- Offer opportunities as a family to practice charity and help others
- Encourage each family member to find productive "work"
- Offer your children opportunities to learn about management of money
- Create clear values about the family's direction and the purpose of its wealth
- When certain conditions are met, each heir should inherit not just money but also control over his or her wealth, within the agreements that have been made by the family

7.2

The Dilemmas of Acquired and Inherited Wealth

People come to wealth in essentially two ways: They acquire it during their life-time through effort or chance, or they inherit it from someone else's reserve. The way in which a person comes into wealth is an important determinant of how wealth affects his or her personality and character. This selection explores the experiences of those who acquire wealth, looking at how they must come to grips with their good fortune and how they raise their children under new circumstances. We also examine the very different experience of inheritors, who are raised with wealth and who come into the world surrounded by the benefits and drawbacks of upper-class life.

This selection was written with James Grubman. This and the next selection are revised from a longer article, "Acquirers' and Inheritors' Dilemma: Discovering Life Purpose and Building Personal Identity in the Presence of Wealth," published in The Journal of Wealth Management, fall 2007. Consult the article for more-detailed references and more-extensive accounts of the research and conceptual models described here.

How does the presence of wealth in one's life shape one's personal sense of self, through the creation of one's personal identity as a wealthy individual, during one's developmental life journey, and in the legacy that families pass on to their children? Family wealth has the potential to help family members of several generations achieve a strong and positive life purpose that integrates one's self with one's wealth.

We begin by making a distinction based on how one comes into wealth—by acquiring it or inheriting it. **Acquired wealth** can be defined as a significant rise in one's socioeconomic level within a single generation. As such, a hallmark of the process of acquiring wealth is the psychological and sociological sensation of *transition*. The individual achieving wealth status travels not across distance but across socioeconomic classes, setting out from blue-collar or middle-class culture toward the promised land of wealth. This journey may be arduous, extending over years of entrepreneurial labor, or it may be a sudden leap produced by the right sequence of Powerball numbers. Either way, acquired wealth involves navigating a change from one social class and culture to another, with all the attendant pleasures, stresses, losses, and new language this change brings. Acquirers of wealth are like immigrants, undergoing the life-changing experience of traveling from their homeland to another country, in this case, a land of more affluence.

Acquirers come to their new status having already developed much of their personal identity in the economic culture of their birth. Since personal identity is formed largely in the culture and economic class of one's childhood, adults who become wealthy as adults must undergo an adjustment in their sense of who they are. This is not true only for someone who achieves wealth later in life: Many aspects of the personality of an individual who achieves wealth early (in his or her 20s and 30s) have already been set by the formative experiences of youth. With acquired wealth, *one's identity is established before the wealth occurs*. We view this as **The Acquirer's Dilemma**—the sometimes-arduous process of incorporating wealth into the personal identity already in place.

Inherited wealth, by contrast, describes that of those who are born into an upper-socioeconomic level. The inheritors are the natives of the land of wealth, the children, grandchildren, and succeeding generations of those who first made the journey to riches. While the acquirer's experience is one of transition in socioeconomic class, the inheritor's experience, rooted as it is in multigenerational wealth, is of *maintenance* of one's class, not *transition*. Inheritors may be fortunate enough to improve their wealth status by their own efforts, thereby achieving that rare combination of being both inheritors and acquirers. More often, wealth maintenance occurs through the skillful resources of the family's wealth managers. Some transitions in wealth status may conceivably bring the individual or family to an even more rarefied level of wealth, as in the transformation of a merely rich, $15-million family to an ultrarich, $500-million family. However, this is not the situation for most heirs, and if there is a fear common to them it is not that they won't vastly increase their family's wealth, but rather that they may lose it and transition downward in socioeconomic class. This downward slide in class may be likened to being expelled from the land of privilege. The risk of precipitating such a fall gives rise to many of the stresses and anxieties reported by heirs, most of whom probably see their primary responsibility as preserving one's wealth and the family's position in the wealth class into which they were born. Successfully fulfilling this responsibility is itself no easy task.

Another key distinction between acquired and inherited wealth is that for inheritors raised with wealth, *the wealth is present before the individual*. It exists in the environment, in the home, and in the childhood circumstances enveloping the heir. Compared with acquirers for whom wealth comes after establishment of identity, inheritors begin life as new individuals within the background of Old Money. Young heirs know little of economic cultures other than the land of their birth. Their identity, therefore, is immersed in wealth throughout childhood. Although there are many benefits to this, there also are toxic elements. This is **The Inheritor's Dilemma**—the daunting task of growing a strong responsible identity out of the environment of wealth.

The Dilemmas of Acquired Wealth

When a person comes to wealth, he or she experiences a shift from one social class and status to another. In the shift, these individuals are seen differently by others. They have access to new opportunities and options as well as relief from the burdens of a financially strained life. Like the immigrants to a new land to whom we compared them above, they must confront new situations, expectations, demands, responsibilities, and possibilities. Moreover, those who come to wealth in a public way are perceived as changed people. Their place in their community may be disrupted as other people rearrange their expectations to match both reality and the stereotypes of "the Rich."

The psychological makeup of wealth creators is highly relevant both for their own personal adjustment and for the interpersonal dynamics in first-generation families of wealth. Many founders and owners of family businesses are entrepreneurs with creative characteristics that affect every aspect of their lives. Many feel that success has come at least partly because of their ability to keep things under their control. They tend to see success as not due to luck but to their own efforts. They may feel entitled to respect for their efforts and may have become used to getting their way because of their wealth. Once they are successful, they are proud of the wealth they have created and want only the best for their families.

Taken to an extreme, however, some controlling or charismatic owners demonstrate a deep vein of self-centeredness or narcissism, contributing to their success but making life difficult for their families. As Ivan Lansberg notes,

> *Narcissism is often a reason why entrepreneurs choose to blaze their own trails. Once family business founders have succeeded, however, the stature and privilege success bestows can create an unhealthy narcissism…characterized by a craving for attention and approval, a fixation with success and public recognition, and a lack of empathy for others. If not understood, this dark side can threaten the health of the business and the competence of would-be successors.*

The acquisition of wealth is often seen as an end in itself by those struggling to get there, never thinking deeply about what will happen at the journey's conclusion. Wealth acquisition does not complete personal development, however. It requires even more, since identity is challenged to incorporate the transition. Having gained surprising wealth, the newly wealthy need to figure out how to live a life that includes their wealth in a positive way. Lives constricted by work pressures may be transformed in early retirement to seek new purpose through philanthropic foundations and pursuits embracing deeper human meaning. Life's choices are broader when a person is rich, but the criteria for what a person should do, and what will motivate one's actions, are more elusive.

The Acquirer's Dilemma is essentially the choice faced by all immigrants: whether and how much to assimilate. One may wish to fit into wealth's desirable characteristics of comfort, security, prestige, independence, and freedom. One may also wish to avoid the more undesirable attributes of the culture: snobbery, entitlement, superficiality, temptation, and disconnection from responsibility. Several stresses can arise as the newly wealthy attempt to integrate their identities as outsiders with the reality of their new surroundings in the culture of wealth. This psychological adjustment depends on many factors, one's age, the number of socioeconomic classes skipped on the way to success, preexisting money, personality, and the speed of wealth acquisition.

Acquired wealth is very different at age 55 than at 25. Both require integration of the fortune into one's personality, but personality at 55 is more established and grounded in experience than it is during the formative years of young adulthood. High-net-worth individuals in middle age tend to be more conservative, cautious, risk-averse, savings-aware, altruistic, and philanthropic, often with a history of more-stable family life and greater life satisfaction and spirituality. Their primary concerns are preserving their identity as middle-class individuals despite their wealth, assuring that their money does not contaminate their children's development, and protecting their assets from taxes, disability, disaster, or dissolution upon death—or all of these. Their personal identity may remain remarkably untouched by their transition to wealth.

A common sentiment voiced by individuals with acquired wealth is, "This is not me." They may have worked hard to achieve security, independence, and freedom from worry. Yet, it is hard to feel totally comfortable alongside "the rich folks" they once envied or disdained. They also cannot quite go back to their roots. With even minimal time to adjust, they find themselves no longer fitting in comfortably with their old friends and activities. Even if they feel at ease with those from their past lives, they may encounter the unearned resentments, jealousies, or adoration of the rich still held by those friends they once held dear.

Coming to Terms with New Wealth:

Resolving the Acquirer's Dilemma

The acquisition of wealth is powerful and life-changing, a unique experience in an individual's life. Resolving the dilemmas of acquired wealth is more complex than society typically understands or accepts. Acquirers may have little sympathetic assistance in their task, because they consider it embarrassing or socially unacceptable to feel conflicted. Through supportive friends, competent therapists, or peers in similar circumstances, they may be able to adjust their self-conceptions, integrating their new status. At the center of the process can be the person most connected to both the wealth and the acquirer: the thoughtful and trusted adviser. By understanding the many facets of wealth acquisition and adjustment, the skilled financial adviser can see the client as a whole person and thus help him or her in a variety of areas rather than simply advising on business issues. This understanding of the client also allows the adviser to individualize the client relationship, adjusting his or her work to the client's unique needs rather than simply offering cookie-cutter ideas and procedures.

After establishing a new personal identity, an acquirer who is a parent adds a second element: concern for what life will be for his or her children. The parents' experience of not having been wealthy will not intuitively be understood by their children. How, then, can parents pass on positive values and the motivation for work and success to the next generation?

The Dilemmas of Inherited Wealth

Inherited wealth offers many things; opportunity, leisure activities, travel, social status, power, and inordinate influence. Like being born with great beauty, it can automatically make someone special without his or her having done anything to earn it. However, as we consider the research and personal accounts of people who inherit wealth, we learn that wealth is far from an unmixed blessing. The presence of money from birth appears to create certain common dilemmas during inheritors' growth and development and to add another layer of complexity to the normal developmental journey every person must navigate.

The omnipresence of wealth while one is growing up has a secondary effect not experienced by individuals who come to wealth as adults. Multigenerational wealth often influences parenting and can lead to unintended effects on a child's development. Too often, what parents fear most comes to pass. Their well-intended child-rearing efforts can make it difficult for children to mature emotionally, experience a sense of efficacy and self-worth, feel positively connected to others, and develop fulfilling work. Growing up very wealthy can delay or retard the process of maturing, sometimes preserving dependency long into adulthood.

Inheritors have a different task. Rather than incorporating new wealth into an already-formed identity, the inheritor must create an effective and versatile individual identity that is strong enough to be separate from the massive power of wealth and at the same time must be secure enough to integrate wealth into her identity without diminishing her sense of self. **The Inheritor's Dilemma** is how to construct one's identity in this way. Along with our metaphor of the acquirer's being an immigrant to the land of wealth, we view the inheritor as the native-born citizen of the land of comfort and exemption from financial worry. The heir grows up surrounded by the language, activities, attitudes, and unconscious beliefs of upper-class culture. The inheritor must still accomplish the task of any individual: to grow a productive, responsible, and well-adjusted identity within the environment of one's birth. People tend to underrate how difficult it can be to grow this identity when the land of one's birth is wealth.

The very nature of the environment makes this growth a uniquely daunting task. Inheritors face challenges from having wealth. These range from the heavy weight of unhealthy parenting practices to the mixed messages about wealth that are often given by both parents and society. An additional issue is the inherent challenge of finding a life purpose when one's life is financially set.

The Developmental Experience of Inheritors

A core theme in the literature on inheriting wealth is that a personal struggle often takes place within each person raised with substantial wealth. Many individuals must come to terms with the mixed blessing of their wealth. For example, one may have to reconcile a sense of entitlement about money with the opposing belief that extreme riches put one in debt to the world. Reconciling opposites is never easy. Some heirs succeed and come to live good, fulfilling, and effective lives, while others simply fail to thrive, caught up in destructive relationships and dysfunctional behaviors. Some initially struggle but are able to achieve positive balance later in life through a process of difficult and painful learning. Each individual must ultimately understand the value of living a meaningful life and discover how to use his or her personal resources to do this.

What causes this internal struggle? First, upper-class parenting is heavily influenced by the source of the parents' wealth. Each type of acquired wealth leads parents to communicate certain messages about money to their children and to have different expectations about how the next generation will use their wealth. Indeed, a source of great concern for parents with acquired wealth is how to raise responsible children who are happy and productive. (The selection "Overcoming Entitlement and Raising a Responsible Next Generation," later in this section of the book, offers some suggestions for doing this.) Families with new fortunes lack a tradition of how children are raised with wealth and how wealth is passed on.

A family with recently acquired wealth may therefore treat their children differently than does a family who has had wealth for generations. Many newly rich parents feel caught between the fear that wealth will harm their kids and a desire to give their kids the best. They may see their wealth as an obstacle rather than an asset in this task. This ambivalence may confuse their children and lead to contradictory messages about wealth. Sociologist Paul Schervish, who has spent many years researching the experience of newly rich parents, aptly describes this dilemma:

> *Especially for the entrepreneurial wealthy—but for those with family wealth as well—the quandary is how to teach their children the responsibilities of wealth while also providing for their needs. Having gone through hard times, they do not want their children to face the same insecurities. As a result, they furnish a life of affluence for their children while at the same time attempting to instill frugality, humility, and responsibility. ... the problem is that once he chose an affluent neighborhood in which to live, his children automatically became exposed to an environment that threatens to make them materialistic.*

Second, powerful forces operate inside the family systems of multigenerational wealth to affect the growth and identity of inheritors. Despite the envy of those peeking into gated communities and stealing glimpses into the lives of the rich and famous, growing up within an ultrawealthy family has a definite downside. These forces range from the personalities of the parents to the cloistered and sometimes oppressive nature of exceedingly good fortune.

Children may respond to the emotional deprivations of narcissistic parents (e.g., parents who have an exaggerated sense of their self-importance and a limited ability to empathize with other people, such as their children) m in several ways. They can take on similar qualities in their own lives, expressing arrogance, entitlement, and insensitivity to others. Alternatively, they can feel chronically impaired, unprepared for their lives, and conflicted about their wealth.

Researcher John Levy, interviewing 30 heirs as well as psychologists and wealth advisers, uncovered several themes in the development of wealthy young people:

- Inheritors are often delayed in their emotional development, lack adequate motivation, and have difficulty with self-discipline
- Self-esteem is often inadequate and many inheritors are bored with their lives
- Many have difficulty using power effectively
- Inheritors often suffer from guilt and alienation

- Suspiciousness is almost inevitable
- Male and female inheritors face different problems

Wealth consultant Joanie Bronfman, after interviewing nearly 100 heirs for her doctoral dissertation, *The Experience of Inherited Wealth*, provides a rare portrait of the lifestyle and experience of wealthy people, along with their struggle to develop comfort and satisfaction with their money and their lives. Her dissertation and similar accounts by others in the past 20 years illuminate several common stresses that accompany multigenerational wealth.

Common Stresses in Families with Multigenerational Wealth

Lack of intimacy and contact with parents.
Parents are busy—with their business, social events, traveling—and don't have much time for their children. They delegate child rearing to servants and caretakers of mixed levels of warmth, competence, and caring. To deal with their guilt, parents may shower their children with "things" to supplement their deficient contact. Added to that, caretakers may come and go, so that young people may learn to embrace money as a source of nurturing. They grow to resent the lack of contact with their parents and to feel entitled to material possessions as substitutes for what they didn't get within the family. Many of Bronfman's respondents spoke about feeling like "poor little rich kids" and longed for a more-normal, less-privileged life.

Parents using money to control their children.
Wealthy parents may be used to being in control and having other people listen to them. They may use money to control others not only at work but at home. This habitual style may sow the seeds of rebellion, passivity, or self-destructive behavior in some heirs who may later re-create similar relationships with their partners. Parents reward "proper" behavior, and the spoken or unspoken threat to cut children off from the family money can have a chilling effect. Threats by working-class or middle-class parents to disinherit a disobedient child carry little weight, so those parents must use a broad range of methods to express anger or extract compliance with their wishes. Wealthy parents can not only use this threat, they may need no other. This control often extends not just to daily behavior but to schools, careers, mates, and other life choices. Arenas in which inheritors can exercise their own will may be much more limited than those avail-

able to children growing up in nonwealthy families. Furthermore, this may create a reverberating pattern of intergenerational conflict: parents overcontrol their children's choices and then later bemoan their offsprings' lack of initiative, decision-making skills, and ability to take risks. Some children get worn down by this; others choose to rebel in self-defeating ways.

Family isolation and distrust.

The wealthy family may see themselves as inherently special and may distrust others, fearing they will take advantage of them. Children hear messages that lead them to distrust others. Given society's attitudes toward the wealthy, there is some validity to this suspicion. However, this blanket suspicion negatively affects a young person by inculcating in him or her a generalized distrust of others without at the same time imparting the social skills that would enable her to trust other people or take care of herself in relationships. How can an heir know if someone cares about her for who she really is? Heirs tend to construct often-elaborate defenses and schemes to discover the true feelings of friends, lovers, and acquaintances, instead of trying to recognize and constructively manage their own deep feelings about being exploited and taken advantage of.

Very wealthy children also keep to themselves. Raised in large estates, they may have few other children to play with and may be kept to a very small circle of family and friends. Like members of a royal family, wealthy children go to exclusive schools or are tutored at home and have few peers to play with.

Entitlement amid luxury.

Young affluent children live in a world of plenty with little understanding of where their possessions come from, what they are worth, or how they come to be there. Harvard psychiatrist Robert Coles coined the term *entitlement* to describe the expectation of children from wealthy families that the world will always provide heirs with the very best. Inheritors grow up with a lifestyle that they expect will continue, even though they often have no idea how (other than with their inheritance) they might sustain such a lifestyle. Deep down, they frequently feel anxious about what would happen if the money went away.

Dependency and lack of knowledge.

Many wealthy families tend to be secretive about their wealth. It is considered vulgar to discuss money openly. Hence, it is something of a mystery to youngsters, who feel they cannot ask questions about this taboo subject. By avoiding communication, families fail to prepare their offspring for—or even to inform them about—the demands, pressures, responsibilities, and potential power of their inheritance. Later, the convenience of a trust fund may take away the necessity for the heir to understand or complete basic financial tasks. This is especially common for heirs who are women, who may not be expected to become wealth producers. The lack of financial skills and awareness can lead heirs to feel inadequate, confused, and afraid in relation to their money. They are not prepared to deal with the money they inherit and may feel dependent upon advisers whom they fear, resent, or distrust. They also delay or neglect to develop the personal qualities and skills necessary to work, take care of themselves, raise a family, and perform other basic life tasks. Such heirs can be both privileged and impaired as they remain "children" far into adulthood.

Confusion about career and life purpose.

Coming from wealth and expecting to inherit it can hamper a young person's motivation to earn a living or consider a career. Many heirs find it hard to develop interests or sustain involvements. They don't know what they want in their lives, and they are confused about the very notions of career and life involvement. In the face of so much money, they are not sure what to do with their lives or how to develop the discipline to stick to something. While the wealthy person is essentially defined by being in the enviable position of not having to work for money, this may not have an entirely positive effect. Without an inherent economic inducement to stick to something or to sustain focus, heirs may drift untethered through their lives. Many wealthy people have an extended late adolescence, embarking on endless journeys to discover themselves.

Anxiety about fulfilling the family legacy.

Inheritors may feel dominated and stifled by the legacy surrounding their money. A family's tradition around wealth can come across as a deep and limiting set of obligations. The magnitude of their parents' success makes doing anything of significance difficult for some heirs who think they are expected to attain this same level of success or match their elders' achievements. The burden of living up to this may be overwhelming, intimidating, perhaps even paralyzing. Often these heirs think that not only their own family but also society is scrutinizing their every move. Other heirs may feel pressured to follow a specific career path or to participate in a family business. It may not be permissible—or they may think it is not permissible, within the family code of values—to choose alternate ways of making a difference in the world. Instead of being an individual, an heir may feel an oppressive obligation to act "properly" as part of the family and to live up to the family name, even if she is less than clear about just what this means. One heir noted that he lived in continual fear of doing something that would result in his losing the money. This fear in turn led him to avoid any behavior that might be risky or controversial.

Several personal accounts of wealthy women overcoming adversity in family business support these findings. Novelist Sallie Bingham, the eldest daughter in a Southern family media empire, achieved notoriety when her father suddenly sold their businesses out from under her and her brother, who were locked in conflict around her desire to have him buy out her share. After being fired from the board by her family—long before the sale—she had gone public with revelations about growing up female in a family of wealth, weighed down by excessive constraint and WASP values. Raised to ignore her feelings and taught that as a woman, she had little to contribute, she writes movingly about the damage this dealt to her self-esteem and her efforts to make a place for herself in the world.

Similarly, Katharine Graham was the lineal heir to *The Washington Post*, the renowned newspaper built largely by her father. When her husband, organizational heir apparent to the newspaper, committed suicide, Graham refused conventional advice to sell the newspaper empire. She instead took over as CEO, ultimately growing the business into an even more renowned, profitable, and politically influential corporation. Her story of overcoming obstacles describes the lack of preparation, deep and formidable self-doubt, and social disapproval she had to face being a female heir, not just to wealth, but to the more substantial personal strengths of power, purpose, and identity.

Preventive Medicine: Raising Responsible Children with Wealth

It is clear that many factors cause inheritors—natives born into the land of wealth—to face difficulty in their personal development. The bounty of their birth puts them at risk for a syndrome of maladjustment that may last well into adulthood. Unless steps are taken to prevent this syndrome or resolve it once it has developed, inheritors are predisposed to two unfortunate outcomes:

- Traveling through life experiencing only glimpses of the freedom and power of wealth
- Perpetuating the same conflicts and ambivalent reactions upon the next generation, re-creating the pattern through the parenting mistakes they experienced themselves

If they are to inherit and use money wisely, children in wealthy families must develop a well-grounded set of skills and understanding about money along with their grounding in general personality. In his insightful analysis of money maturity, financial planner George Kinder offers a developmental approach to this process. He proposes that people transit through a number of incremental stages in their relationship with money. In this gradual progression, a person proceeds from a childlike innocence about money to a competent knowledge of financial matters through various other stages until ultimately, having put in the necessary effort, one can arrive at a visionary understanding about money's power and limitations. The stages, or styles, Kinder has identified are universal: In defining them, he does not refer specifically to people of wealth, however, having an understanding of the ways in which people in general approach wealth helps us recognize factors essential to the development of the ability of the person of wealth to confidently and compassionately craft a successful future—or conversely, to recognize those factors that hinder this development, so one remains in a state of childlike ignorance, incompetence, and inability to empathize with others.

One style some people use in relating to money, according to Kinder, is "innocence" (not knowing or caring what it is and how it works); another is "pain" (one's money decisions or awareness inspires negative reactions and bad feelings in oneself). Pain arises when something disrupts one's comfortable life—a financial reversal, realization, or another painful life event—reminding the individual that he or she does not live in the Garden of Eden. Through pain a person finds that he or she has to learn to become more active in defining her life and getting what she wants. Individuals progress first toward a basic knowledge of money matters, then toward true understanding of financial principles. If they continue to advance, creating within themselves the capacity to persevere to achieve goals, they may ultimately develop a vision of how money can be integrated into their lives. Mastery of one's relationship to money is therefore a reflection of one's personal maturity and requires a sophisticated grasp of money values and power and their complicated connections. Unfortunately, much visible power in the world derives from wealth rather than competence and often lack of money precludes one from achieving a position that in itself commands respect. Understanding that these connections are not reflections of objective truths but of social constructs is a step toward a healthy relationship with money and wealth. Sadly, the very wealthy often are stuck in innocence or embroiled in pain, with remarkably little true knowledge or understanding to accompany their riches.

What makes the difference between heirs who are able to find a place in the world and those who stumble? While not all responsibility can be heaped on parents, it does appear that the conscious involvement of parents in raising children with wealth is a critical factor in the degree of turmoil the inheritor feels about his or her wealth.

Recent books by Lee Hausner, Joline Godfrey, and Jon and Eileen Gallo offer several common messages for wealthy parents:

- Early attachment and secure love from parents during early childhood (ages 1 through 5) are fundamental to personal identity. Parents must be physically present and emotionally available. Attend to the child, and the child will feel safe and secure in the world. Very early childhood development encourages money maturity later in life only if parents help their children craft the basics of good personality in general.
- Initiative, responsibility, and appropriate discipline during middle childhood (ages 6 through 12) are necessary for self-esteem and later autonomy. Parents must require effort by their children, allow struggle, and encourage action. Children need to be given visible chances to lead and take center stage in front of family and friends, so they gain mastery over risk, learn to manage fear, and taste achievement.
- Increased responsibility must be tempered by consequences and limit setting in adolescence (ages 13 through 18) to offset entitlement and to help the adolescent develop a personal and social conscience. Parents should encourage independence and social responsibility while enforcing consequences.
- Financial literacy must be taught *throughout* childhood in age-appropriate steps in order to create financial competency in adulthood. Young people must be prepared to understand and make basic choices about money by the time adulthood arrives. Waiting till age 18 doesn't work and creates major problems.
- The allowance is a major method by which financial literacy can be taught. Allowances are neither entitlements, reimbursement for doing chores, nor easy sources of punishment for bad behavior. They are parents' best means of teaching money skills and money attitudes consistently over time in a progressive way.
- At a very young age, individuals should start participating and sharing in philanthropic activities, not just by giving money but through active, hands-on efforts.
- Parents must be in control of their own individual and collective behaviors about money, since children learn the most from watching and sometimes must choose between what parents say and what they do. As wealth counselor Thayer Willis observes, "The most important values in life are caught, not taught."

Other useful lessons include encouraging parents to be open about family finances in ways that are appropriate to each stage of early development, involving children in giving to charity by example rather than just by exhortation, and challenging children to think about doing real work in their lives despite their financial security.

The thoughtfulness and care with which parents teach their children seems to be connected to the parents' own stage of development and self-understanding. If parents have progressed to a more mature view of money and wealth, they are able to convey it to their children, who might otherwise find themselves confused or caught up in a consumer society. In the final analysis, the best way to raise responsible children with wealth may be to first make sure we are responsible adults with wealth.

7.3

From Conflict to Clear Life Purpose: Coming to Terms with Family Wealth

We have noted how effective parenting activities can forestall the personal de-railing endemic to inherited wealth. But what of those who are raised with deficient parenting in wealthy circumstances? This selection explores how inheritors can get personal development back on track after damage has occurred. We propose that development of an individual's wealth identity moves through stages, ranging from innocence of the power and pain of wealth through a level of conflict over the wealth to the achievement of a sense of reconciliation with wealth and integration of it into one's self.

This selection was written with James Grubman.

We of course know that many inheritors are able to accept their wealth, take up their roles in life, and remain unconflicted about their fortune. Many heirs do not experience much conflict from having wealth and reach adulthood without significant conflict because they received healthy parenting that instilled good values. But as we suggested in the previous selection, the presence of family wealth may trigger deep personal conflicts in some inheritors that must be resolved if they are to grow and thrive. Something happened in the childhood of such people, or as they matured, that set up a conflict or disjunction between themselves and their wealth. They may observe people who are poor or needy; they may be singled out negatively or positively for their wealth; or they may become confused about what it means to be so fortunate. Instead of feeling comfortable and satisfied, they are plagued by self-doubt, disquiet, and questions—triggered by ways in which others treat them or by what they see in the world. These doubts in turn disturb their personal development, complicating their choice of career and lifestyle, and impeding the development of intimate relationships outside their family.

When this inner conflict arises, the inheritor goes through a cycle of personal development that has several stages:

- Conflict about how wealth fits into his life
- Acceptance and reconciliation with his wealth
- Discovery of altruistic life purpose that includes his wealth

The literature on the personal development of those raised with wealth suggests that the commonly cited disorders of narcissism, passivity, dependency, entitlement, and immaturity accurately represent signs of the Conflict phase of psychological adjustment, a common phase from which many inheritors never advance. This level of wealth maturity is marked by some form of painful conflict in which wealth has overwhelmed and possibly contaminated the development of a strong individual identity. The Conflict phase is characterized by a lack of integration of identity and wealth, in which The Inheritor's Dilemma remains partly or wholly unresolved.

Fortunately, the Conflict phase does not have to remain an end point. It often becomes a wake-up call, leading one to make some decisions and set out on a personal journey that results in the development of a positive relationship to one's wealth. The conflict can be a way station along the journey to a second phase of acceptance, reconciliation, and integration with wealth. Individuals reaching reconciliation with their wealth are no longer hobbled by the guilt, shame, fear, grandiosity, or insecurity prominent when wealth and identity conflict. In Steven Rockefeller's monograph *Family Philanthropy and Creative Democracy: One Family's Experience* in which he chronicles the evolution of the Rockefeller family over five generations, he includes a personal statement of the necessity for such a journey to self-identity:

> *A person will not be really happy in the midst of wealth, finding an enduring sense of satisfaction and meaning, if as a consequence of having it, his or her unique individuality has gone undeveloped for whatever reason. Furthermore, if people do not feel that what they are doing proceeds from free choice and is a way of developing and expressing their own creative abilities, the benefits of their work to others will be limited.*

This comment touches also on the potential of a further phase we shall explore, one in which the heir reaches a stage of commitment to an altruistic life purpose.

Reconciliation with Wealth Through Personal Recovery

Many heirs seek out and benefit from psychotherapy, personal coaching, or some form of personal and spiritual practice as an aid on their journey toward a better adjustment. In the Conflict phase, therapy can help members of enterprising families come to terms with their mixed feelings about wealth and begin to find some balance in their relationships with parents and family. It can also help them make effective life choices and career decisions.

Adjunctive to therapy, in the past two decades groups of inheritors have come together to share their common experiences and concerns. These personal support groups, with names like "giving circles," seek to stay private, out of the limelight, and to provide a safe, understanding, and confidential environment for this work. The growing body of literature that uses interviews with heirs identifies the many elements needed for them to help each other. A prominent example is The Inheritance Project, created by several heirs in the early 1990s as a research and educational center. It has produced a series of monographs (www.inheritance-project.com) that discuss overcoming common challenges in developing a positive personal identity and life path for inheritors.

Paul Schervish and his colleagues coined the term *hyperagency*, the special responsibility that those of exceptional fortune experience as a result of being wealthy, as a key aspect of their lives. Hyperagency is a form of social and psychological power whereby, having wealth, the individual has an extreme level of "the ability to determine conditions and circumstances of life rather than merely living with them." In their life stories reported in the research, the wealthy defined themselves as having overcome significant obstacles in order to use their wealth in a productive way, as part of a good life.

Several books by wealthy inheritors document the struggle to develop a sense of positive self-worth. This struggle is especially common in women inheritors. Jessie O'Neill's account of pain, self-doubt, and self-destructive behavior, *The Golden Ghetto*, was an early account of the parental dysfunction often inherited with wealth. Her description of parental neglect, alcoholism, and isolation, subsidized by vast family wealth, used the term *affluenza* as recognition of wealth's insidious influence, its ability to be passed on from one generation or family member to another, and its capacity to infiltrate an otherwise healthy individual with distressing consequences.

Thayer Willis, who like O'Neill became a wealth counselor, suggests, "If you have inherited substantial wealth, then you know that it is harder for you than for most people to achieve a sense of purpose and competence." She has written about how the heir's struggle must begin with facing the "dark side" of wealth, where wealth that is intended as a gift of infinite promise and possibility is experienced as stifling, confusing, scary, and painful. Her unique contribution is the emphasis that spirituality and religious devotion can provide a path to overcoming the identity conflicts inherited with wealth. This devotion assists in achieving balance, acceptance, and purpose. She is particularly effective in showing how an heir, while not having to work for money to survive, must nonetheless find ways to do something worthwhile, often in the form of a career in social service, arts, or social action. The process of growth involves moving money from the foreground to the background in identity, using wealth mainly as a resource for achieving one's goals and life purpose.

The Role of Philanthropy and Social Purpose in Resolving Conflicts Around Wealth

For acquirers and inheritors who are able to reach reconciliation with their wealth, life achieves a sense of balance and purpose. Unburdened by having to earn money to support living, the wealthy individual may find commitment to paid or unpaid work, a good marriage, responsible parenting, and community service or philanthropy consistent with personal and family values. This is life with purpose, an admirable achievement for anyone.

Philanthropic activities are a natural part of healthy adjustment to wealth. On a practical level, philanthropy can serve as a useful activity as well as a means of integrating the benefits and responsibilities of wealth. The transition from individual and family self-interest to concern for others helps an individual overcome some of the ambivalent feelings of guilt and shame that accompany a fortune. By doing something to give back to society, wealth's immigrants and natives can each come to terms with the emotional struggles about being very rich. As part of this shift, the individual may become more comfortable choosing a lifestyle of affluence with less doubt or anxiety. As the money gains purpose, so does the individual. He or she becomes involved in careers in social activism, philanthropy, community service, and the arts.

Philanthropy can also be a career path for the heir who does not need to earn money and who cannot outdo his or her parents as wealth creators. When a family has a great fortune well-managed internally or by outside advisers, family members may not be motivated to generate more money for the family. Many heirs have neither the inclination nor the talent to be successful entrepreneurs, certainly not at the level of the wealth-creating generation. In some of the wealthiest families, development of an heir's personal identity is associated with participation and leadership in the family philanthropy. This path has many positive effects. Heirs can find their own productive purpose and career with the added benefit of not feeling competitive with their wealth-creating parents. Families can also come together in mutual collaboration across generations, as first-generation entrepreneurs see their children and grandchildren taking on careers and giving away some of the wealth that has been earned.

Abby Stranahan, who worked with her family's philanthropy, expresses aptly the mixed feelings of many heirs about not doing paid work and not creating wealth, the benchmark in society for being productive and therefore worthy:

> *I know I'm doing important work, but I still would like to have a paid job. I don't want my whole identity tied up with doing things that only someone with money can do. The third generation in this family has had more trouble with money and careers than the second generation had. We work hard, but we're not making money.*

Stranahan emphasizes that participation in the family foundation was instrumental in her personal development:

> *Knowing we had a foundation that had a clear purpose, that I agreed with its goals, and that I was genuinely encouraged by the board to participate in the foundation, gave me a different perspective on my family's position. I could feel okay about having money because we were giving it away and doing good things with it.*

Beyond the pragmatic level of philanthropy lies another stratum of the integration of identity and wealth. For some, the melding of self and wealth forms a creative power turned outward to the world in altruistic service to humanity. It is, in essence, *Purpose* with a capital *P*, beyond the individual sense of purpose achieved with normal integration with wealth. This degree of wealth adjustment may represent not just an answer to The Acquirer's and Inheritor's Dilemmas but a wonderful rearrangement of the pieces themselves.

In a study of 100 wealthy donors, Francie Ostrower reports the vast majority felt that giving back was not only a personal choice, it was an obligation. Donors mentioned the usual benefits of giving, that it is a means by which heirs can come to terms with guilt, make their wealth become acceptable to society, and manifest values that are important to pass on to the next generation. For some, however, philanthropy was seen as not only a social obligation but a spiritual one as well, embracing the highest values of self, society, money, and service. She found that those who were part of a religious or spiritual group were more likely to emphasize giving and stewardship as important life tasks.

Paul Schervish, Platon Coutsakis, and Ethan Lewis describe the developmental path some acquirers and inheritors take as they move from being empowered in their individual efforts to working from a broader focus on their potential role in and impact on society:

> *If the first phase of psychological empowerment revolves around feeling entitled and efficacious in regard to one's interests, the second entails self-reflective attention to the source and quality of those interests. At this second level psy-*

chological empowerment becomes characterized by a set of orientations related to what psychologists call self-actualization and what spiritual traditions refer to as holiness or wisdom. ... the capacity of the wealthy to turn their attention inward in an effort to evaluate the spiritual or moral quality of their interests and propose to themselves a less self-centered set of priorities. Those who do so may be described as having learned the spiritual secret of money. The scope of their self-interest increasingly broadens and deepens to include a greater diversity of people and needs. If in the first phase of psychological empowerment the wealthy base their public behavior on their private interests, in the second they base their personal concerns on public needs.

Religious organizations and philosophies have long supported wealth's responsibility and opportunity for advancing social welfare. In the secular realm, Lynne Twist has written a powerful book about the nature of money and philanthropy, *The Soul of Money*, which offers one of the most complete and provocative presentations of this spiritual perspective. Her book contains many accounts of the rich who realize their wealth has led to their impoverishment in the realm of human relationships. Twist shows these people discovering the spiritual nature of wealth and money's true potential for both making a difference in the world and opening doors to situations in which the wealthy can become genuinely involved with other people. As individuals use their money for socially engaged goals, they truly "inhabit their wealth." She presents a compelling argument for altruistic purpose being the most fulfilling energizer in the journey toward integration of self and wealth.

Many of the special challenges wealth puts in the path of those who possess it come from the inordinate freedom it grants them, the surplus of resources available beyond what is required to fulfill ordinary human needs, and the ability to manage the world around them in ways not possible for others. As difficult as the challenges experienced by the wealthy are, these same hurdles are present in different ways for those with lesser means; they are essentially the challenges of life. Developing a healthy personality, achieving the attitudes and skills necessary to attain money maturity, finding purpose in one's life, and parenting children in a loving yet still disciplined way are all universal tasks. Nevertheless, wealthy individuals and families have unique life journeys, requiring that they accomplish these developmental tasks laboring, as they must, under the weight of both the powerful benefits and the heavy burdens of great fortune.

7.4

Overcoming Entitlement and Raising a Responsible Next Generation

Not too long ago wealthy parents' greatest concern was that their wealth would act as a negative force for their children, causing them to feel entitled and preventing them from engaging in productive work and livelihood. Since the financial crisis, many of these families are experiencing a change in the availability of their assets—or even a substantial loss—and thus a change in current and future wealth. This inflection point has created an opportunity for them to examine how they want to raise their children vis-à-vis wealth. For some families, the financial meltdown requires they also take a hard look at their present lifestyle and make certain changes. What happens when you continue to live and feel affluent when in fact your net worth may have been reduced by a quarter, a half, or more? Is the potential negative force of wealth still great when the expectation may be present but the full asset availability is not? What changes when the assets a young person felt entitled to no longer exist in the same fashion? This selection presents some ways that families can adopt stewardship principles within the family so that each generation can find positive and creative ways to continue the family legacy and sustain (or even increase) the family wealth.

This selection was written with Fredda Herz Brown of Relative Solutions.

While raising children is always a challenge, a family with substantial wealth faces some special hurdles because of their good fortune. Typically these enterprising families are aware of the challenges as well as the opportunities generated by their wealth. While parents who have created substantial family wealth are proud of what they have done and want to share it, they also want to make sure that their children develop a work ethic and do something special with their lives. Although no parent can guarantee a positive outcome of his or her parenting, we have identified some common practices parents can take advantage of that create conditions for their children to succeed, even as they experience changes that may have come with the financial crisis.

Family wealth has a different meaning for different generations, as we saw in the preceding two selections. Wealth creators may remember coming from modest life circumstances, and they know what it means to work hard. They know where wealth comes from and are confident that if their wealth were to disappear, they could make more. In many cases, they were driven by the desire to make a difference, not by the prospect of achieving great wealth. Many entrepreneurs have experienced cycles of financial distress and affluence. While they may enjoy the fruits of success, the focus of their energy has been as acquirers rather than as consumers.

Their children often have a different experience of wealth. Family wealth has been present in their lives from birth (though older children may remember times when the parents struggled). They likely grew up around other wealthy families, in an environment where things were plentiful, and they felt valued and special. They experienced wealth as spenders. With few experiences of work in their early years, children of wealth often have a foggy notion of earning and of where wealth actually comes from.

Entitlement refers to the sense that one is special and expects to experience this sense of specialness as he or she moves through life. It is an experience most young people have and must master as they move through late adolescence and into young adulthood. Although it is a typical mind-set for young people, it is perhaps particularly entrenched in those young people who grow up in a very affluent environment. They tend to live a Garden of Eden–like existence, and they have to emerge from an expectation that they can get everything they want and that they will be treated as special. In addition, they may be so sheltered that they don't see how this "entitledness" appears to others who do not have their privilege.

For both wealthy parents and their offspring, the current downturn in the economy seems to have begun to challenge the view that their wealth will always be there and they will always have it. It has shattered the senior generation's confidence that they can provide the necessities, much less a large enough cushion, for their offspring, since their cushion was severely diminished if not totally eliminated. If young people are to succeed in the world on their own, they need to develop the motivation to overcome obstacles, the skills to get things for themselves, and a sense of their own abilities.

While it may seem that the wealthy family's challenge is how to avoid creating a sense of heightened expectation and entitlement (and in part it is), the real challenge is to help their children move through life and develop a more-mature and more-active sense of their life path and purpose. Wealthy parents may increase their future parenting challenges when they reinforce their younger children's feelings of specialness and privilege without balancing these with a sense of responsibility. By providing a life in which the children have little experience differentiating need from want and little involvement with others who do, parents may be making the challenges of late adolescence and early adulthood more difficult. For example, a young person may "need" a car to get to a volunteer experience or may "want" one because he or she doesn't want to take the school bus. The young person must both understand the difference and participate in some sort of giving before getting the car.

Another way a family often unwittingly (and often with all good intentions) reinforces heightened entitlement, rather than helping their children overcome the sense of entitlement that all children feel, is by not talking within the family about the reality of wealth. They may feel that if the family doesn't talk about it, their children won't know about it or will not experience the specialness that accompanies it. Unfortunately, they are forgetting about the many messages that come from around them telling them that they are privileged and special. In school, in the community, and through the media, children discover that not everyone has as much as they do. They may feel special because they have more, but also awkward because they aren't quite sure how to deal with it. Parents who won't discuss their wealth openly with their children leave the children to draw their own conclusions about the family's means and about what they can expect in the future. Often the children's conclusions reinforce their sense of specialness. Thus, thinking that reality may be too much for their children to understand, parents inadvertently foster in them the belief that "what we have is what you have." The current economic situation provides ample opportunity for families to be more open and transparent not only about the impact of the recent changes on their own and other families' fortunes, but also about their wealth in general, opening the door to direct and honest family conversations.

Some enterprising families who aren't comfortable having such conversations about their wealth still think they should communicate some message to their children, so they give lip service to the fact that the children can't expect to live a life of privilege and affluence forever. At the same time, they give their children everything they want. Without being aware of what they are doing, they are giving the children mixed, or double, messages.

Clearly wealth enables families to offer more opportunities to their children. Education is one such opportunity; children of wealthy families are often able to attend the best schools, and unlike many other children in our society, to leave school without debt. Some families have a tradition of working during high school and college, sometimes in the family business, but most wealthy families do not encourage their children to work while in school. Rather, like many other parents, they offer their children ways to improve their education and broaden their college choices by providing them with extracurricular activities, lessons, and enriching travel and learning opportunities. In most cases, children in affluent families come to expect these things; they no longer view them as special opportunities that carry with them a responsibility and a sense of accountability.

Yet, when asked, these same families will often express a desire to develop in their children a sense of the importance of their creating their own achievements and accomplishments. They want them to develop fulfilling and remunerative careers. They do not want the family wealth to support their children, but rather to supplement their incomes so that they can live well.

However large it seems, the family's wealth is limited. The fact is, while the family wealth can grow, the family itself is growing geometrically, and over two or three generations family members cannot expect to have the same level of wealth unless they continue to generate it. Yet as we have seen above, children are often raised to believe that what they have is what they can expect and that family money is their money. For many families of wealth that expectation is being challenged. Clearly the goal for even a wealthy family with regard to the next generation is to help them develop the capability and skills they will need to be independent and take care of themselves. This independence is the opposite of being entitled.

So the life task for all young people is to grow beyond feeling protected, special, and entitled and to see that their lives can be richer, and they can be stronger, if they develop their own abilities to do something that makes a difference. Building the confidence to make it on one's own without the protection of one's family is part of becoming a productive young adult with a work ethic. If parents (or parental resources like money) are always behind a young person, it is harder for him or her to learn to take independent action. If a young adult never has to be responsible for his own welfare, and thus never has to make choices that have real consequences, he may never learn to think critically or to identify the factors essential to making a decision. Not having ever had to think for himself, he may make poor lifestyle choices; dangerous lifestyles may not seem so dangerous when one has the safety net of one's family to catch him. And although he may not be afraid to make choices that could end up harming himself, he may be afraid to take risks in the world of work, believing it is safer to accept the protection of his parents than to attempt to make his way in the workplace and fail. However, the greatest learning comes from failing, so parents are cheating their children of critical building blocks toward individuation if they protect them from this experience.

The entitled young person may have begun to believe that the family's wealth belongs to him or her. But is wealth really a possession, something that one "owns"? Some families begin to teach that the wealth is not an individual possession, but something that the family can draw on with limits. These are the concepts of stewardship. They also teach that each family member should expect to go out and support him- or herself and work toward personal goals, with very limited support from the family after a certain point. Some families may say this even though their behavior suggests that it is not really so. It is hard, for example, to ask a young person to train for or seek an entry-level job when the family trust fund could support that person with a good income. Individuals need help to develop the motivation or incentive to see that work is a learning and personal development experience as well as a means of survival. We suggest this is something a young person must come to understand through witnessing give and take in the family over a period of time, not by just listening and absorbing.

The more substantial the family wealth, the harder it may seem to make a case that a young person has to add to the family wealth. A young person may even feel overwhelmed, wondering what difference his or her contribution will make when the family has so much. There are stories of a young person whose motivation to prove value to the family, or to outdo elders, causes him to make risky or foolhardy decisions about family assets that lead to losses. Yet, when a young person can successfully make his or her own money, he feels a sense of personal achievement that is not conditional on the amount he makes. By being rewarded for doing something on his or her own, even something as simple as finishing a project, an individual grows and develops outside the family. Even if the individual doesn't "need" the money, she needs the learning and the sense of productivity and self-worth that work provides.

This idea of encouraging a family member to do something on her own can be extended into the years between high school and college and those years right after college. Some families begin to build expectation of one's own capability and competence by planning that for a period of time each family member will work on her own and not be supported by the family. Some do this by not distributing trust money until a certain age, except for specific purposes such as education and emergency health care. The expectation that a person support him- or herself for at least a period of time—or at least that she learns to live on what she earns—is important for every young person, but we believe it is an especially necessary step for the most wealthy as they grow into adulthood. Successful personal development seems to demand a personal journey in which the individual separates from the family, and does something real, visible, and important on his or her own.

Another important element of becoming independent is learning to make decisions. For wealthy families, decisions are often complex and intertwined with other people, such as nonfamily advisers. Thus, offering a young person a specific opportunity to contribute, to have a voice, and to vote on family affairs is important. If a person is not involved in the family's wealth by being informed or making decisions about it, then family wealth becomes passive and in the background, not active and needing tending. The next generation may become entitled rather than empowered.

Offering young people pathways to learn, develop skills, and become decision makers in areas regarding the family money can start initially in a limited way. For example, they might be invited to serve on a family committee, helping to plan an annual family meeting, or to attend a seminar on the family finances. Then other opportunities appropriate to their age and maturity can be developed. Finally, there are ways that family members from the next generation can become increasingly involved in family decision making by becoming active participants in family leadership and governance positions.

Pathways to Responsible Adulthood

Clearly, a family cannot guarantee responsible adulthood for their children, but they can certainly make it more likely. We offer some core principles and activities that help a wealthy family make it more likely that their offspring become productive and independent.

Inform.

The first activity for a family is to tell their children not just what they have, but what that means and what they can expect. Given the chance that they may give their children a mixed message, or that other people may say things that confuse their children, at least the family can talk about their wealth and what it means to them. This is not a one-time activity but must be revisited in different ways if the message is to get across. These conversations can probe the children's assumptions and expectations, and challenge or clarify misconceptions as they arise.

Several types of information are needed. First of all, the young people have probably not seen the family earn its money, so they must learn about where it comes from and what it took to get there. It is important for the family to look beyond the wealth generators in this history lesson so that the children get the sense that all family members are valued, even those whose contributions were not financial and did not generate more wealth. This is the family's history, and it is a wonderful experience for young people to hear this from the family elders while they are able to tell the tales.

Second, they must learn about the values and expectations that are attached to the wealth. Many family founders have expectations that are neither clear nor explicit. If family members are expected to work for a living, this should be a topic of conversation as they are growing up. They should know what they can and cannot expect from the family. A good beginning in this area is for young people to have a sense of what it costs to provide them with their life style and how that is paid for. They may also participate in developing their own personal budget.

Third, as they grow up they should learn, in an age-appropriate way, what there is in the family resources and how it can be accessed. When it is age-appropriate, they should learn about family trusts and the difference between being an heir and having control. The family should initiate the conversation and over time, make sure that they prepare the young people with increasingly full disclosure and discussion of the rules and expectations. If there are restrictions on accessing their money, they should learn why that is. This is a good time to teach the concept of *stewardship*, holding the wealth for the benefit not just of their own generation but of generations to come.

Engage.

Too many families put great stock in informing but do so in a way that is excessively formal or that comes across as telling, rather than as inviting others to participate in an exchange. Worse yet, some families have their financial advisers do presentations or send financial statements without offering any opportunity for the young people to respond or ask questions. This is a mistake. Many young people hear the words, but they don't understand what they mean. They are afraid to ask questions and appear stupid. The competence of their parents and the pressure to appear smart causes some children to be uneasy about asking questions. They may even hide behind a veneer of maturity and knowledge, which can appear as arrogance.

The concept of family engagement refers to sharing information in a way that invites the young people to share in return. They may ask questions, voice concerns, or even express frustration or disagree with what they learn. For example, one young person hearing about trusts for educational purposes looked at the enormity of the choices he could make and wondered aloud how he could possibly figure out what he wanted to do for a living. Another was clearer about his choice but worried that his family might not approve of his desire to travel with his rock band.

The issue for parents is whether they are willing to hear things from their children that they do not agree with. Parents have a hard time allowing their children to have their own values and ideas, make their own mistakes, and acquire their own learnings. When family wealth is involved, too often the family puts so many strings on it that the young people are not allowed to explore or learn on their own. The arguments over politics and lifestyle that take place in so many families are important stepping-stones to growth. They help the young people learn to define their own ideas by experimenting with possibilities. If a young person does not feel heard or respected (not necessarily agreed with), he or she will simply turn off communication and apathy can set in.

Model.

Children learn about money and wealth not by hearing rules but by seeing their parents in action. In one family, the parents talked about being frugal while their lifestyle was the epitome of opulence. Why would the message of frugality mean anything to their children who lived in such splendor and whose friends were so impressed by it? Many of the challenges of entitlement come from the disjunction between word and behavior.

Simply stated, children imitate what they see and forget what they are told. If the family physically sets an example of service by doing things to help others, the children will learn. A family who wants to set an example of giving for their children cannot just write checks to good causes; they need to arrange to visit them and learn about their work firsthand.

Modeling also involves helping children move out of their protected "bubble" to experience how other people live. While they may initially feel special when seeing less-privileged areas, by observing their parents showing empathy and respect and by going through "leveling" experiences their parents have provided for them, children can learn to develop empathy for others.

Teach.

Learning about money is not just learning about how much is there. Managing money is a complex process, and the more there is, the more complex the process. A young person growing up in a wealthy family with trusts and multiple investments has to learn more than how to balance a checkbook. In order to be a steward of the family's investments, and an inheritor of substantial wealth, a young person has to have an advanced financial education.

Some of this can come from school, but it needs to be supplemented. Some families with a family office or operating business offer internships for young family members. Others design a financial seminar in which young people can learn about the nature of their family enterprises and the skills they need to master to understand the information. Yet others develop an educational seminar on financial skills to be offered to the younger generation at their annual family meeting. Such practices send a message about the responsibility each family member has to be informed.

Family financial seminars have benefits that might not be immediately apparent. As members of the extended family's younger generation, the cousins who are growing up in separate households or branches learn about their common legacy and how to work together as a team. They see that, unlike other families, they are joined by financial and other enterprises and they will have to work together to manage them. As they grow up and discover opportunities for themselves in family governance, they go from being students and learners to becoming participants more actively engaged in decision making. This is training for responsibility. Some families have added Action Learning projects to seminars. In these projects, groups of young people work together in activities like service projects or, for example, are given a pile of real money to invest. By learning to make choices and decisions, and seeing the results of their actions, young people can learn and develop financial acumen.

Empower.

In their desire to make sure that young people do not squander the family's money, family elders sometimes create a structure that does not allow a young person to ever grow up. Trusts often make them permanent beneficiaries, always under the benevolent guidance of a trustee. While this protects the family wealth, it does not promote adulthood in the family member. If there is no way that the young person can ever become able to make decisions about the family's wealth, that person will never feel that the money is truly his or hers. Therefore, as a dependent, the family member will never be able to take care of or build the family wealth and will have no way of expressing him- or herself other than through spending.

When they reach young adulthood, family members need to be able to make their own decisions about their money, and each must have a role as a "citizen" of the family. Families are understandably reluctant to give young adults this responsibility, fearing that they may not act wisely. But by providing opportunities for the young people to experiment with decision making, to have a chance to make mistakes, and thus to learn to cope with the results of their own errors, families can offset the possibility of capricious actions later. There comes a time when young people must have the power to take care of their own money, even if some strings are attached.

If a young person is prevented from ever trying anything, he or she can become excessively cautious and unable to act. Raised with the internal lesson that the worst thing a person can do is make a mistake, an individual grows up afraid of risk, not able to test himself, and paralyzed when confronted with the need for action.

Families often try to enshrine their values by creating trusts that limit a young person's ability to use resources. This is good practice to avoid liability and protect assets. However, it can have the unexpected consequence of limiting the young person's ability to experiment, take risks, and learn from experience. Every young person needs to have this learning experience, and the family may be able to protect the family assets while still allowing the young person to experiment and learn. Offering the young person a graded amount of money to control, a family can help the person shift from an attitude of consumption to one of stewardship by teaching her to sustain and even possibly add to the family assets.

To support risk taking and entrepreneurial development of young people, some families have developed a "family bank," in which family funds are reserved for new ventures. A family member can ask for support for a profit-making venture or, perhaps, a philanthropic project. The family member applying for the funds is required to present to the family a case for the new venture or endeavor, and if supported, is accountable for the results promised. Family members can learn from each other and even generate positive competition for excellence.

By providing a network of family connections and mechanisms for decision making in family governance, the family can also provide a backdrop for a young person's education and involvement.

A Time and Opportunity

The path to developing young people who are able to sustain and act as stewards of family wealth is complex and multifaceted. It begins with a realization of the complexity of the challenge and an understanding that all affluent children naturally develop a strong sense of entitlement. While we are a culture that has spawned entitlement in all our children, there is a special challenge for a child from a very wealthy family. We are also a culture in which a wealthy family has the unique opportunity to examine what it has done and implement a variety of steps along a developmental pathway to reverse this process.

A young person's developmental path must take him or her through a series of educational experiences, dialogues, and challenges that help him begin to move beyond the seductive safety of entitlement. This is a matter of continual engagement and active involvement by parents, not a question of setting up trusts, hiring people to speak at family meetings, or telling young family members what is expected of them in relation to their consumption of their wealth, their spending habits, and other behaviors. These are all important, but the overall family process for moving from entitlement to stewardship comprises many activities and requires a great deal of work.

We have heard many families describe the experiences they are having with their children regarding the financial crisis and its impact. An affluent young mother we met at a conference told us that her son was worried about his best friend's father who was now unemployed after having been very successful in one of the financial services firms. Her son wondered what they could do to help his friend's family and whether this could ever happen to their family. While his mother hesitated to offer too much reassurance, she did tell her son that it was unlikely but also that they always had to be prepared and should use times like this to think about what really counted in life. She suggested that they invite the friend over for dinner since that seemed to help calm her son.

This is a time of opportunity; there is a window available to educate our young people about the transience of money and the need to develop the ability to rely on oneself. Many young people's worlds are being shaped by the current financial crisis. For them, the experience may be similar to that of those who were very young during the Great Depression. They may grow up in a different way than did their parents, who are mainly baby boomers who thought they were invulnerable and wanted more. If these young people are given help thinking about the current economic conditions and forging a set of principles for the future based on the learnings they are gleaning from living through this period in history, they may be able to grow beyond their sense of entitlement quickly and perhaps without a great deal of angst or anger. This may encourage them to raise more questions, be more empathetic, understand more clearly the circumstances of others, and become more self-sufficient. These are all good things; the young people just need some guidance from their parents and their family adviser, who must create an environment of trust in which the young people can resolve their age-appropriate entitlement dilemmas.

7.5

The Power of Giving as a Shared Family Activity

This selection looks at various ways a family can come together to be involved in shared charitable and philanthropic ventures, ranging from passive to active. It also looks at the option of individual giving and explores ways a family philanthropy can have the impact the family desires. It presents a number of ways enterprising families can create and maintain their societal capital.

A recent study forecasts that in the next two decades, more than $40 trillion will pass between generations. While some wealthy families have already created patterns of philanthropy, the amount of new wealth that is being transferred suggests that many more families will, perhaps for the first time, begin to consider how they want to use their surplus wealth to make a difference in the community and the world. Much philanthropy is supported by tax advantages, but there are many more-persuasive reasons for families to share their money.

After they achieve business and financial success beyond their expectations, enterprising families begin to focus not only on managing their businesses and shared assets, but also on how their wealth can be used to make a difference in the world. In fact, increasingly the focus shifts from the family business to how the whole family can use its wealth to make a difference. A family must make many family, strategic, and structural choices—from among such projects as individual gifts to the creation of large family foundations—if their giving is to have the impact on society, and on their family, that they desire.

Just as the market calls into being businesses that respond to certain needs, so too philanthropy creates an alternate market, supported indirectly by tax laws that encourage it, for individuals of wealth to use some of their money to make the world a better place for others. There is a long tradition of people giving back to the community. The practice of tithing grew up as a way for the fortunate to help those who are less fortunate and to support their deepest values. People of wealth have always taken leadership in supporting the arts, social welfare, education, and other activities that enrich the community.

As people amass great wealth, their reputations are increasingly tied to their giving rather than their acquiring. Andrew Carnegie, in his classic essay *The Gospel of Wealth*, preached of the responsibility of those of great wealth to give substantially back to the community, which he did. The wealth accumulated so quickly by Bill Gates has recently been used to create one of the largest foundations in the world.

Philanthropy can do many things for the family who practices it. In addition to doing good, visible philanthropy has been used to improve the communities in which families have their businesses. Some entrepreneurs have shifted their focus in later life to philanthropy, and there is evidence that some of today's new wealthy are making that choice as well. They find that giving money away can be as creative and fulfilling as creating wealth. In creating their businesses, they focused their energy along a very narrow path. Yet in their experience as philanthropists, they are exploring more deeply human needs and societal issues.

As young people grow up in a wealthy and successful family, they face many personal dilemmas. The business cannot accommodate many next-generation candidates, and many young people do not have the skills or interest to join the company. Given that they will inherit substantial wealth, the question of what they want to do with their lives does not include having to make a living. So what can they do to develop a sense of personal identity, to fulfill themselves? For many third-, fourth-, and nth-generation heirs, the answer is to become involved in giving. There are networks of donors that offer not just access to philanthropic resources but also personal support (for example, the Tides Foundation or The Philanthropic Initiative).

Giving can be an individual or a whole-family pursuit. Both directions have value. Individual giving allows a person to put his or her own stamp on her gift, to do what fits her own ideals or ideas. Each family member has his own personal values and experience that can be expressed in giving. He may give to causes that he is personally involved in or through giving may become more active with a cause. In fact, many donors have chosen to become more hands-on, actually working with an organization they support, rather than just handing over a check.

But giving collectively has other advantages. For one thing, by pooling resources a family can have a greater impact than they can as individuals. A family foundation or large gift can make a clear difference in the community, whereas smaller gifts to several groups may not.

Pathways for Giving

There are five pathways that family members can embark upon for their giving:

Shared giving.
A family can allocate a certain amount for giving and meet together to decide on what to support. Each member may have some say or a portion to allocate. The family might share the impact of past giving and look after their portfolio of gifts. In addition to giving, the family has an opportunity to teach and learn from each other and to do something together that matters and in which each member has a voice.

Family foundation.
Foundations are very popular because they allow a family to retain control of the assets—often stock in family companies—while offering the benefits of the profits to a cause. A family foundation can take many forms. It can be an operating foundation that uses its funds for a specific purpose. It can have a theme or focus area, such as supporting child development in the community where the family is located. In addition, the family may use some of the foundation's resources to determine how best to accomplish its objectives. Family members can participate in various leadership roles, from membership on the board to more-active involvement as staff.

Community leadership.
The most common way wealthy family members give to the community is to combine donations with active involvement in various community groups, serving on an organization's board, for instance, or participating in its activities or operations. Through active service a donor can exercise visible leadership; by combining the two—funding and activity—the family can help determine the direction of institutions and participate in the growth and development of the community. Many next-generation family members find their lives enriched by community leadership. Although this can be a vanity pursuit, in which awards, testimonials, and elegant events overshadow the act of giving, in fact, the exercise of informal community leadership can have an impact on the community that is as greater or greater than that which the family had acquiring its wealth. In addition, family members can express their individual preferences and use their unique talents in many ways.

Donor networks.

While family giving most often supports charitable institutions that already exist, some heirs want their wealth to make radical changes in society. In the 70s, groups of donors formed several networks in which they could pool their resources to create the leverage needed to make a major impact in society. These groups—such as the Haymarket People's Fund, in Boston, and the North Star Fund, in New York, both of which are members of the Funding Exchange—created an infrastructure that uses wealth for optimal social impact. The Funding Exchange, whose organizers coined the slogan "Change Not Charity," emphasizing that they are committed to transformative change, using their giving to make a real impact on the world through efforts such as the eradication of poverty, illiteracy, and other social ills. Young adults in multigenerational enterprising families donated inherited wealth as the seed money for virtually all 16 of the member funds. The Funding Exchange also offers personal support for donors and brings them together as a learning community to develop their capability to make a difference. Also, it offers a public platform for members to advocate their views and recruit additional support.

Public service.

Public service used to be more highly valued and respected than it is today. An heir could give back to society by assuming political office or taking a role as a professional in a nonprofit institution. In fact, many leading political figures (whatever we think of their motivation or their politics) are able to work in that capacity because of their family wealth. The notion is that because they are already wealthy, they can serve without being susceptible to temptation. Public service can also take the form of leading an educational, advocacy, or service organization. Leadership can take several forms. An individual can be a leader by directing a service, chairing a board, or serving as a board or staff member. One can take on a more-limited role by leading a project or an initiative. Heirs have found that active service—as a teacher, a writer, a service provider, or an advocate—can be more meaningful than giving financial support.

Too many families see their philanthropy simply in terms of writing a check and taking a tax deduction. But with actively participating in the operations of an institution like a community center, neighborhood theater, or local park or garden, family members and entire families together can discover far richer, more-efficacious, and more-engaging means of giving that allow them to have a greater impact on the community than just signing checks. Furthermore, because of the current economic crisis, their efforts are needed now more than ever as the government and nonprofits can no longer afford to fund many educational, art, and athletic programs in low-income neighborhoods. Families have preserved such programs not only by providing funding but also by providing teachers, poets, artists, and musicians from within their own ranks as teachers and administrators. As a family finds they have far more wealth than their members and their heirs need to live full lives, they can shift their focus to giving and provide an effective and positive outlet for their energy, vitality, and creativity, enriching their own communities and the world at the same time.

7.6

The Serious Business of Family Philanthropy

Over generations, the focus of the family legacy can pass from operating a family business to management of the family philanthropy. This transition offers an opportunity for several generations of the family to work together. But the creation of a substantial family philanthropic effort is often, like the family's legacy business, the sole purview of the wealth creator. Just as succession is an issue in the family enterprise, succession and governance are issues for the family foundation. This selection explores some of the common challenges families face as they shift from creating wealth to giving back to the community.

This selection was written with Sam Davis of Relative Solutions.

Many people think of philanthropy as offering an easy means for bringing together multiple generations and branches in a common cause. Enterprising families and the professionals who advise them often seem to agree that philanthropy provides a low-risk opportunity to unify families.

In reality, family philanthropy is a complex undertaking and is not a guarantee of family unity. As Patricia Angus and Fredda Herz Brown found in their 2002 study of family foundations, the process of giving back can lead to family divisions if the impact of family dynamics on the foundation and the need for governance structures are not considered.

Look at the case of a third-generation family foundation. Established by the grandfather to provide educational opportunities for the children of workers in the family's manufacturing business, the foundation foundered after his death as his children fought to assert their own philanthropic priorities. Lacking an effective governance structure or professional staff, the foundation became a source of family debates over social and geographical interests. A generation later, third-generation cousins prevailed on their parents to retain a consultant to assist them in restructuring the foundation and rebuilding family relationships.

Similarly, one previously close-knit family nearly came apart when the adult children in the second generation contested their parents' support for grants made to organizations sponsoring the expansion of settlements in Israel's East Bank. A three-year impasse was overcome only when the parents agreed to provide their children with the same number of board seats as they had and to divert one-half of their foundation's annual grants to organizations supported by their children.

Like the families in these two examples, others have assumed that philanthropy would serve as a ready means for bringing members together only to learn the hard way that differences in value sets between generations and other conflicts can present barriers to family unity. Some well-intentioned families have made the mistake of providing their next-generation adult members with relatively small sums of money to give away only to learn that their adult children felt marginalized, a process Sharna Goldseker of the Samuel Bronfman Foundation's 21-64 program calls "keeping them at the children's table." Families who have taken unstructured approaches often discover that family philanthropy is replete with the same power and control issues found in their other family enterprises.

Causes of family conflict experienced by those enterprising families who take informal approaches to philanthropy include the following:

- The absence of a structure and guidelines for intergenerational family decision making
- Failure to engage and educate the next generation about the family's philanthropic heritage and initiatives
- Differences in values between the generations and branches
- Lack of experience and professionalism in dealing with the often-complex details related to philanthropy

Although philanthropy can serve to bind a family to its core values and become one of the defining features of a family's legacy, many families fail to treat family philanthropy with the same level of professionalism they afford their operating businesses or investments.

What steps might families of wealth take to remedy this, giving their family philanthropies the same professional commitment they do their business and investments? Following such steps can go far in ensuring family unity.

The philanthropic legacies of many families emerge from their ownership of a business. Just as these families found that defining their family mission and values helped them focus their business efforts and build family unity, they can use the family's charitable legacy to affirm their philanthropic values and mission. To undertake this, the family might explore its multigenerational legacy by telling family stories and reviewing articles, pictures, and the family's history of contributing to the community and giving to others. Even if the family has never previously engaged in a structured approach to philanthropy, a review of the family legacy will almost certainly reveal key themes and values that will inform the thinking of future generations as they advance along the path toward defining the family's philanthropic purposes and goals.

To overcome differences in values, passions, or interests that may emerge between generations or family branches in discussions about the direction of a family philanthropy, families can benefit from defining a shared vision for the future of their philanthropic endeavors, similar to that which they would develop for their family businesses. A well-thought-out and carefully crafted philanthropic vision statement can guide the family's charitable giving and volunteer efforts for years to come. While a concise statement of a shared vision can serve as a family touchstone, the process of developing and discussing multigenerational scenarios, or stories of what the family wants to achieve, can be even more important in reaching consensus within the family and forestalling potential differences before they arise.

Once a family has affirmed its philanthropic legacy and vision for the future, the family will benefit from having an effective means for making philanthropic decisions if conflicts are to be avoided. In family businesses, the board and shareholder governance structures serve as decision-making forums for the family. Philanthropic enterprising families can establish similar multigenerational governance structures to serve their philanthropies. For example, rather than simply spreading philanthropic resources among individual family members in an informal, mostly unsatisfactory manner, families can use their governance structures to decide how much of their grant making they want to share and how much they will allow family members to distribute individually.

Some families go to great lengths to avoid situations in which strong feelings, disagreements, or other family dynamics are on display. However, giving back to the community and to others is an inherently emotional endeavor that requires an understanding of and trust in family relationships. Rather than stifling authentic passions of individual family members, families can invest in learning how to best manage the dynamics of family relationships and build on the individual and collective strengths of family members. The development of the family's human capital (see "True Wealth: The Stewardship of Family Capital," in Part I to learn more about human capital) can prove to be a huge benefit in sustaining its philanthropic legacy. By training future leaders and planning for succession, the family can ensure success for its philanthropic ventures in future generations.

Families who treat philanthropy as serious business engage members of their next generation at early ages and provide them with opportunities to learn from others. Grant making is the aspect of philanthropy that tends to draw the greatest interest from family members, and families often find it a good place for younger members to begin. Some families require younger members to give back to their communities through volunteer activities and site visits before they are invited to participate in giving money to nonprofit organizations. This process allows next-generation members to develop their own philanthropic interests and share them with the family. Other families use outside advisers to teach younger members about the management of philanthropic funds and the development annual grant-making budgets. Some families favor "junior boards" or other means for introducing next-generation members to governance responsibilities. Families who engage next-generation members at early ages tend to experience smoother leadership transitions when the time comes to pass the torch.

Still, it is only by applying the same level of accountability to their grant making that they do to their business and investment activities that families receive full satisfaction from their philanthropic efforts. Families that simply follow their hearts when engaging in philanthropy often find they have spread their charitable funds too thin and are unable to make the kind of impact they desire. It's only when a multigenerational enterprising family engages in the process of prioritizing its interests and establishing measurable goals that it can become truly strategic in its grant making. The added benefits of taking these businesslike steps are likely to be an increase in family engagement, a reduction in conflict among family members, and an increase in satisfaction from having brought tangible benefits to others.

For families who have undertaken philanthropic work in an informal manner for a long period of time, it may not seem worthwhile to take a more businesslike approach. However, if such families begin to think of philanthropy as one of their valuable assets to be passed to succeeding generations, they may take a different approach. Often it is young family members of the next generation who call their families to account for the performance of their philanthropic efforts. If families respond to such inquiries by inviting the next generation into a process for engaging in philanthropy, they can find important allies in the strategic management of an important part of the family's heritage.

Philanthropy offers no guarantees of maintaining family unity. However, families who provide their philanthropic endeavors with the same level of professional attention they give other assets are able to continue to enhance their legacies while avoiding family conflict. Family philanthropy is serious business and should be treated as such.

Putting it All Together: How You and Your Family Can Move Forward

This book is a call to action for your family. I hope you have used it as a guide to explore the topics and areas that especially concern your family now or that you expect to face in the future. You may be feeling a bit overwhelmed as you see the array of choices that your family may face and the tasks that you must accomplish if your family is to remain vibrant and unified. The challenge of keeping an enterprising family together over multiple generations may feel nearly impossible. This coda offers a few ideas designed to help you think through the decisions you need to make and challenges you must confront if you are to move forward effectively and efficiently.

First, you are not alone. Every family who has created a successful family business, or garnered substantial family wealth, must look ahead at the challenges I've presented in this book. It is part of the price of success, and as families tell me, "We are privileged to be facing these challenges."

Second, it is important to understand that although you may not be able to predict *when* they will occur, the major family transitions, those that all families face, are predictable—in fact, most are biologically based—and therefore you can be certain *that* they will occur. With this knowledge, you can proactively rise up to meet and work through them.

This book was written to help you address the increasingly complex challenges facing enterprising families as they transition from one generation to another in a global environment, providing you with a road map to help you clearly identify **where you need to go** (to most effectively satisfy both the will of the family and the desires of the individual members) **and what steps you need to take when you get there** (to ensure the family remains sustainable, robust, and successful across generations). Not only are you not alone on this journey, but you may benefit from exploring the experiences of others. The cases and stories I've shared here include those of a few groundbreaking families who have developed successful systems of governance, leadership development, and family collaboration. Others have experienced missteps and sidesteps that have caused existing family and business disputes to become even more deeply entrenched. They too are worth examining.

It is important to keep in mind that good intentions on their own will not lead your family to success. One of the most differentiating characteristics of successful enterprising families is that they put aside the time to do the required work. Of course, any successful family is composed of people who are busy and in demand. Yet to succeed in the activities outlined here, a family must make a clear commitment to each other to meet, to work, and to develop plans that do not sit on a shelf but actually get implemented. Success is a lot of hard work. This may mean travel and scheduling meetings way in advance, but it has to be done.

You can choose your friends and your spouses, but your family is largely predetermined. However its success isn't. For a family to succeed, you need to actively commit to working together to openly and transparently address often difficult and contentious issues. You need to spend time with each other to develop respectful relations so that when stark disagreements arise—as they do in all families—you can deal with them directly, honestly, and with a sincere desire for a productive resolution. This requires finding a way to get the most-resistant and most-difficult family member into the process, which can be a challenge on its own. While other families can get away with avoiding tough issues and troublesome family members, when you are joined in great financial, philanthropic, and organizational ventures, you cannot push things under the rug.

In addition, you must think ahead, consider predictable events like births and deaths—the biologically based transitions we referred to above—and unpredictable ones like business challenges, and you must create a plan for the future. As noted in many of the selections, this cannot be done by a single family leader on his or her own. The future is a collective creation, comprising the family in its entirety, the ownership of its shared assets, and the development of its next generation. As well as creating a plan, the members of the whole extended multigenerational family—what practitioners in this field call a clan—must create together a set of activities, gatherings, rules, and agreements that help them move forward.

Families who are also major financial entities must progress beyond their personal relationships to create organizational and management structures that are accountable to the entire family. An enterprising family must learn how to act not just as an extended family, with informal bonds and social contact, but also as a disciplined financial and business entity, with boards, defined leadership, accountability, and strategic goals and direction.

The tasks outlined in the book are **all about people** and the **development of empowered and informed leaders** with the temperament, the capability, and the commitment to take on roles as stewards of the family wealth. Although each nuclear family is responsible for raising its own children, it will help the entire family—and its individual members—move successfully into the future if the combined family, including subsequent generations and multiple family branches, work together to define shared values and establish plans for developing these values and the skills to manifest them. Articulating values, purpose, and principles, and finding ways to embody them in the work of the family, helps develop good citizens and new leaders. To succeed as a family, you have to produce successful, prepared, and motivated adults in the next generation. And to ensure that the next generation's adults act with diligence, discipline, and imagination, the family might offer individual coaching, family-education programs, and other creative and purposeful activities that give the youth a deeper understanding of the family and an awareness of the outside community, including corners of the world or of their own locales not marked by wealth and privilege. Together these will help create a next generation of strong, but versatile and compassionate, family leaders.

You and Your Family: First Steps

You can begin to undertake these tasks in two ways: first, as an individual, reflecting on your own role and on how you might be able to help the family, as a nuclear family or as an extended clan. You can make some decisions on your own and for yourself, for instance, whether you want to become involved in attempting to move the family forward or trying to engage others in working on these issues together as a whole family. You can also try to identify a way to begin to untangle difficult relationships with other family members. The materials here can help you craft a personal plan for your own development and also help you decide how to approach and work with individuals in your family.

At some point, however, and probably sooner rather than later, you will want to raise key issues with others. You may start with a single person—your spouse or one of your siblings whom you especially trust. Then you may want to explore the issues with your nuclear family—your spouse and children. Finally you may cast your net wider and invite into the conversation all the extended families that grew from the generation who first created the shared family wealth.

Eventually your family will have to discuss and participate in most of these activities together. Sooner or later, probably sooner, you will have to raise the question of whether to work on these issues as a whole extended family. This means that your family has to develop a pattern of openness, transparency, and collaboration. For some families, as has been shown, this is a significant challenge.

The process outlined here usually begins with a meeting of family members. It can be a meeting of everyone or of key individuals. Often the process begins when one family member becomes aware—by reading a book like this or attending a workshop or seminar—of things that an enterprising family can do to strengthen itself and bring those learning to others. The first group can be the key family leaders, your parents, and your siblings, or it may include others. As the group gets together, its participants begin to become aware of the myriad possibilities open to the family. The group then has the task of awakening the family to what is possible, and why it is needed.

There are many ways to start to raise issues. The first hurdle is to develop trust so that family members are comfortable telling the truth to each other. One activity I find useful is for family members to anonymously send articles or even sections from this book to each other, as a way of broaching an issue.

One of the most important principles to remember when calling the family together is to move slowly. It is counterproductive to try to push the family to do something quickly. I find the saying "Go slow to go fast" instructive here. A family meeting doesn't have to start as a meeting with everyone. You can start with a meeting of your siblings or your cousins, as a generation. Tell family members that the first family meetings are to learn and talk about things, not to take actions or make decisions. This will take the pressure off. Then you can ask family members to discuss particular selections or a specific question such as, Why do we stay together as a family enterprise? Some family members may find such ideas as collaboration, governance, strategic planning, and leadership development unusual, surprising, or even threatening.

Another helpful first step is for some family members to together attend a family-enterprise workshop, lecture, or presentation. Many communities have family-business networks, often connected to the local business school, that sponsor events that focus on the topics you find in this book. These workshops are important—especially for family members who do not see the need for such work—in two ways: They provide information about best practices, often with a presentation by members of a local family whom you know and respect. You hear what other families have done, and you see a model for what you can do, presented by people whom you know. These events also allow informal exchange between families. They are attended by families, like yours, who face similar issues.

Meeting and exchanging with other families gives you the opportunity to see how other families have done what you are considering doing. After hearing the experience of another person who has shared your reality, and who has created governance or educational programs, you and your family members may more fully understand what these programs and structures mean and how they can positively affect a family like yours. And finally, these networks often organize groups of individuals who meet regularly to offer support and counsel. There are groups for family leaders, for next generations, and for spouses. Usually they are small groups of individuals who share the same perspective in the family and can share experiences and support each other in making change.

Do You Need a Guide? Engaging an Adviser or Consultant

One choice a family may make is to find a consultant or an adviser to work with as they begin to hold family meetings, define their mission and vision, create governance structures and agreements, craft a family-enterprise strategic plan, and develop next-generation leadership and stewardship.

A consultant is a guide who helps the family take actions that are difficult to take on their own. A consultant provides the family the benefit of a neutral party—one who is not an insider with a vested interest—who can help create the conditions for the family to come together. A consultant has two roles: to act as an expert to help the family understand what is possible and what they might do to ensure their future, and to help the family put these things into action. I believe that the expert role, telling a family what they can do, is only of limited value to a family. They may know what they want to do, but they find it hard to get everyone's attention and get people to come together. The consultant has to work with the family as they learn to hold meetings, set up governance structures, and develop leadership-succession practices.

The consulting role for this task, getting people together to work on these issues and deciding together, is **process consulting**. Instead of telling the family what to do, a consultant who has this orientation helps the family work together to decide what they want to do and encourages them to take action. The consultant is also a teacher and coach, helping family members develop the skills to act as family leaders. As the consultant does something with the family, for example, setting up a family meeting, he or she is at the same time helping family members work together—say, to plan the program and to learn how to lead a family meeting on their own the next time (or the time after).

The question your family faces is whether to move forward by working on your own or with a consultant. This book is not intended to be a commercial for family-enterprise consulting, but I have seen that the families who are the most successful at addressing and resolving the most-complex challenges tend to work with consultants. You can determine the degree to which you might profit most from, or even need, the services of a consultant by considering the following factors:

- How complex and large is our family and are our various enterprises?
- How much disagreement, or perhaps even anger and hurt, lies within

the family from past history?
- How urgent is the crisis facing the family now; does it demand an immediate decision or action?

If your family is highly complex, faces significant disagreements or strongly held positions, or is in crisis, you will be well served to get a consultant. If your family is small, doing fine, and does not face a pressing challenge or significant disagreement, then you might be successful convening your own family to work on mission, governance, and leadership.

Final Thought

I am delighted that you have joined me on this journey and that you are considering major steps forward for your family. As a final thought, I would like to suggest that what is recommend here is more than just a good business or financial strategy for sustainable family enterprises, which last through generational transitions. It is a blueprint for taking your family forward so that you can benefit personally as individuals, together as a family, and as one or more shared family enterprises. I would like to hear from you about your experiences and get your feedback about how you and your family have taken this journey together. You can contact me at djaffe@saybrook.edu or www.dennisjaffe.com.

About the Author

Dennis T. Jaffe, Ph.D.

Dennis has been working with family enterprises for more than 20 years. He was one of the founding members of the Family Firm Institute (FFI), where he is a fellow and has served on its board. In 2005, he received the Institute's Richard Beckhard Award for contributions to the practice of family business consulting. He was also one of the creators of FFI's certificate program in Family Wealth Advising. For 25 years, he has been professor of organizational systems and psychology at Saybrook University, where he co-founded and leads the doctoral program in Sustainable Organizational Systems.

Dennis was a regular columnist for *Families in Business* at its inception and for a number of years and has contributed several family profiles and has written two cover stories for *Worth Magazine*. He is co-author of two of the foundational works about family business, *Working with the Ones You Love: Building a Successful Family Business* and *Working with Family Businesses: A Guide for Professional Advisers,* as well as co-designer of the assessment tools Aspen Family Business Inventory and Aspen Family Wealth Management Inventory. In 2007, he was awarded the Editor's Choice Award for his article on family-business strategic planning for the *Journal of Financial Planning.* He conducted a research project on best practices for family wealth management for JP Morgan Private Bank, and he is the co-principal investigator of a study of women and wealth for Campden Conferences.

He has written 20 books, including *Getting Your Organization to Change; Rekindling Commitment; Take This Work and Love It; Managing Change at Work; Empowerment, Self-Renewal: High Performance in a High Stress World;* and *Organizational Vision, Values and Mission,* and more than 100 management articles. His learning tool, the Values Edge, has helped families and organizations explore their personal, group, and organizational values. He co-authored *Beyond the Term Sheet,* a study of governance in venture capital startup firms, of which portions appeared in several journals and in an article in *The Wall Street Journal.*

Dennis is the creator of many corporate training programs, including Leading Change and Managing Change, that help leaders engage their teams and move organizations in new directions in times of great transition. He was a founder and vice president of content for MemeWorks, which provided Web-based executive development tools to companies. He was the founder of the consulting firm Changeworks Global. His video, *Managing People Through Change*, was voted one of the Best Products of 1991 by the magazine *Human Resource Executive*. His work has been featured in *Inc.* magazine, *Entrepreneur, Nation's Business, Time,* and *The Wall Street Journal,* and he has been profiled in *People* magazine.

He has been a board member and fellow of the Center for Mind-Body Medicine, World Business Academy, and Saybrook University, as well as the Family Firm Institute. He is a licensed clinical psychologist. He is a professional member of the Collaboration for Family Flourishing, the Academy of Management, NTL Institute, and the Society for Organizational Learning. He has been president of the Association for Humanistic Psychology and twice was the winner of the Medical Self-Care Book Award.

Dennis received his B.A. in Philosophy, M.A. in Management, and Ph.D. in Sociology, all from Yale University.

He can be contacted at djaffe@dennisjaffe.com, and at his website, www. dennisjaffe.com.

Made in the USA
Lexington, KY
14 April 2016